Praise for *At the Brink*

"Unlike so many, John Lott gets it. He understands precisely how devastating Barack Obama's policies are in every important domestic area—the economy, health care, and crime. Lott also recognizes that Obama, with the help of a protective media, has shrewdly camouflaged his disastrous policies in propaganda and deceived American voters. But Lott is a master of the facts, and Obama's record and propaganda disintegrate when met with facts."
—DAVID LIMBAUGH, AUTHOR OF THE *NEW YORK TIMES* BESTSELLER *THE GREAT DESTROYER*

"John Lott's latest book is chock full of sober, fact-driven analysis that is must-reading for anyone who wants a glimpse of our near future. At the Brink *is destined to become as important a book as* More Guns, Less Crime, *and could just as well be titled* More Government, Less Wealth.*"*
—KEVIN A. HASSETT, PH.D., DIRECTOR OF ECONOMIC POLICY STUDIES AND SENIOR FELLOW, AMERICAN ENTERPRISE INSTITUTE

"America is standing at the precipice, ready to tumble into a pit of high taxes, ever higher spending, and unsustainable debt. Barack Obama has been pushing from behind, with his stimulus, health care law, and now his gun-grabbing. Have we reached the point of no return? With his characteristic attention to detail, John Lott documents how we got here and shows us the way back."
—W. JAMES ANTLE III, EDITOR, DAILY CALLER NEWS FOUNDATION, AND AUTHOR OF *DEVOURING FREEDOM*

"Marshalling evidence on Obamacare, the stimulus and other spending, expanding regulation, gun control, and looming tax increases, At the Brink *paints a compelling and highly readable picture of the Obama administration's policy failures."*
—SCOTT HARRINGTON, ALAN B. MILLER PROFESSOR, WHARTON SCHOOL, UNIVERSITY OF PENNSYLVANIA

"John Lott offers readers an exceptionally clear, understandable, and devastating critique of President Obama's leading policy initiatives, from Obamacare to economic stimulus, gun control, business regulation, and tax policy. I particularly enjoyed Lott's rebuttal of Obama's economic stimulus efforts, which is the best and most comprehensive rebuttal to claims of effectiveness that currently exists anywhere. This book should be in the hands of every citizen who knows something is very wrong in public policy today but can't find the words or facts to turn concern into solid argument. The words and facts are here."

—WILLIAM W. BEACH, DIRECTOR, CENTER FOR DATA ANALYSIS, AND LAZOF FAMILY FELLOW, THE HERITAGE FOUNDATION

"John Lott lays out the false arguments used to justify the increased role of government, from health care to taxation and spending. He knows the issues inside and out, anticipates the counterarguments well, and effectively uses both economic theory and data to support his positions. The scariest thing is that voices like his are becoming way too scarce."

—ROBERT G. HANSEN, PH.D., SENIOR ASSOCIATE DEAN, TUCK SCHOOL OF BUSINESS, DARTMOUTH COLLEGE

"John Lott explodes every myth on which the president has built his domestic policy. Numbers don't lie, and Lott's analysis is indispensable for understanding how Obama has brought America to the brink of disaster."

—DAVID HARSANYI, SENIOR REPORTER AT *HUMAN EVENTS* AND AUTHOR OF *OBAMA'S FOUR HORSEMEN*

AT THE
BRINK

AT THE
BRINK

WILL OBAMA PUSH US OVER THE EDGE?

JOHN R. LOTT JR.

Since 1947
REGNERY
PUBLISHING, INC.
An Eagle Publishing Company • Washington, DC

Cataloging-in-Publication data on file with the Library of Congress
ISBN 978-1-62157-051-6

Published in the United States by
Regnery Publishing, Inc.
One Massachusetts Avenue NW
Washington, DC 20001
www.Regnery.com

Manufactured in the United States of America

10 9 8 7 6 5 4 3 2 1

Books are available in quantity for promotional or premium use. Write to Director of Special Sales, Regnery Publishing, Inc., One Massachusetts Avenue NW, Washington, DC 20001, for information on discounts and terms, or call (202) 216-0600.

Distributed to the trade by
Perseus Distribution
250 West 57th Street
New York, NY 10107

To my mom

Contents

INTRODUCTION

Now and then a tremendously charismatic leader arrives on the political scene. Barack Obama is such a person. Starting out largely as an unknown, he has been able to talk his way into the hearts of the American people.

Yes, he came across as a caring, likable man. But few bothered to delve into his voting record or the precise nature of his views. Little was known about Obama's brief tenure as a senator from Illinois. It was as if he were beyond reproach—it was largely taboo to question his integrity or his commitment to the principles on which this nation was founded.

The tone of the debate changed only after millions of Americans had lost their jobs and the recession had dragged on for years. Many voters were disappointed. Obama's campaign promises simply hadn't come true. Yet with his charisma and the added power of incumbency, he managed to win reelection.

There is a tendency to happily explain away Obama's many failures. After all, politicians always exaggerate during their campaigns. But the "Blame it on Bush" excuse is starting to wear thin, several years after the financial crisis.

Yes, President Bush does deserve some of the blame. He increased the deficits beyond the levels necessary to finance wartime spending after 9/11. And the push for home ownership by those who couldn't afford it started back in the Clinton administration.

Nevertheless, there is something different about this president. George W. Bush and other presidents lacking the line-item veto were often reluctantly dragged into spending more than necessary by interest groups and a spendthrift Congress. Mr. Bush had a particularly hard time saying no. But President Obama, who campaigned in 2008 to cut "net government spending" and then promised that his massive increases were only temporary, has fought relentlessly for new spending, all under the pretense of stimulating our sluggish economy. Isn't a time of financial hardship a time when all of us, including the government, should be tightening our belts? Unfortunately, the government doesn't have to balance its accounts as you and I do. It can just create money out of thin air.

What makes Obama different is that he truly believes that the government is the solution to our problems. He actually wants more government spending, more regulations, more gun control. He simply does not rate individual freedom very highly.

Can we blame Obama's dismal economic record on his misguided economic principles? Sure we can. President Reagan, who said government is the problem and not the solution, was able relatively quickly to get America out of a recession that in many ways was even worse than that of 2008.

Like so many other politicians, Obama is a lawyer by training. He tends to see new and expanded laws, not fewer laws, as the solution. Still, the Obama I knew nearly fifteen years ago,when we were both teaching at the University of Chicago, was far to the left of most lawyers.

Unfortunately, Obama's lack of private-sector experience and lack of training in economics are abundantly clear. He believes that the federal government can micro-manage business decisions, that the economy is something you can "jump-start" with more government spending, that speculators are bad guys, and that doctors can easily be made to provide the same care at lower cost simply by cutting how much they are paid. The list goes on.

The fact is that Barack Obama is an incurable left-winger. Why he believes what he does is not really too important. What is important is that we try to mitigate the consequences of a second term that is likely to be even more disastrous than the first. Now that Obama will not have to face the voters again, we will surely learn even more about the true nature of the president's agenda.

This book deals with the economic realities of Mr. Obama's first term and why his policies did more harm than good. We aren't going to "search our hearts" for answers to issues such as gun control, welfare, and health care. Our hearts can be deluded by charismatic politicians like President Obama, so let's use our brains instead.

The president has been able to endlessly misconstrue the facts about the economy, the health insurance industry, and every other important issue. He has got away with it largely because the media and many voters are so enchanted with the youthful, optimistic president. Armed with the facts, we might be able to challenge

Obama's new proposals for additional regulations, taxes, and mandates.

It's reasonable to approach a book titled *At the Brink* with a measure of skepticism. But I hope that in the chapters that follow I will convince you that that's exactly where we are.

The American health care system has been the envy of the world. Despite the popular impression that the system as a whole is badly flawed, a huge majority of Americans are satisfied with the care that they themselves receive. Americans' satisfaction with their health care is higher, in fact, than that of Canadians, whose socialized system is supposed to be a model for their unenlightened neighbors to the south. Even the Achilles' heel of U.S. health care—the legions of uninsured—turns out, upon closer examination, to be less severe a problem than the masters of public opinion have convinced us it is. Instead of gradually and cautiously reforming this flawed but marvelous system, President Obama went at it with a machete. His greatest legislative triumph—the Patient Protection and Affordable Care Act—will soon be an irrevocable part of American life. Almost every feature of Obamacare is misbegotten, and it will inflict incalculable damage on the health care system itself and on the nation's finances.

The administration's policies have made the economy dramatically worse. Obama inherited a severe recession, as he has been known to remind us. His apologists like to suggest that because the recession was caused by a "financial crisis," it was mysteriously immune to the medicaments of enlightened economic theory. The reason for the failure of the United States to recover from the recession that began in December 2007 is the doctrinaire Keynesianism that the Obama administration—with huge Democratic majorities in Congress—has applied to its ill patient. I will lay out compelling evidence that the spectacular "stimulus" spending with which

Obama launched his presidency not only has failed to help the economy—it has poisoned it, slowing the recovery.

The last year of Obama's first term ended with the massacre of twenty six- and seven-year-olds at Sandy Hook Elementary School, along with six women who tried to save them, a reminder that the nation's woes are not limited to the economy. This slaughter—so sickening, so unthinkable—renewed and intensified the sense that something is deeply wrong. Although the atrocity at Sandy Hook was not unprecedented—these psychopathic mass shootings have become distressingly regular—the tender age of its victims invested it with a special horror. More than after Columbine or Aurora, the public was seized with the conviction that *something must be done*.

Something must be done, but not what Obama is pushing. The immediately obvious response to Sandy Hook was "take away the guns." That's understandable. People see something bad that happens with guns and they think that if we only take away guns, those bad things won't happen.

If only things were that simple. The problem is that there's no evidence that tighter gun control would prevent another massacre. All the evidence, in fact, is to the contrary. Mass shootings almost always take place in "gun-free zones" like Sandy Hook Elementary School or Aurora's Cinemark 16 movie theater, where the murderer is assured of no armed interference.

President Obama, however, has never let reality get in the way of his ideological agenda. Just as he used the financial crisis of 2008 to push governmental intervention in the economy to a previously unimaginable level, he took advantage of the fear and outrage after Sandy Hook to pursue a goal he has cherished for many years—the disarmament of American civilians. I do not exaggerate. Back at the University of Chicago, Barack Obama told me, "I don't believe that people should be able to own guns."

Obama's most powerful weapon in transforming America will be the federal judges he appoints who share his radical philosophy. He will have the opportunity to populate more than half of the federal judiciary and could radically alter the Supreme Court before his presidency is over. If the Republican opposition in the Senate fails to make a stand against judicial radicals, Americans' liberty and prosperity could be eviscerated within eight years.

This president does not like businessmen, whom he demonizes as "speculators," while denying the critical role of entrepreneurs in creating wealth ("You didn't build that!"). Obama is the most heavy-handed regulator in American history, and he has saved the worst of it for his second term. He doesn't believe that incentives affect people's behavior, nor does he appreciate that businesses learn firsthand through hard experience what their customers really want and what it takes to grow a successful company.

The first transformational president of the left, Franklin Roosevelt, secured his countrymen's acquiescence in the New Deal with the disarming reassurance that "the only thing we have to fear is fear itself." The supremely canny politician Barack Obama uses similar tactics of persuasion.

America is at the brink. There are things we should be afraid of. We should open our eyes before it's too late.

CHAPTER ONE

THE LOOMING OBAMACARE DISASTER

A n exchange on MSNBC's *Morning Joe* a few days after Obama's reelection between host Joe Scarborough and Karen Mills, head of Obama's Small Business Administration, perfectly captures the mess we're in:

> *Scarborough*: But we do hear from business owners—I am sure that you do too—that are now contemplating after the election. Certainly I hear from a lot saying, "Gosh, I am going to have to keep people under thirty hours.... It is only a matter of time before I go out of business. I can't afford the cost of what this new regulation puts on me." First of all will you explain to us—because we keep hearing "thirty hours, thirty hours"—explain that

cut off. What do you tell those business owners? Why are
they wrong?

Mills: You know, I travel all around the country, every
week I go to a different part of the country. I'm with small
businesses. And I'm not hearing that.

Scarborough: You have never heard that?

Mills (shaking her head and indicating "right"): I will tell
you what I have heard.

Scarborough: You need to talk to your staff to tell them to
get you out of the bubble.[1]

Obama's reelection extinguished any hope of stopping Obamacare. Whether we like it or not, it is going into effect in a series of
stages. Immediately after the election, firms around the country
started laying off workers or cutting back their hours. Few responded
as dramatically as Henry Hamilton, a business owner in Key West,
Florida, who committed suicide two days after the election.[2] Hamilton's body was found next to a living will that read, "Do not revive!
(expletive) Obama!" He was reportedly worried that his tanning
salon business wouldn't survive the government's 10 percent special
tax on tanning.

In 2014, small businesses across the country with at least fifty
full-time employees are faced with either paying a fine of $2,000 per
employee or providing health insurance that for an individual will
cost at least three times that amount.[3] The Congressional Budget
Office (CBO) claims that the tax will raise $10 billion,[4] though this
is really just a guess. They make lots of assumptions, including the

notion that these taxes won't change how companies act. But for many of these companies the rational thing to do will be to turn full-time employees into part-time ones, or simply to fire them, and the most dispensable employees are going to be those with the lowest wages (because they'll have the highest spike in the cost of employing them).

Take Apple-Metro, a company that owns forty Applebee's restaurants in the New York City area.[5] Each restaurant employs between eighty and three hundred people, and they could face hundreds of thousands of dollars in new taxes. Zanr Tankel, the company's president, noted just days after the election that the tax means, "there goes the profit in your restaurant."[6] He warned, "in a best-case scenario, we only shrink the labor force minimally." Clearly many firms will think twice before adding that fiftieth employee.

Papa John's CEO John Shattner "expects franchise owners will be forced to cut employees' hours because they can't afford the costs of health insurance plans."[7] He estimates that the new law will cost his company between $5 million and $8 million a year and add approximately 11 to 14 cents to the price of a large pizza. "That's what you do, is you pass on the costs. Unfortunately, I don't think people know what they're going to pay for [Obamacare]."[8] Other companies such as Red Lobster and Olive Garden face similar undesirable choices.

Not understanding the notion that there is no such thing as a free lunch, comedians Jon Stewart and Stephen Colbert, liberal columnists, and leftwing blogs like the Daily Kos slammed Shattner for his wealth and refusing to absorb the higher costs of Obamacare.[9] Stewart sneered that Papa John's could afford to give away two million free pizzas, but couldn't cover employee health insurance premiums. But of course, the giveaway was a promotion, a form of advertising, which companies use to increase sales, which in turn can lead to hiring more employees. Obamacare, on the other hand, is a tax that many companies can't afford on their profit margins.

Some high-tech firms, like Boston Scientific, Stryker, and Medtronic have announced thousands of layoffs. Obamacare subjects their products to a new medical device excise tax.[10] The tax, which is expected to raise $20 billion in revenue, won't just reduce employment, it is going to reduce these companies' incentive to innovate and produce better medical devices in the future.[11] Former Democratic Senator Evan Bayh, who voted for Obamacare and now regrets it, wrote, "It will also stifle critical medical innovation in the industry that gave us defibrillators, pacemakers, artificial joints, stents, chemotherapy delivery systems and almost every device we depend on to save lives.... Who knows what lifesaving devices that might have been developed will fall victim to this tax?"[12]

The special tax on tanning, like the 10-percent tax that was almost imposed on plastic surgery, was motivated to discourage behavior that Democrats don't like.[13] Some pushed the tanning tax because of concerns that tanning could lead to skin cancer.[14] But the medical device tax is particularly strange, as new devices are necessary for improved health care.

It isn't just "greedy" for-profit companies that are cutting back employee hours. The Community College of Allegheny County got some attention for publicly announcing cuts. If the college is to pay for this mandated health care, it must cut classes or employee hours. After the election, the college's four hundred part-time employees learned that they were being cut back to twenty-five hours per week.[15] Clint Benjamin, an adjunct instructor at CCAC, has been buying health insurance out of his own pocket for the last six years. He explained to *Inside Higher Ed* that the reduction of his course load will cut his pay by six hundred dollars a month and make it more difficult to keep buying his own insurance.[16]

Unfortunately, these levies on firms are not the only costs. Obamacare will raise costs, increase the ranks of the uninsured, and give the federal government control of how doctors treat even privately insured patients. In short, it will do all the things President Obama said it would not do. More than that, the federal government, through its subsidies and taxes and regulations, will strictly limit the competition of ideas in medical care.

Fudging the Costs

From the beginning, Democrats tried to cover up the true costs of Obamacare. Then Speaker of the House Nancy Pelosi actually delayed the release of the Congressional Budget Office estimates of its costs—which, by House rules, had to be released three days before voting on the bill—in order to find a way to revise the cost estimates below a trillion dollars. When Democrat number-crunchers were done, they had brought down the estimated cost for the final bill (covering 2010–2019) to $940 billion.[17]

But no one really believes that the CBO equations accurately measure the costs of the health care bill. The true costs will obviously be higher, if for no other reason than that in order to keep the figure below a trillion dollars, parts of the law were delayed to push their costs outside the 10-year window.[18] And other numbers were fudged as well.

One important piece of "creative accounting" was to assume that seniors' medical care would not suffer from the $500 billion in cuts to Medicare that were to finance about half of Obamacare's cost over its first decade. Obamacare supposedly manages to cut payments to doctors and hospitals without reducing the quality of services. But the law doesn't explain how it does this. It simply states that all benefits are guaranteed: "Nothing in this Act shall result in the reduction or elimination of any benefits guaranteed by law to participants in Medicare Advantage plans."[19]

Over the next decade, this Obamacare cut will reduce expenditures on Medicare by about 10 percent.[20] Doctors and hospitals taking Medicare and Medicaid patients already get reimbursed at rates that do not cover their costs. Even lower reimbursement rates mean that payments from other patients and their private insurers will have to rise to offset those losses—or they could go out of business. Cuts in Medicare mean, de facto, higher premiums in private insurance. As costs rise, more people will opt out of buying insurance. But the CBO estimates ignore this.

Immediately before the House vote, the Medicus Firm (a physician-recruiting agency) conducted a survey of doctors. The results showed that 46.3 percent of "primary care physicians (family medicine and internal medicine) feel that the passing of health reform will either force them out of medicine or make them want to leave medicine."[21] This is something else the CBO estimate ignores—that Obamacare might actually shrink the pool of doctors and hospitals. Fewer doctors and hospitals mean higher health care prices. And it means less service for Medicare patients. One of the largest physician surveys ever conducted in the United States, the Physicians Foundation survey of 13,575 doctors in September 2012, found that 52 percent of doctors had already limited their Medicare services or were planning to do so.[22]

The CBO estimates swept quite a lot under the rug. For example, despite repeated requests by Senator Tom Coburn (a physician) and other Republicans, the CBO never analyzed the effects of banning insurance companies from considering pre-existing conditions,[23] because that ban will obviously raise the cost of private insurance and hence reduce the number of insured people.

Shortly before the House health care vote, President Obama explained, in an interview with Fox News's Bret Baier, why he thought that his health care bill was necessary: "Well, if [the health care bill] does not pass, I'm more concerned about what it does to families out there who right now are getting crushed by rising health care costs and small businesses who were having to make a decision, 'Do I hire or do I fix health care?' That's the reason I make these decisions."[24]

Unfortunately, he was wrong. Two things are certain. First, Obamacare has already increased medical costs—and this will only get worse as more of its provisions go into effect. Second, the CBO cost estimates, even if large, have underestimated the true costs of the health care bill.[25]

Some former Obama administration officials have slowly come to the same conclusions. David Gamage, who worked on implementing Obamacare while he was working at the Treasury Department during 2010–2012, was rather blunt: "I have been researching Obamacare and assisting with its implementation, and have come to this realization: Without further reforms, the law will create unnecessary costs for working-class Americans."[26] As so often happens, government regulation creates problems that generate calls for yet more government regulation. Obamacare is going to be no different.

The massive costs threaten to bankrupt the nation, dramatically raise insurance premiums, and leave tens of millions of people left uninsured. Adding another layer of government bureaucrats to our health care system will improve neither costs nor quality. Instead, Obamacare will be the destruction of a health system that has been the envy of the rest of the world, and what that means to individual patients is more health care headaches, lower life expectancy, and needless deaths—something pro-Obama voters probably didn't bargain for.

Three Big Lies

When Barack Obama campaigned for the presidency in 2008, he promised to provide health insurance for the uninsured at a cost of about $50 billion a year.[27] What started off as a relatively modest program gradually turned into a gigantic attempt to completely redo the entire health care system. Addressing Congress on September 9, 2009, President Obama said, "The plan I'm announcing tonight would meet three basic goals. It will provide more security and stability to those who have health insurance. It will provide insurance to those who don't. And it will slow the growth of health care costs for our families, our businesses, and our government."[28] Each one of these claims—that Obamacare would reduce costs, lower

FIGURE 1

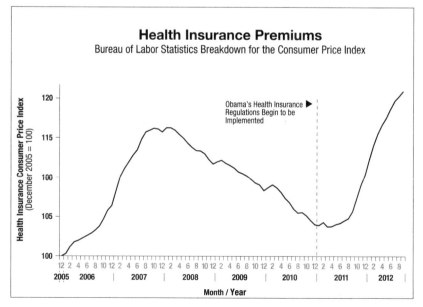

insurance premiums, and ensure health care coverage for all Americans—was false.

On July 24, 2012, the Congressional Budget Office revised its estimates of Obamacare's costs. It now estimates that over a ten-year period, from 2013 to 2022, Obamacare will cost an astounding $1.67 trillion.[29] Unfortunately, the federal government is not the only one facing increased costs. Private health insurance costs are also soaring, increasing by an incredible 16.4 percent from January 2011, when Obamacare insurance regulations first started going into effect, to September 2012 (see Figure 1).[30] Compare that to the fact that health insurance costs dropped from the beginning of 2008 to 2010[31] and we can see that Obamacare not only dramatically increased rates but undid progress in lowering insurance costs.

According to the Congressional Budget Office, in 2015 there will be 36 million Americans uninsured.[32] By 2022, the CBO estimates that 30 million will still be uninsured. So while the number of uninsured Americans might be reduced, such a reduction is coming only at an enormous cost.

Before Obamacare was passed, there was no shortage of experts who would give rosy predictions. Professor Jonathan Gruber, the MIT economics professor who designed both the Romney health care plan in Massachusetts as well as Obamacare, was one of them. Before the law was passed, Gruber testified before the U.S. Senate that Obamacare would guarantee "[s]izeable premium savings for [the] young .... Even larger premium savings for older individuals.... Also large premium savings for a family."[33] He told the *Washington Post*, "What we know for sure the bill will do is that it will lower the cost of buying non-group health insurance."[34]

Gruber's predictions, however, became much more pessimistic once Obamacare had been passed.[35] He is now charging state governments to forecast how Obamacare will change insurance premiums in their state. His predictions for three states—Wisconsin, Minnesota, and Colorado—have been publicly reported.[36] In Wisconsin and Minnesota, Gruber is predicting average premium increases for the individual market of 30 percent and 29 percent, respectively, by 2016—annual increases that will likely be several times greater than the inflation rate. For Colorado, the increase would be 19 percent.

But looking at the average increase in premiums is somewhat misleading. In Wisconsin, for example, few people will see their rates go up by precisely 30 percent.[37] Many people in the individual market will see their health insurance rates soar even more: 13 percent of them could see their rates fall; but 31 percent could see their rates increase by 25 to 50 percent, and a full 41 percent can expect to see their premiums increase by more than 50 percent. And Gruber's estimates might be optimistic. The state of Ohio hired one of the world's largest actuarial firms, Milliman, to assess the impact of Obamacare. The Milliman report stated that by 2017 "individual health insurance market premiums are estimated to increase by 55% to 85% above current market average rates (excluding the impact of medical inflation)."[38]

How does anyone think that these numbers fit with Obama's frequently repeated promise, "Now, let me just start by setting the record straight on a few things. . . . Under the reform we're proposing, if you like your doctor, you can keep your doctor. If you like your health care plan, you can keep your health care plan?"[39] Increasing insurance premiums by more than 50 percent doesn't leave you with the "same plan"; it gives you a plan you might no longer be able to afford. These increased costs make a mockery of then Speaker Nancy Pelosi's promise of "universal, quality, affordable health care for *all* Americans" that "lowers costs for *every* patient" and "reins in premiums."[40] Ironically enough, Obamacare's official title for the House version of the bill is the "Affordable Health Care for America Act." But in fact it will make health care harder to afford for most Americans.

Even Jonathan Gruber, in a January 2012 report to the State of Colorado, warned that his own estimates of projected increases in health care premium costs could understate the case because "we cannot incorporate the effects of the ban on pre-existing conditions," which will inevitably drive up insurers' costs. It could do more than that. It could unravel the whole insurance system if people wait until they get sick to get insurance. Insurance will no longer be insurance; the cost of coverage will have to cover the entire costs of an illness.

Obamacare also limits insurance rates for coverage of pre-existing conditions. What insurance companies lose on those who wait until they are sick to buy insurance they will have to make up through higher premiums from those who carry insurance continuously whether healthy or sick. The result is a vicious circle—as rates rise, it becomes even more attractive for people to delay coverage until they are sick, leaving fewer individuals to pay the higher average premiums.

After the November 2012 election, when he could not be accused of trying to influence the results, Mark Bertolini, the CEO of Aetna, America's third-largest health insurance company, warned about "premium rate shock" when Obamacare's major provisions take effect in 2014. "We've shared it all with the people in Washington and I think it's a big concern," the Bertolini said. "We're going to see some markets [especially small businesses and individual buyers] go up as much as 100 percent."[41]

Choosing Your Own Umpire

The Congressional Budget Office is often appealed to for an objective measurement of a law's financial impact. But the CBO may not be as impartial as you think. For example, the economist who helped construct the economic models used to estimate Obamacare's impact, Melinda Beeuwkes Buntin, previously served as Obama's director of the Office of Economic Analysis and Modeling (under the National Coordinator for Health Information Technology) in the Department of Health and Human Services, a political appointment.[42] She had also donated over $26,000 to Democratic politicians, including the maximum $2,300 donation to Obama in 2008.[43]

The CBO ignored the higher costs of all the new benefits under Obamacare. And there are plenty, as the president himself boasted:

> They will no longer be able to place some arbitrary cap on the amount of coverage you can receive in a given year or a lifetime. We will place a limit on how much you can be charged for out-of-pocket expenses, because in the United States of America, no one should go broke because they get sick. And insurance companies will be required to cover, with no extra charge, routine checkups and preventive care, like mammograms and colonoscopies—because there's no reason we should not be catching diseases like breast cancer and colon cancer before they get worse. That makes sense, it saves money, and it saves lives.[44]

If covering the cost of those routine checkups really saved money, no one would have to force the companies to cover them. These benefits are nice, but they aren't free. Mandating lower co-payments will raise insurance costs for two reasons: First, insurance companies have to pay more money as the patient contributes less. Second, patients will have an incentive to consult a doctor for trivial ailments, undeterred by the out-of-pocket expense.

The Congressional Budget Office estimates that in 2015, Obamacare will cause twenty million people to purchase insurance. That number is crucial to its cost estimate because fines and insurance premiums are supposed to cover the program's costs. That number is also completely unrealistic. Higher insurance premiums will cause more people to drop their insurance. The ranks of the uninsured may actually increase.

The lever with which the law would expand coverage is the so-called "individual mandate"—a fine (or "tax," as the Supreme Court prefers to think of it) imposed on those who fail to buy health insurance.[45] There are two serious problems with this mechanism. First, it will be nearly impossible for the Internal Revenue Service to collect the tax on the uninsured.[46] The health care law expressly rules out the measures by which the IRS enforces compliance with tax laws—imposing liens, seizing assets, freezing bank accounts, and charging civil and criminal penalties. All the IRS can do is withhold your tax refund, which you can mitigate simply by reducing the amount withheld from your wages. The CBO expects citizens to comply with the mandate simply because it is the law.[47] How many motorists comply with highway speed limits when they think no cop is watching?

Second, even if the individual mandate could be enforced, Obamacare creates a powerful incentive to drop your health insurance and pay the fine. Consider some numbers. In 2012, the average price of an individual insurance policy was $5,615 for a single person and $15,745 for a family of four.[48] Remember that the law prohibits "discrimination on the basis of pre-existing conditions, or other health status–related factors."[49] You can now wait to purchase insurance until you have been diagnosed with an illness or become pregnant. You will have to pay a fine for being uninsured, but it is small compared with the price of the insurance. The fine is a flat fee plus a percentage of your income.[50] The penalty will increase between 2014 and 2016. After that, it will be indexed for inflation.

Households earning twice the poverty level—that is, about $22,000 for an individual and about $46,000 for a family of four in 2012—or more will face insurance premiums that exceed the penalty for not buying insurance.[51] For example, in 2016, the fine for being uninsured will be $695 plus 2.5 percent of income over $10,250. So if you earn $50,000, your penalty will be $1,689. That's just 30 percent of the average premium for an individual policy in 2012. But premiums will have risen dramatically by 2016, making the fine trivial compared with the cost of buying insurance. For someone earning $100,000 a year, the Obamacare fine would be $2,939, just over half the premium for a typical individual insurance policy. According to one study, the difference between the cost of premiums and the Obamacare fine can reach about $16,000 for a family of four with parents who are fifty-five years old. Even for individuals, the gap can reach over $7,000.[52] For all but the highest earners, then, it will make sense to skip the insurance and pay the fine.

Americans will be able to save thousands of dollars, every year, by waiting to buy insurance until they are seriously ill or pregnant. Although not everyone may feel comfortable dropping his insurance, especially someone with at least some minor health problems, many people will. And more and more will do so as the price of the "same" insurance increases.

Imagine if you could buy auto insurance *after* you had an accident and you could drop it again once your car was repaired. Everyone can understand that that's not how insurance works. The "insurance" premium would soon equal the price of repairing your car plus the administrative costs of handling your policy.

Unfortunately, that's how we're going to treat health insurance. The more people shy away from buying insurance when they are healthy, the higher the price of insurance will be for those who buy it when they fall ill. The insurance system will quickly unravel as everyone realizes that now you need to buy insurance only when you are really sick. Insurance companies, of course, will stop insuring people, and health care will be transformed into a fee-for-service system. All the estimated costs of Obamacare assume that people will ignore these financial incentives and not gradually shy away from buying insurance.

Who came up with such a plan? Obama assembled a group of very bright policy experts who had little or no experience outside of academia or government—a group of elitists who think they know what is best for others and are unabashed about micromanaging other people's lives, even down to the most basic and personal issues of health care.

Take Lawrence Summers, secretary of the Treasury under President Clinton, former president of Harvard, and chief economic advisor to the president in the first two years of the Obama administration. Explaining why universal health insurance would not increase the federal deficit, Summers said on NBC's *Meet the Press* in April 2009 that the government needed to step in and reduce the number of surgeries. He declared: "Whether it's tonsillectomies or hysterectomies . . . procedures are done three times as frequently [in some parts of the country than others] and there's no benefit in terms of the health of the population. And by doing the right kind of cost-effectiveness, by making the right kinds of investments and protection, some experts that we [sic]—estimate that we could take as much as $700 billion a year out of our health care system."[53]

Summers seemed unconcerned that surgeries are often performed for reasons other than increasing life expectancy. Tonsillectomies are performed primarily to alleviate acute or chronic throat pain.[54] Where to draw the line between pain and surgery is a choice we have traditionally left up to patients. Unless you know the patient, it is very difficult to conclude that a surgery was a "mistake."

Summers's plan sure sounds like rationing. Total health care expenditures in the United States in 2008 came to $2.4 trillion, so Summers must believe that proper regulations can cut health care expenditures by almost 30 percent. That's a lot. Summers hedged his extravagant claim by adding that, for the time being, the government would not have to cut expenditures by more than a third of that $700 billion.

Obama revealed his faith in central planning during the health care debate when he complained that private insurance is more expensive than government insurance simply because private companies have to add on profits.[55] And Obama takes a dark view of profits. He lashed out at doctors numerous times, accusing them of preferring to amputate a foot rather than carefully treat diabetes because they can earn more money from the amputation.[56] And if a patient has "a bad sore throat," if he has allergies, Obama charges that the doctor will think to himself, "I make a lot more money if I take this kid's tonsils out."[57] The president forgets that the desire for higher profits drives down costs, including administrative costs.

Ever wondered why grocery stores are very seldom run by non-profits? By Obama's reasoning, non-profit grocery stores, with no profits to earn or federal taxes to pay, should drive down the price of food. But non-profits lack the incentive to search every corner to drive down costs and to increase quality of their products and services to woo the consumer. That's why non-profits do not take over the grocery-store market. But in Obama's view, such incentives are not particularly important; experts in Washington can run things more intelligently than greedy investors who have their own money at stake.

The Attack on Religious Freedom

The insurance company—not the hospital, not the charity—will be required to reach out and offer the woman contraceptive care free of charge, without co-pays and without hassles. The result will be that religious organizations won't have to pay for these services, and no religious institution will have to provide these services directly. Let me repeat: These employers will not have to pay for, or provide, contraceptive services. But women who work at these institutions will have access to free contraceptive services, just like other women, and they'll no longer have to pay hundreds of dollars a year that could go towards paying the rent or buying groceries.[58]

PRESIDENT OBAMA, REMARKS BY THE PRESIDENT
ON PREVENTIVE CARE, FEBRUARY 10, 2012

With regard to the assault on the Catholic church, let me make it absolutely clear, no religious institution, Catholic or otherwise, including Catholic Social Services, Georgetown Hospital, Mercy Hospital, any hospital, none has to either refer contraception, none has to pay for contraception, none has to be a vehicle to get contraception in any insurance policy they provide. That is a fact.[59]

VICE PRESIDENT JOE BIDEN, VICE PRESIDENTIAL DEBATE,
OCTOBER 11, 2012

This is quite a cynical ploy. Obama's Department of Health and Human Services initially ruled that all employers must include free contraceptive coverage (including abortifacient "morning after" and "week after" treatments) in their health insurance policies or pay ruinous penalties. The regulation provided a narrow exception for places of worship, but religious organizations such as hospitals and schools were subject to the mandate. Understandably, the Catholic Church and a multitude of other religious organizations were up in arms. Obama responded with the promise that he would impose the mandate only on insurance companies, not on employers, supposedly solving the dilemma.

The president's moral reasoning satisfied his fans in the media— "quite clever" is how some have described the proposal[60]—but it failed to impress the opponents of the HHS mandate, who know a logical sleight of hand when they see it. Are religious organizations supposed to feel better if insurance companies are told what they must sell rather than customers told what they must buy?

Another problem with the administration's "compromise" is that many religious institutions are self-insurers. The requirement that insurance companies provide free contraceptives outside employers' plans solves nothing, since the employer and the insurance company are one and the same.[61] Obama's only response to these institutions is that they can stop self-insuring and buy group insurance for their employees. The more affordable option of self-insuring is therefore unavailable to religious employers with moral scruples about abortion and contraception.

There is another line of reasoning that the Obama administration wants us to swallow. A cost really is not a cost if a gain of some sort outweighs it. Yes, the HHS mandate may cost the insurance company or the employer something. But pregnant employees would cost *even more*. Jack Lew, Obama's chief of staff, claimed on *Meet the Press* that the HHS mandate would lower health care costs—a win-win result.[62]

Two problems. The first and most important is moral. A religious organization's objection to the contraceptive mandate is not based on the cost but on the requirement that it participate directly in an immoral act. Second, it is in fact doubtful that contraceptive coverage would reduce costs. If it would, why would the government have to mandate such coverage? Insurance companies would happily include coverage that both lowers its costs and increases benefits to its customers.[63]

The Obama administration's tactic—largely successful—has been to frame the debate as a question not of religious freedom but of whether contraception will be available. As Jack Lew put it, "There are some who just oppose [the idea] that women should have the right to contraception. We do not agree with that."[64] But it is not a question of whether contraception—such as condoms—is available, though that's what the administration wants everyone to think. No *free* contraception supposedly means no contraception at all. The argument may be absurd, but it has political appeal.

The contraceptive mandate is typical of the president's plan. Obama always pretends that his transfer schemes are really creating cost savings all around. Obamacare promises lower insurance costs while mandating all sorts of new coverage.

How the Sausage Was Made

Remember all that talk about the uninsured? That is how it started. People without health insurance, Obama suggested, do not get medical care. But we can provide coverage for all, he promised, and at the same time reduce the overall cost of health care. As usual, it was a win-win proposition. In reality, however, Obamacare is an expensive monstrosity, and it is now clear that many of the members of Congress who gave it life did not understand what they were voting for.

John Conyers, a Democrat from Michigan who was the chairman of the House Judiciary Committee, explained the process best when he was asked whether his fellow legislators had read the Obamacare bill before voting on it:

> I love these members that get up and say, "Read the bill." What good is reading the bill if it's a thousand pages and you don't have two days and two lawyers to find out what it means after you read the bill?[65]

Obamacare passed by a narrow vote of 219 to 212 after much arm-twisting. A change of just four votes would have meant defeat,[66] and it is easy to find four congressmen who have expressed regret over supporting the bill. Like other pro-life Democrats, former Pennsylvania congresswoman Kathy Dahlkemper, who was defeated in 2010, felt betrayed: "I would have never voted for the final version of the bill if I expected the Obama Administration to force Catholic hospitals and Catholic Colleges and Universities to pay for contraception."[67] There were other reasons for regrets. A 2012 headline in *The Hill* read, "Democrats expressing buyers' remorse on Obama's healthcare law."[68] The story quoted retiring Democratic congressmen Brad Miller of North Carolina, Dennis Cardoza of California, and, surprisingly, even arch-liberal Barney Frank of Massachusetts, as saying it was a mistake to pass the law. "Such members can afford to be more candid in speaking their minds without offending their leadership," the story noted, "but are also likely to reflect the feelings of other lawmakers in the House and Senate."

The vote was even closer in the Senate, where the change of only one would have killed Obamacare. Former senator Evan Bayh, a Democrat from Indiana, had second thoughts about his vote by late 2012, worrying about the damage the law's taxes would do to the economy.[69] Writing in the *Wall Street Journal*, Bayh apologized for his vote this way: "As a Chinese proverb says: It is better that wisdom comes late than not at all."

During his 2008 presidential campaign, Obama flatly ruled out raising taxes on middle-class families: "I can make a firm pledge. Under my plan no family making less than $250,000 a year will see any form of tax increase. Not your income tax, not your payroll tax, not your capital gains taxes, not any of your taxes."[70] Part of that pledge was a specific promise not to tax the lavish health insurance plans—so-called "Cadillac" plans—enjoyed by many union households.[71]

And what did we get? First, there's the "individual mandate"— the tax on those who don't buy health insurance. Then there's a 40-percent tax on individual plans costing more than $11,500. Both of these clearly violate Obama's promise.[72] Many union workers whose families make less than $250,000 participate in "Cadillac" plans, as do people with chronic health conditions and other risk factors, and the individual mandate applies to families earning less than $250,000. Other violations of the pledge include reduced medical itemized deductions and medical device excise taxes.

Faced with charges that Obama had broken his campaign promise, the administration began to tinker with the definition of a tax.[73] Austan Goolsbee, the chairman of Obama's Council of Economic Advisers, asserted that the individual mandate was a "penalty," not a tax, because when the uninsured require medical care, the costs are imposed on everyone else.

Of course, by Goolsbee's logic, gasoline taxes are not really taxes because drivers are using public roads. Virtually anything we normally call a "tax," even the income tax, could instead be viewed as a type of user fee. After all, income taxes are used to finance such public goods as national defense and a judicial system.

The administration pushed Goolsbee's "penalty" argument before Obamacare was passed but switched its stand as soon as lawsuits challenging the act's constitutionality were filed. The federal government has the constitutional power to *tax* individuals, but it lacks the authority to penalize persons who refuse to purchase particular goods or services. Fortunately for the Obama administration, the Supreme Court decided that the penalty is in fact a tax, even though the law explicitly stipulates that it is not a tax.

The extraordinary effort to secure Obamacare's passage bordered on corruption. In exchange for Senator Ben Nelson's vote, Nebraska received an extra $100 million in Medicaid funding—the infamous "Cornhusker kickback." Senator Mary Landrieu sold her vote for an additional $300 million in Medicaid funds, the so-called "Louisiana Purchase."[74]

The frantic deal-making continued right up to the final vote. Eleven states and the District of Columbia secured $8.5 billion in special federal funds to provide health care coverage. A last-minute deal increased Oregon's Medicare reimbursement rates. And Tennessee received an additional $100 million to run hospitals.[75]

The buying and selling was not limited to medical issues.[76] Additional water supplies for central California bought the votes of Representatives Dennis Cardoza and Jim Costa. And Representative Luis Gutierrez of Illinois accepted the president's promise to support citizenship for illegal immigrants.

At an earlier stage of his political career—when he was running for president—Barack Obama professed his support for transparency in American politics: "That's what I will do in bringing all parties together, not negotiating behind closed doors, but bringing all parties together, and broadcasting those negotiations on C-SPAN so that the American people can see what the choices are, because part of what we have to do is enlist the American people in this process."[77]

Faced with the challenges of enacting his unpopular federal takeover of the health care system, however, Obama's views changed. Presidential press conferences disappeared. The few press conferences that were granted were conducted by his spokesmen. More specifically, the health care debate took place almost exclusively behind closed doors. C-SPAN did not broadcast the negotiations. Only one proceeding, the Health Care Summit of February 2010, was ever broadcast. It was hardly a "negotiation"—the Democrats held the floor more than twice as long as the Republicans.[78]

How American Health Care Stacks Up

How can we evaluate the quality or effectiveness of health care? Many ways of measuring it have been proposed, but it can't be expressed in a single figure. The temptation is to give too much weight to the qualities that are more easily measurable. Life expectancy, for example, is easily measured, though it depends on far more (e.g., exercise, nutrition, sanitation, lifestyle risks) than the quality of medical care. The waiting time for treatment is another easily quantifiable aspect of health care.

Other factors are more difficult to measure, such as how doctors treat their patients—politeness, willingness to offer explanations, and so on. Do patients feel like valued customers, or is their experience like a visit to the Department of Motor Vehicles? Measuring the quality of care is tricky and must rely on polls. Such measurements, nevertheless, are extremely important.

Life Expectancy

We spend one and a half times more per person
on health care than any other country,
but we aren't any healthier for it.

PRESIDENT OBAMA IN HIS ADDRESS TO A JOINT SESSION
OF CONGRESS ON HEALTH CARE ON SEPTEMBER 9, 2009

If you were seriously ill, what country would you want to be in? That seems like the most obvious question for comparing health care in different countries, yet it is seldom asked. Instead, Obama talks about life expectancy. In that address to Congress, he assured the nation, "These are the facts. Nobody disputes them."

The media have repeated that refrain over and over again. A column in the *Washington Post* asserted in September 2012, "Our health care system has a whole lot of problems. We spend much more than other countries on health care—a third of it on stuff that doesn't make us healthier—and don't really see better outcomes."[79] Paul Krugman wrote in the *New York Times*, "European countries spend far less on health care than we do."[80] But the administration then hides from a serious discussion of where we could cut back.

When I contacted the White House, Obama's press office pointed me to the Commonwealth Fund or the United Nations' World Health Organization (WHO). Both of these organizations use life expectancy at birth as the primary measure of health care quality. As usual, the UN manages to put the United States in a bad light. In its "Overall Health System Performance" report, the WHO purportedly measures how the health care system "contributes to good health." The report is mostly based on guesses of how long a newborn in each of 191 countries will live but also includes other factors, which I will discuss later. After the number-crunching, the WHO concluded that U.S. health care ranks thirty-seventh in the world—behind Chile, Colombia, Cyprus, Dominica (a small island in the Caribbean), Malta, Morocco, Portugal, and San Marino. America's overall score is similar to that of Costa Rica, Cuba, and Slovenia.

Does anyone take the WHO index seriously? Would the international bureaucrats who pay lip service to these rankings prefer to be in an accident in Morocco or in the United States? If they were seriously ill, would they travel to Portugal or to America? To its credit, the WHO lists the many factors that were used in constructing its "Overall Health System Performance" ranking, so we can pick those measures we consider more reasonable and overlook the rest. Some measures are more closely related to health care itself. One such factor is the "overall level of health system responsiveness," defined as "a combination of patient satisfaction and how well the system acts."

By that measure, the United States ranks first. That top ranking is not surprising, as polls show that about 90 percent of Americans are happy with their health care. And as we shall see, even the vast majority of uninsured Americans are happy with their care.

The United States ranks much lower in other areas, in particular life expectancy. The WHO first estimates average life expectancy and then adjusts it so that a year lived suffering from a disability counts for less than a healthy year. The Commonwealth Fund reports life expectancy without making the adjustment for disability.

Adjusted or unadjusted, the measure of life expectancy reflects many factors besides the delivery of health care. Life expectancy can be dramatically shortened by smoking, obesity, accidents, and murder. Thus, while emergency medicine can save the lives of many car crash victims, even the best health care system cannot be blamed for the crashes happening in the first place.

Lifestyle risks vary considerably across developed nations, as shown in Table 1 on page 27, compiled by the Organisation for Economic Co-operation and Development (OECD). Obesity, for example, is ten times as frequent in the United States as in Japan or Korea. Americans are about three times as likely to be obese as Austrians, Dutch, Finns, French, Italians, Swedes, and the Swiss. On the other hand, we smoke less.

According to these numbers, obesity and smoking reduce life expectancy by about the same amounts.[81] In other words, on average, being obese is as risky as being a smoker. As our problem with obesity outweighs the benefits of our relatively low rate of smoking, Americans are, on balance, leading a less healthy lifestyle than the OECD average. Only the Greeks, with their heavy smoking, get a worse score for obesity and smoking rates taken together (see the first two columns of Table 1). At the opposite end, the Swedes have the healthiest lifestyles, with low rates of obesity as well as smoking.

Americans spend a lot of time driving, so we die in auto accidents more often than people in other OECD nations, except again for Greece. The automobile death rate in the United States is about 72 percent higher than the average for other countries. Since the victims of auto accidents are often quite young, these deaths have a considerable effect on average life expectancy.

And then there's murder. America's murder rate is above the OECD average. Again, these victims often are young, so the murder rate has an outsized effect on average life expectancy.

Even indicators that are more closely linked to the effectiveness of the health care system—infant mortality, for instance—can be heavily affected by outside factors. While infant mortality in the United States is extremely low from a historical perspective, many other developed countries enjoy even lower rates. But their lower rates may be the result of behavioral differences, including drug use during pregnancy.

The WHO, rather arbitrarily, does not count all individuals equally but takes away points in its index when life expectancy varies among different racial groups. Naturally, this approach penalizes the United States with its racially mixed population. It should be obvious that the quality of the health care system is not solely responsible for all the differences across groups. African-Americans,

Table 1: Some Behavioral Differences across Countries for 2006*

Countries	Percent of population that is obese**	Percent of population over 15 that consumes tobacco	Car accident fatalities per 100,000 people	Intentional homicides per 100,000 people
Australia			8	
Austria	12.4	23.2	8	0.7
Belgium		22.0	10	
Canada	15.2	17.8	9	1.9
Czech Republic	17		10	1.3
Denmark	11.4	25.0	6	0.5
Finland	14.3	21.4	7	2.1
France	10.5	25.0	8	
Germany			6	0.9
Greece	16.4	40.0	16	1.0
Hungary			13	
Iceland	20.1	19.3	8	
Ireland	15		9	1.6
Italy	10.2	23.0	9	1.1
Japan	3.4	26.3	6	
Korea	3.5			
Luxembourg	20.4	21.0	8	
Mexico	30		12	11.0
Netherlands	11.3	31.0	5	1.0
New Zealand		20.7	10	1.1
Norway	9	24.0	14	0.7
Poland			12	1.3
Portugal	15.4	19.6	10	2.2
Slovak Republic	17.2	25.0		1.2
Spain	14.9	26.4	9	0.8
Sweden	9.6	14.5	5	1.3
Switzerland	8.1		5	0.8
Turkey		33.4		4.1
United Kingdom	24	22.0	6	1.4
United States	34.3	16.7	15	5.6
Average for Countries other than the U.S.	14.1	24.0	8.7	1.8

* Data on Obesity and Tobacco use are from the OECD. Car accident fatality data are primarily from "Road Accident Statistics in Europe," European Commission, April 27, 2007. Data on intentional homicide rates are from the Tenth United Nations Survey of Crime Trends and Operations of Criminal Justice Systems, covering the period from 2005 to 2006, United Nations Office on Drugs and Crime.
** While most of this data is for 2006, there are a few observations for obesity and tobacco use that are obtained by interpolating the values for 2005 and 2007 or for taking the 2005 values.

particularly women, are much more likely to be obese than are other racial groups. Likewise, murder is more common among African-Americans: despite making up only 13 percent of the population, African-Americans account for as much as 50 percent of murder victims.[82] Whatever accounts for these differences, they certainly are not the fault of the local doctor or hospital.

If we reject these measures, how can we evaluate the quality of the health care that Americans receive? An alternative is to compare survival rates for patients diagnosed with a particular disease. Take the eight types of cancer listed in Table 2 and their survivor rates in the United States and Europe, respectively (all survivor rates are age-adjusted). An American has a higher probability of surviving every type of cancer for five years. Men especially fare better in the United States, with a 40 percent greater likelihood of surviving for five more years.

Table 2: Five-Year Cancer Survival Rates for the U.S. and Europe (survival period data for 2000–2002, age-adjusted survival rates)

Type of Cancer	Survivor rate for the U.S.	Survivor rate for Europe	How much higher is the U.S. survivor rate?
Prostate	99.3%	77.5%	28.13%
Skin melanoma	92.3%	86.1%	7.20%
Breast	90.1%	79.0%	14.05%
Corpus uteri	82.3%	78.0%	5.51%
Colorectum	65.5%	56.2%	16.55%
Non-Hodgkin lymphoma	62.0%	54.6%	13.55%
Stomach	25.0%	24.9%	0.40%
Lung	15.7%	10.9%	44.04%
All malignancies (men)	66.3%	47.3%	40.17%
All malignancies (women)	62.9%	55.8%	12.72%

Table obtained from Samuel Preston and Jessica Ho, "Life Expectancy in the United States; Is the Health Care System at Fault?" University of Pennsylvania Population Studies Center, 2009, http://upenn.edu/egi/viewcontent.cgi?article=1012&context=psc_working_papers.

Table 3 provides a country-by-country comparison of cancer survival rates along with the WHO ranking of each country's health care system. Despite its lower WHO rating, the United States has a higher cancer survival rate than any of these other countries. For colon, prostate, cervical, and thyroid cancer, the better the WHO rating the lower the survival rate. This result suggests that the WHO measurements tell us little about the effectiveness of health care.

If you were seriously ill, what country would you want to be in? The answer is pretty clear. The American health care system is second to none. But you cannot blame the health care system for the choices that some Americans make. I can use the figures in Tables 2 and 3 to show the number of premature deaths that would result from moving the United States to a European model of health care.

Some think the solution is to alter Americans' lifestyle choices by imposing high taxes on guilty pleasures like sodas and gasoline. Fewer calories and more walking would reduce obesity. But presumably

Table 3: Five-Year Cancer Survival Rates for the U.S. and by Country in Europe (age-adjusted survival rates)

| Country | WHO Rating | Cancers for Men | | | Cancers for Women | | |
		Colon Cancer	Lung Cancer	Prostate Cancer	Breast Cancer	Cervical Cancer	Thyroid Cancer
United States	37	61.7%	12.0%	81.2%	82.8%	69.0%	95.9%
White		62.5%	12.0%	82.7%	83.9%	71.8%	95.7%
Black		52.6%	12.0%	69.2%	69.2%	55.6%	93.0%
France	1	51.8%	11.5%	61.7%	80.3%	64.1%	81.0%
Italy	3	46.9%	8.6%	47.4%	76.7%	64.0%	77.0%
England	18	41.0%	7.0%	44.3%	66.7%	62.6%	74.4%
Switzerland	20	52.3%	10.3%	71.4%	79.6%	67.2%	78.0%
Sweden	23	51.8%	8.8%	64.7%	80.6%	68.0%	83.7%
Germany	25	49.6%	8.7%	67.6%	71.7%	64.1%	77.0%
Denmark	34	39.2%	5.6%	41.0%	70.6%	64.2%	71.7%

U.S. National Cancer Institute (2003). Survival period data for 1991 to 1993. International Agency for Research on Cancer (2003). Survival period data for 1990 to 1994.

Americans drive because we like living in the suburbs and having yards. We may also drive to save time.

The attempts of President Obama and Mayor Michael Bloomberg to reduce obesity through government regulation demonstrate the importance of recognizing personal preferences. New York City has banned sugary drinks larger than sixteen ounces, and Obama tries to control what children eat in school, limiting calories and salt and making sure they get more vegetables.[83]

In theory, these regulations should make it more costly for people to consume more calories and thus should reduce obesity. The problem is the ready availability of close substitutes for the forbidden foods, which makes it difficult to change people's behavior.

If the regulation of diet can work any place, it ought to be public schools, which hold their students captive for much of the day. But even detailed regulation of school lunches and vending machines appears to have little effect. Students simply consume more sugary drinks *after* school. According to an article in the *Journal of Nutrition Education and Behavior* analyzing data for Maine, "keeping such drinks out of teenagers' reach during school hours may not be enough."[84]

Another study, published in the journal *Sociology of Education*, examined school bans of junk food and reached the same conclusion: "Whether or not junk food is available to them at school may not have much bearing on how much junk food they eat."[85]

It is really very difficult to force people to live more healthily than they want to because there are so many ways to take risks. The federal government has mandated safer cars, but research has consistently shown that such mandates lead people to drive more recklessly.[86] The number of accidents actually increases after safety features such as seat belts are mandated for cars. True, the occupants of a given car are more likely to survive an accident, but the number of accidents increases enough to offset the safety benefits. Cars strike more pedestrians and bicyclists, moreover, as the drivers become more reckless. The same goes for NASCAR drivers.[87] And bicyclists are more likely to be hit by cars when they wear safety helmets.[88] Again, the reason is that they feel safer.

The unintended effects of safety regulations show up in other areas, such as childproof medicine bottles. Childproof caps cause parents to store medicine in places that children find easier to reach, thus offsetting the benefits of the caps.[89]

Barack Obama and Michael Bloomberg may not approve the choices people make, but individuals are in the best position to make decisions about what they like to eat and where they like to live.

Quality from the Patient's Perspective

One man from Illinois lost his coverage in the middle of chemotherapy because his insurer found that he hadn't reported gallstones that he didn't even know about. They delayed his treatment, and he died because of it. Another woman from Texas was about to get a double mastectomy when her insurance company canceled her policy because she forgot to declare a case of acne. By the time she had her insurance reinstated, her breast cancer had more than doubled in size. That is heart-breaking, it is wrong, and no one should be treated that way in the United States of America.

PRESIDENT OBAMA IN HIS ADDRESS TO A JOINT SESSION OF CONGRESS ON HEALTH CARE ON SEPTEMBER 9, 2009[90]

These emotional stories proved to be powerful rhetorical weapons in the health care debate, enabling Obama to demonize the greedy insurance companies. But Democrats had to cull through millions of cases from three large insurers for a five-year period to come up with these two examples.[91] Both had become staples of Obama's speeches well before his address to Congress.[92] But neither case was as egregious as he made it out to be. Obama's repetition of these two stories well after it was clear that his facts were wrong suggests that he couldn't come up with any other good examples.

Yes, the Illinois man, Otto S. Raddatz, did lose his coverage, but Obama conveniently omitted several key facts. Raddatz's insurance was rescinded because his medical history showed that he had previously been diagnosed with an aneurysm and gallstones yet had not disclosed those diagnoses when he applied for insurance. Raddatz's doctor stated that he had never informed him of these illnesses. The Illinois attorney general's office informed the insurance company of the oversight, and the policy was reinstated within a couple of weeks.[93] Given the seriousness of Raddatz's pre-existing conditions, it seems likely that he had been informed but that his doctor claimed responsibility so that Raddatz's insurance coverage would not be affected.

More importantly, Raddatz did not die because of his insurance problem. He got the surgery he needed and lived for three and a half more years before dying of unrelated causes. Obama's misrepresentation of the facts is inexcusable because Raddatz's sister had corrected the account three months earlier in Congressional testimony.[94]

The woman from Texas, Robin Beaton, is still alive and also testified before Congress.[95] Her treatment was indeed delayed by several months, but contrary to Obama's account, the initial surgery was canceled because her doctor had listed her condition prior to the delay as "precancerous" rather than as "cancerous."[96] After the surgery was delayed because of the doctor's inaccurate report, the insurance company discovered that Beaton had failed to disclose a pre-existing irregular heartbeat and had knowingly underreported her weight. Despite all that, she still got the treatment she needed.

If Obama and his Democratic sleuths could not dig up any better horror stories, there probably aren't many to be found. Nevertheless, the public has somehow been convinced that the system is not working.

We don't have to rely on anecdotes to know whether our health care system works. Shortly before the November 2006 election, the Kaiser Family Foundation, in conjunction with *USA Today* and ABC News, released the results of a survey of health care consumers. It found that 89 percent of Americans who were insured were satisfied with "their own personal medical care." Ninety-three percent of those who had recently been seriously ill were satisfied with their medical care, as were 95 percent of those who suffered from a chronic illness.[97] Despite these extremely high rates of satisfaction, only 44 percent of the respondents were satisfied with the "overall quality of the American health care system."[98] The logical explanation for this discrepancy is that most people, despite receiving good care themselves, believe others must not be getting what they need. In particular, people are concerned about the uninsured.

Now that we are moving closer to something like Canada's single-payer, government-run health care system, we should compare recent health care satisfaction surveys in both the United States and Canada. We can then ask who is most satisfied with the access to and quality of health care: uninsured Americans, insured Americans, or Canadians.

We will use surveys taken before Obama's changes to the health care system to better gauge what Americans will be giving up. The two surveys for the United States and Canada are rare in that they ask a wide range of identical questions. The findings undermine the assumption that "universal coverage" necessarily translates into higher rates of satisfaction with a health care system.

American Satisfaction

*It is a common finding in public opinion research.
People are satisfied in the small, but dissatisfied in the
large. People are satisfied with their child's teachers
or school, but dissatisfied with schools generally. . . .
They are satisfied with their doctor or their last visit to
the hospital, but they are dissatisfied with what they
perceive is happening with medical care as a whole.
This finding is just one additional example.*[99]

HENRY AARON, SENIOR FELLOW FOR ECONOMIC STUDIES
AT THE BROOKINGS INSTITUTION, FROM A CONVERSATION
THAT I HAD WITH HIM IN JUNE 2009

A common assumption is that insurance does not work well for the seriously ill. As Al Hunt, the executive director of Bloomberg News, observes, "It's tough to find a family with a severely ill or injured child that doesn't despise its private health insurer."[100] Hunt's assertion, though, does not square with what respondents told Kaiser about their insurance carriers. Fifty percent of those who suffered a serious illness while insured rated their overall insurance coverage as "excellent" and 40 percent rated it as "good." Among those who contracted a chronic illness, 50 percent rated their coverage "excellent" and 42 percent "good."[101]

The results of other polls are similar. An ABC News/*Washington Post* poll from 2003 found that 82 percent rated their own health coverage positively, but the majority of Americans were "dissatisfied with the overall quality of health care."[102]

Actually, few services receive such high satisfaction ratings.[103] The American Customer Satisfaction Index (ACSI)[104] has conducted a large number of surveys concerning various categories of products and services. Remarkably, no other category has exceeded the 85 percent satisfaction level reported for health care in the ACSI survey in 2007.[105]

Only personal care and cleaning products achieved that same high level, with pet foods and soft drinks both tied for second, at 84 percent. The average satisfaction level across the survey's forty-three industries was 76 percent—the lowest being a 62-percent satisfaction rate for the cable and satellite television industry. Only when studying the performance of different firms can one find satisfaction levels that are higher, but it is rare. Among the 222 individual firms for which customers were surveyed, only the H. J. Heinz Company obtained a satisfaction rating as high as 90 percent. The second-highest was Amazon.com, at 88 percent.[106]

The Insured and the Uninsured

There's no real question that lack of insurance is responsible for thousands, and probably tens of thousands, of excess deaths of Americans each year. But that's not a fact Mr. Romney wants to admit, because he and his running mate want to repeal Obamacare and slash funding for Medicaid—actions that would take insurance away from some 45 million nonelderly Americans, causing thousands of people to suffer premature death.[107]

PAUL KRUGMAN, *NEW YORK TIMES*, OCTOBER 14, 2012

It's a common assumption that an uninsured person has no access to health care. Indeed, Senate Majority Leader Harry Reid's claim that "there are 45 million Americans without health care" is typical.[108] Paul Krugman implies the same thing, and if there were any doubt what he meant, his column is titled "Death by Ideology."[109]

Table 4: Insurance and Income Percent Uninsured by Income			
Income	Insured	Not insured	Percentage of population in survey with that level of income
Less than $20,000	64.5	35.5	16.4
$20,000–$35,000	78.8	21.2	17.3
$35,000–$50,000	85.3	14.7	17.8
$50,000–$75,000	94.6	5.4	17.4
$75,000–$100,000	97.0	3	13.0
Over $100,000	98.9	1.1	14.9
Refused to answer	86.2	13.8	3.1
Overall incomes	86.9	13.1	100

Source: Kaiser Family Foundation health care poll, conducted September 7–12, 2006

Senator Reid should have said that forty-five million Americans do not have health *insurance*. Many uninsured Americans do see a doctor and get other forms of health care, often paying for it out of pocket, and there are many sources of free health care for those who have trouble paying. In fact, estimates indicate that the uninsured spend, on average, 60 percent of what the insured spend on health care.[110]

Yet 52 percent of the insured Americans surveyed by Kaiser believe that becoming uninsured poses a "critical problem," 36 percent view the threat of losing their insurance as "serious but not critical," and another 7 percent see it as a "problem but not serious."[111] Only 4 percent view loss of insurance as "not much of a problem."

How many people are uninsured? How satisfied are they? According to the Kaiser Family Foundation survey, 13 percent of U.S. residents (both legal and illegal) were uninsured in 2006.[112] Having insurance is closely related to level of income. As Table 4 shows, over a third—35.5 percent—of households earning less than $20,000 a year are uninsured. The rate falls to 21.2 percent for the

	2006 Kaiser Family Foundation Survey		2003 ABC News/*Washington Post* Survey	
Please tell me whether you are very satisfied, somewhat satisfied, somewhat dissatisfied, or very dissatisfied with:	Percentage who are very dissatisfied	Percentage who are either dissatisfied or very dissatisfied	Percentage who are very dissatisfied	Percentage who are either somewhat dissatisfied or very dissatisfied
The quality of the health care you receive?	2.3	3.9	2.5	4.9
Your health care costs, including both expenses not covered by insurance, and the cost of your insurance, if any?	7.8	10.3	7.9	10.95
Your ability to get a doctor's appointment when you want one?	2.9	5.5	3.2	5.5
Your ability to see top-quality medical specialists, if you ever need one?	4	5.2	4	7.4
Your ability to get the latest, most sophisticated medical treatments?	4.6	5.1	2.9	6.6
The quality of communication with your doctor?	1.3	3.0		
Your ability to get emergency medical care?	3.8	5.4		
Your ability to get non-emergency medical treatments without having to wait?	4.2	7.2		

**Table 5: The Uninsured
Percentage of U.S. Residents Who Are Both without Health
Insurance and Dissatisfied with Their Medical Care**

Sources: Kaiser Family Foundation health care poll, conducted September 7–12, 2006, and ABC News/*Washington Post* poll, conducted October 9–13, 2003.

$20,000–$35,000 bracket and goes down to 14.7 percent for the $35,000–$50,000 bracket. Beyond $50,000, the problem is miniscule as the percentage of uninsured falls to low single-digits.

Only 2.3 percent of U.S. residents are *both* uninsured and very dissatisfied with the health care they receive, as indicated in Table 5.[113]

The percentage that is uninsured and somewhat dissatisfied is 3.9 percent. The earlier (2003) ABC News/*Washington Post* poll showed similar results.[114]

The surveys indicate that only a very small percentage of U.S. residents who are uninsured have trouble getting a doctor's appointment, seeing top-quality medical specialists, receiving the most sophisticated medical treatments, or getting emergency or non-emergency medical care. Nor do physicians appear to treat their uninsured patients differently from their insured patients—only 1.3 percent of Americans were both uninsured and very dissatisfied with their communication with their doctors.

The only area in which the majority of the uninsured are very dissatisfied with their care is cost. Yet, those costs do not seem to be so large as to cause the uninsured to be dissatisfied with the overall quality of their care.

What about the Canadian System?

I suspect that we're going to have continued vigorous debate. I suspect that you Canadians will continue to get dragged in by those who oppose reform, even though I've said nothing about Canadian health care reform. I do not find Canadians particularly scary, but I guess some of the opponents of reform think that they make a good boogeyman. I think that's a mistake.

PRESIDENT OBAMA, AUGUST 10, 2009[115]

Through regulation and the gradual unraveling of our insurance system, Obamacare has put the United States on the path to a government-run health care system like those in so many other countries. Do they run better? Canada, because of its similarity to the United States, provides the best comparison.

Twenty months after Kaiser surveyed Americans, the Institute for Policy Innovation sponsored a similar study of Canadians.[116] The questions about the quality of the heath care system and the quality of individuals' treatment are virtually identical, except that the Canadians were also asked about the speed with which they were able to obtain treatment. (The Kaiser survey did not ask about speed of treatment, an omission that probably reflects Americans' assumption that they will not have to wait in a queue for health care.)

Table 6 on page 41 allows us to compare how U.S. residents and Canadians rate the quality of their medical care. Canadian satisfaction levels are always below those of all U.S. residents, whether you look at how many say that they are "very satisfied" or satisfied (either "very" or "somewhat" satisfied). There are eight concerns:

- "The quality of the health care you receive."
- "Your ability to get a doctor's appointment when you want one."
- "Your ability to see top-quality medical specialists, if you ever need one."
- "Your ability to get the latest, most sophisticated medical treatments."
- "The quality of communication with your doctor."
- "Your ability to get emergency medical care."
- "Your ability to get non-emergency medical treatments without having to wait."
- "Your ability to see top-quality medical specialists, if you ever need one quickly."

Let's consider the first seven questions, which were identical in the U.S. and Canadian surveys. The results are striking. The most likely answer of insured U.S. residents to every question is "very satisfied." For every question, substantially fewer Canadians are "very satisfied" with their health care than insured U.S. residents. Actually, the Canadians' answers are indistinguishable from those of *uninsured* U.S. residents.

For those who are either "very" or "somewhat" satisfied, the differences are less striking but still clear. Canadians are substantially happier than U.S. residents in only two areas. On the other hand, insured U.S. residents are happier than Canadians in five areas.

The eighth and final question reinforces this pattern. Since the Kaiser survey did not ask U.S. residents if they were able to get access to top-quality medical specialists quickly, the best we can do is to compare the Canadian answers to question 8 with the U.S. answers to question 3, which is the same question, though it does not qualify for speed. With that comparison, Canadians are again much closer to uninsured U.S. residents than they are to the insured.

What Types of People Are Happiest with Their Health Care?

When we try to assess the satisfaction of different groups of people—the insured and the uninsured, Canadians and Americans—we need to make sure that we are comparing apples with apples. If the wealthy were much more satisfied with their health care than the poor, for example, our conclusion that the uninsured are as satisfied as the insured might be invalid. So I have accounted for such demographic differences as level of education, age, marital status, income, sex, political views, race, and geography.[117]

U.S. residents are strikingly uniform in their satisfaction with the health care they receive. Blacks are just as satisfied as whites—and this continues to hold true if we refine the divisions and compare blacks and whites with insurance or blacks and whites without

	United States			Canada	Are the differences significant?	
Table 6: Who Are Happier with Their Health Care? U.S. versus Canada						
	Insured	Uninsured	Total	Total	Comparing U.S. uninsured to Canadians	Comparing U.S. insured to Canadians
(1) How satisfied are you with the quality of the health care you receive?						
Very satisfied	56%	28%	52%	39%	No	Yes
Total Satisfied	93%	62%	89%	86%	Yes	No
(2) How satisfied are you with your ability to get a doctor's appointment when you want one?						
Very satisfied	55%	30%	51%	33%	No	Yes
Total Satisfied	87%	57%	82%	68%	No	Yes
(3) How satisfied are you with your ability to see top-quality medical specialists, if you ever need one?						
Very satisfied	50%	14%	45%	17%	No	Yes
Total Satisfied	84%	44%	79%	58%	No	Yes
(4) How satisfied are you with your ability to get the latest, most sophisticated medical treatments?						
Very satisfied	42%	11%	38%	16%	No	Yes
Total Satisfied	83%	47%	78%	58%	No	Yes
(5) How satisfied are you with the quality of communication with your doctor?						
Very satisfied	59%	36%	56%	48%	No	Yes
Total Satisfied	90%	68%	87%	82%	No	No
(6) How satisfied are you with your ability to get emergency medical care?						
Very satisfied	55%	20%	50%	26%	No	Yes
Total Satisfied	88%	54%	83%	64%	No	Yes
(7) How satisfied are you with your ability to get non-emergency medical treatments without having to wait?						
Very satisfied	39%	17%	36%	23%	No	Yes
Total Satisfied	77%	41%	72%	60%	Yes	Yes
(8) How satisfied are you with your ability to see top-quality medical specialists, if you ever need one quickly? Since this question wasn't asked of the Americans, the Canadian answers are compared to those provided by Americans for question #3.						
Very satisfied				14%	No	Yes
Total Satisfied				45%	No	Yes
Unweighted N	1200			1022		

Sources: Kaiser Family Foundation health care poll, conducted September 7–12, 2006; Institute for Policy Innovation poll, conducted May 8–13, 2008. The notion of statistical significance here is defined as whether it is greater than at the 5-percent level for a two-tailed t-test.

insurance. Those with incomes greater than $100,000 have similar levels of satisfaction to those making less than $20,000.

Differences in level of education, marital status, sex, or political beliefs have little effect on people's satisfaction with health care. Those who dropped out of school before high school and those who had some high school are as satisfied as those who graduated from college. Liberals are only very slightly less contented than conservatives. The only factor that accounts for significant differences in satisfaction is age, and here there is no consistent pattern. Americans over seventy are happier with their health care than Americans in their thirties or fifties, but they are not happier than those in the twenties, forties, or sixties.

The same general uniformity is seen among Canadians. The one exception is geography. Canadians living in Manitoba are the most satisfied with their health care, followed by those in British Columbia. The least satisfied Canadians are those who live in the eastern provinces of Newfoundland and Prince Edward Island. Canadians living in Manitoba are five and a half times more likely to be satisfied with their health care than those living on Prince Edward Island.

The conclusion to be drawn is that residents of the United States have been better off with respect to health care than Canadians. As the U.S. system deteriorates under Obamacare, we may want to remember this when we debate the next round of fixes.[118]

American Health Care Isn't So Bad after All

Few people in the United States are *both* uninsured and dissatisfied with the health care they receive. This is not to deny that many of the uninsured face problems of cost and access when seeking medical care, especially if it is very expensive. But those problems are less pervasive than one might assume, affecting only 2 to 4 percent of

the population. The vast majority of U.S. residents, insured and uninsured, enjoy timely access to quality care with which they are satisfied.

Many people concede that Canadian-style national health insurance creates access problems and waiting lines, but they assume
that the advantage of universal coverage is worth the tradeoff. Measurements of satisfaction call that assumption into question. Canadians have been experiencing satisfaction levels much closer to those
of uninsured U.S. residents.

The Cost of the Uninsured

Virtually every hospital in the country is required to treat people
who need care regardless of their ability to pay.[119] There is a cost, of
course, for this "free" care, and hospitals have to cover it by charging
their paying patients more. The cost of care for the indigent is a big
problem for hospitals in poor neighborhoods. But do the uninsured
really impose a heavy burden on the American health care system
as a whole? Lots of people think so. If everyone were insured, they
argue, health care costs would go down substantially for the rest of
us. Obama himself has frequently made this argument.

The annual cost of medical care for the indigent, the administration tells us, is $43 billion. That figure, which comes from the liberal
advocacy group Families USA,[120] rests on faulty assumptions. Most
of the uninsured not only pay for their own care but pay *more* for it,
because they don't receive the discounted prices negotiated by insurance companies.[121] The Families USA estimate also prorates ability
to pay based on the portion of the year that someone is uninsured.
But people often wait until they are insured before they undergo
expensive medical procedures.[122]

The Kaiser Family Foundation, using the Department of Health
and Human Services' Medical Expenditure Panel Survey, puts the

cost of indigent care closer to $8 billion, just one-third of one percent of total annual health care expenditures in the United States.[123] The 215 economists who filed an amicus brief with the Supreme Court in 2012 estimated the cost of the uninsured to hospitals at a maximum of $16 billion.[124]

Ironically, federal involvement in health care drives up costs far more than the uninsured do. Medicare and Medicaid already pay hospitals and doctors less than their costs, forcing them to charge private patients more. Studying data from California, Stanford's Dan Kessler finds that the cost-shifting from government insurance programs is already eight times larger than the costs of the uninsured.[125] Obamacare's cuts to Medicare—$716 billion over the next decade—will make that gap even bigger.

The burden that the uninsured impose on the health care system is relatively light primarily because most of them are young people who are in good health and only temporarily uninsured. Just before Obama became president, two-thirds of the uninsured were between eighteen and thirty-four years old.[126] According to the Congressional Budget Office, 86 percent of them reported that they were in good or excellent health.[127]

About 30 percent of the uninsured are eligible for Medicaid, which provides coverage for the poor, but have not enrolled. (Pre-existing conditions do not exclude someone from Medicaid.) They have not enrolled because they don't want to pay Medicaid's small monthly premium. As a result, many who are eligible for Medicaid wait to enroll until they need care. These people are thus effectively insured at all times, even when they are not formally enrolled in the program, and we can exclude them from our calculations. Nearly 70 percent of the remaining uninsured people only lack insurance for less than four months. Many of these temporarily uninsured are simply switching jobs and do not get coverage because they are in good health.

What about the uninsured who are not poor enough to qualify for Medicaid? Most are not in dire financial straits. After all, almost 60 percent of the uninsured have household incomes of more than $50,000.

True, there is a group of people who are bordering on poor but not eligible for Medicaid, but the group is relatively small. Many (if not most) of those people are most likely illegal immigrants.

The truly uninsured are largely young people who can afford insurance but who voluntarily go without it as they move between jobs. They are overwhelmingly uninsured by choice and only for a short time.

Other Excuses for Obamacare

The Threat of Monopoly

Consumers do better when there is choice and competition.... Unfortunately, in 34 states, 75 percent of the insurance market is controlled by five or fewer companies. In Alabama, almost 90 percent is controlled by just one company. Without competition, the price of insurance goes up and the quality goes down....
[A]n additional step we can take to keep insurance companies honest is by making a not-for-profit public option available in the insurance exchange....

PRESIDENT OBAMA IN HIS ADDRESS TO
A JOINT SESSION OF CONGRESS ON HEALTH CARE
ON SEPTEMBER 9, 2009

The greed of insurance companies and doctors has been a recurring theme not only of Obama but also of most advocates of Obamacare. Shortly before the crucial vote in Congress, the White House blog ranted, "the insurers' monopoly is so strong that they can continue to jack up rates as much as they like."[128] In the *New York Times* that same month, Paul Krugman attacked what he calls the "vileness" of profit-driven insurance companies.

These arguments were echoed in Congress, resulting in legislation going beyond the Obamacare provisions. Ostensibly to promote competition, the then Democratically-controlled House passed a bill in 2010 to exclude health insurance from the partial antitrust exemption for the "business of insurance."[129] Obama made eliminating the antitrust exemption a top priority as a way to encourage "more competition."[130]

The partial antitrust exemption for insurance companies did not originate as a favor for special interests.[131] In fact, the exemption permits small insurers and employers to share data in forecasting the cost of health benefits. The repeal of the exemption would jeopardize such activity and thus make it more difficult for smaller providers to participate in a market.

Driving out the little guy is what Obamacare is all about. The law is designed to clear the way for a government takeover. The tidal wave of regulations that accompany Obamacare threatens to overwhelm small businesses. Even Jonathan Gruber estimates that most small employers will face higher premiums as a result of the law.[132] A 2011 survey of 1,300 employers by the consulting firm McKinsey found that up to 30 percent of employers are thinking of dropping health insurance coverage when the new regulations start in 2014.[133] A smaller survey of three hundred business owners in October 2012 found that 24 percent were planning to drop coverage, while 39 percent were uncertain.[134] Obama's most famous promise about health care reform looks increasingly empty:

> If you like your health care plan, you keep your health care plan. Nobody is going to force you to leave your health care plan. If you like your doctor, you keep seeing your doctor. I don't want government bureaucrats meddling in your health care. [135]

During the debate over Obamacare, the Democrats threw around a lot of "facts." We have since learned that many of them were simply concoctions based on opinion polls, as Ron Suskind carefully details in *Confidence Men*. "New polling," he writes, "showed that, unlike the debacle of the 1990s, the principal villain in the 2000s was no longer seen as government bureaucracy, but rather insurance profiteering."[136] Obama's top pollster, Joel Benenson, confirmed as much. The administration's goal, he said, was to get people to "think the insurance companies have been the villains here, not the government."[137]

Accounts by Suskind, confirmed by former Obama advisor Peter Dreier, describe how the administration picked the theme of insurance companies as villains.[138] Obama was friendly to the insurance companies at first and struck a "grand bargain" with them. In exchange for not opposing additional regulations, health insurance companies would get more customers at taxpayer expense. But Obamacare's emerging details—its insurance mandate, a tax on certain employer premium payments, the looting of Medicare— began to alienate different groups, even in Obama's base. The White House responded by reneging on the grand bargain. Suskind writes, "Once the White House abandoned that [grand bargain]—its strongest bipartisan stance—the insurers became a convenient scapegoat."[139] The insurance companies, facing "some combination of fear or bribery," agreed to give Obama what he wanted—but when Obama changed the deal and decided to move even farther to the left politically, he decided to make them the villains.[140]

Obama's remarks about competition illustrate how the themes in the health care debate reflected polls rather than facts. The president worked to reinforce various prejudices—that there's little competition among health insurance companies, for example, and that it's important to take the profit motive out of the health insurance business. These are simply myths based on a misinterpretation of the data. In reality, non-profit insurers are so abundant that the largest insurer in virtually every state is a non-profit.

Obama's carefully crafted speeches about competition and greed went over well. Even some moderate Republicans, like Olympia Snowe of Maine, fell for it: "There is a serious problem with the lack of competition among insurers," the senator declared. "The impact on the consumer is significant."[141]

To support its claims about the high "concentration" in the insurance industry, the administration pointed to a 2008 study by the American Medical Association that is easily misinterpreted.[142] It appears to show that one or two insurance companies dominate the market in each state. But the AMA figures omit roughly half of the insurance market—the employer-provided insurance, that is, "self-insured" or "self-funded" plans.

There is much confusion about such plans. Self-insured companies usually hire a so-called third-party administrator, which is often an insurance company, to manage their plan. An employee may be given a card bearing the name of an insurance company, but that company is only the administrator, not the insurer.

Table 7 summarizes the American Medical Association report.

Table 7: States with Most Concentrated "Full" Insurance Market for 15 Most Concentrated States

State	Company with largest share of "full" insurance market	Largest firm's share of "full" insurance market	Company with second-largest share of "full" insurance market	Second-largest firm's share of "full" insurance market	2 Largest firms' combined share of "full" insurance market
(*Bold italics* indicates non-profit organization)					
Hawaii	***Blue Cross Blue Shield HI***	78%	Kaiser Permanente	20%	98%
Rhode Island	***Blue Cross Blue Shield RI***	79%	United Health Group Inc.	16%	95%
Alaska	***Premera Blue Cross***	60%	Aetna Inc.	35%	95%
Vermont	***Blue Cross Blue Shield VT***	77%	CIGNA Corp.	13%	90%
Alabama	***Blue Cross Blue Shield AL***	83%	Health Choice	5%	88%
Maine	WellPoint, Inc.	78%	Aetna Inc.	10%	88%
Montana	***Blue Cross Blue Shield MT***	75%	New West Health Services	10%	85%
Wyoming	***Blue Cross Blue Shield WY***	70%	United Health Group Inc.	15%	85%
Arkansas	***Blue Cross Blue Shield AR***	75%	United Health Group Inc.	6%	81%
Iowa	***Wellmark Blue Cross Blue Shield***	71%	United Health Group Inc.	9%	80%
Missouri	WellPoint, Inc.	68%	United Health Group Inc.	11%	79%
Minnesota	***Blue Cross Blue Shield MN***	50%	Medica	26%	76%
South Carolina	***Blue Cross Blue Shield SC***	66%	CIGNA Corp.	9%	75%
Indiana	WellPoint, Inc.	60%	M*Plan (Health Care Group)	15%	75%

These numbers are of limited use, as they describe less than half of the health insurance market. For most employees, their employer, not an insurance company, pays for any bad health outcomes. According to the federal Agency for Healthcare Research and Quality

(Department of Health and Human Services), employers are the insurer for 55 percent of all employees.[143]

Let's look at Maine, Senator Snowe's home state. According to the AMA, the two largest insurance companies appear to control 88 percent of the market, with WellPoint, Inc. making up most of that—78 percent. But again, these numbers refer only to plans insured, not merely administered, by insurance companies. The AMA figures do not include the majority of people in Maine—52.1 percent—who receive their insurance through "self-insuring" or "self-funding" employers.

In Maine, therefore, WellPoint is not nearly as dominant as the AMA figures suggest. It provides primary, or "full," insurance, to 78 percent of the market *not covered by self-insurers*. WellPoint's share of the entire market in Maine is only 37.1 percent. That sounds a lot less impressive. The second-largest insurance company in Maine, Aetna, controls a mere 4.8 percent of the total market. The two largest insurance companies account for 41.9 percent of the total market.

The situation in all the other states is similar. Even in the fifteen states with the most concentrated markets, those detailed in Table 7, 57 percent of the insured population, on average, participates in an employer-insured plan.

Obama's contention that "almost 90 percent" of the health insurance market in Alabama "is controlled by just one company" is terribly misleading. The accurate figure is only 36 percent. And the second-largest company has just 2.1 percent of the market.[144] (The president even fudged the AMA numbers, generously rounding up from the AMA's actual figure of 83 percent.)

Obama and his supporters also conveniently neglected to mention that the largest insurance company in virtually every state is the non-profit Blue Cross Blue Shield. And Blue Cross Blue Shield's operations are of course non-profit organizations. (See Table 7, with

FIGURE 2

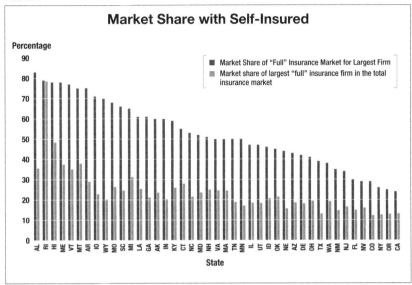

non-profits marked in bold italics.) In only a few states, such as Maine, is the largest one a for-profit firm.

So what about President Obama's claim that in the thirty-four most concentrated states, 75 percent of the insurance market is controlled by five or fewer companies? Since self-insured firms cover 57 percent of people insured in those states, the actual total market share for the largest five firms is only 32 percent. Figure 2 illustrates how dramatically this consideration alters the numbers for each state.[145]

Despite these facts, the Obama administration has sold the idea that the health insurance market is dominated by a few greedy insurance companies. Indeed, the appeal of a government insurance option in Obamacare was that it would take profit out of the picture.[146]

Ironically enough, for all the talk about "market concentration" in the health insurance business, Obamacare will reduce the number of insurance carriers. The rules eliminate competition among differing levels of coverage and enforce uniformity among plans. When every insurance company's plan is identical, fewer insurance companies will survive.

How Much Do Americans Really Spend on Health Care?

*Then there's the problem of rising costs. We spend one
and a half times more per person on health care than
any other country.... [H]ealth care represents one-sixth
of our economy.... Everyone in this room knows what
will happen if we do nothing. Our deficit will grow.
More families will go bankrupt. More businesses will
close. More Americans will lose their coverage when
they are sick and need it most. And more will die as a
result.* [147]

PRESIDENT OBAMA IN HIS ADDRESS TO A JOINT SESSION
OF CONGRESS ON HEALTH CARE ON SEPTEMBER 9, 2009

Obama's above pronouncement that we spend too much money on health care took place when he launched the health care debate in 2009. These higher costs are supposedly the result of our lack of universal coverage. Paul Krugman chimed in, "The United States is the only advanced nation without universal health care, and it also has by far the world's highest health care costs." To the Nobel-winning economist, it was clear that "this combination of broader coverage and cost control is no accident: It has long been clear to health-policy experts that these concerns go hand in hand."[148]

We have seen that Americans get a lot for their health care dollars. Many of the expenditures that the central planners want to cut have produced important medical benefits. Some of those expenditures—what we spend on drugs, for example—have financed research that has benefited people around the world.

You frequently hear that one-sixth of the nation's income is spent on health care. Obama relies on a calculation that in 2007, $2.2 trillion, in an economy of almost $14 trillion, was spent on health care.[149] As with many of the president's statistics, there are problems with this figure. The health care costs cited in the Obamacare debate have been inflated by double counting and further distorted by price controls. The recent growth in U.S. health care expenditures, moreover, has actually been less than in countries where the government pays for most health care.

The $2.2 trillion figure includes not only direct spending by insurance companies, individuals, and the government on health care, but also spending on buildings and medical equipment for doctors and hospitals. It should be obvious that you cannot count both the money paid for an MRI procedure and the money that the hospital paid for the MRI machine. Payments for MRI scans typically cover the cost of the machinery.

According to Dr. Joseph Antos of the American Enterprise Institute, the figure of $2.2 trillion includes all the money "going into the hands of the major actors in the health sector (providers, suppliers, insurers). It is not a measure of the share of the economy going to services actually produced during the year."[150]

There are also accounting problems with the money spent on research. The total health care figure includes the entire budget of the National Institutes of Health and a large percentage of the budget of the National Science Foundation. But much of this money has nothing to do with medical research, and some is recouped through the products the research creates. Some of NIH money goes to the general operations of various universities. Professor Bob Hansen of Dartmouth's Tuck School of Business confirmed for me that "'overhead' rates on grants from places like the NIH [run] close to 50 percent, [and] there is also a lot of funding of general university overhead in the NIH budget. Cross-country comparisons are rendered problematic when we realize that other countries fund their universities through direct payment rather than through the U.S.'s reliance on 'indirects.'"

All this double counting adds up to about $363 billion. The portion of America's GDP going to health care turns out to be about one-eighth, or 13 percent, and the gap with other countries no longer seems as large. France, for instance, spends about 11 percent of its GDP on health care.

The gap with other countries gets even smaller when one takes into account the price controls that many of them impose on products such as pharmaceuticals. Americans spend almost twice on drugs per person than the world average. U.S. drug companies spend vast sums to develop new drugs, and Americans pay market prices for them. Once developed, drugs are reasonably inexpensive to produce. Because of price controls in foreign countries, the prices there often cover only the cost of manufacturing and distribution. Foreign customers get a "free ride" courtesy of the American consumer, who funds research that saves lives around the world.

The debate about drug prices in the United States is perennial, but over the last few years the threat from Obamacare has caused American pharmaceutical companies to slash their research budgets. If Americans spent as much for drugs as other countries do, we could reduce our health care expenditures by another percentage point. But there is a real cost to this. Companies will not develop new drugs unless they can recoup the massive costs of research and regulatory approval. Lives will be lost around the world. Americans might feel justifiably annoyed for picking up this tab for the rest of the world, but instead of putting price controls on our own drugs, the solution might be to get rid of government regulation in other countries.

Are medical costs in the United States in fact out of control? Data collected by the OECD are revealing.[151] During the decade from 1998 to 2007, per capita health care expenditures in the United States rose an average of 7.2 percent per year. In the twenty-four other countries for which data were available, the average yearly increase was 8.2 percent. In fourteen of those countries, health care costs in that decade rose more than in the United States. A similar pattern occurs over the last twenty years.

In the average OECD country, the government accounted for 72 percent of all health care expenditures in 2007. At 45 percent, the United States is tied for the lowest share. The government's share of health care spending was more than 80 percent in about a third of the countries. Making the United States more like other countries and giving the government an even greater role does not seem like a promising way to reduce costs. Indeed, the greater the government's share of health care expenditures, the more medical costs rise. Using all the data available from 1960 to 2007 and accounting for per capita income as well as other factors, each 1 percent increase in a government's share of health care expenditures increases health care expenditures by about 0.4 percent.[152]

Behind all the debate over rising health care costs is a question that everyone ignores—why should we really care? As Americans get wealthier, why should they avoid spending more on bigger houses or nicer cars or better health care? Why not be happy that we can now afford hip replacements in old age and diagnose cancer earlier? In recent years Americans have spent more money on housing than on health care, a fact that by itself tells us nothing about whether we spend too much on housing.

Finally, Obamacare would reduce costs by the brute-force method. Over the next decade, Medicare payments to health care providers will be cut by $716 billion.[153] Supporters of those cuts say that they will merely "improve efficiency," and during the 2012 presidential campaign various "fact checkers" from National Public Radio and the *Washington Post* insisted that those cuts would not affect quality.[154] After all, as FactCheck.org explained, Obamacare "Stipulates That Guaranteed Medicare Benefits Won't Be Reduced."[155]

And if the president signs a law forbidding the sun to set, it will not set.

Obamacare cuts payments to providers but demands that they provide the same level of service. Medicare is already reimbursing less than their costs. The result is the cost shifting that we discussed earlier.

Unfortunately, not even Barack Obama can repeal the law that you get what you pay for. More doctors will decline new Medicare patients. And the doctors most likely to do so are the better ones. Even if patients somehow get the treatment they got previously, they'll have fewer doctors to choose from and the quality will be lower.

How the government will allocate Medicare money between hospitals under the new rules is downright scary. A provision that took effect in October 2012 punishes about two-thirds of hospitals based on their readmission rates.[156] Readmissions are costly—about $17.5 billion a year, so simply reducing readmissions should save money. But what if the alternative to readmission is death? Is readmission or death a better measure of the quality of medical care?

Riskier medical cases, moreover, involve higher readmission rates. The best hospitals often take the riskiest cases. Despite their high quality, they therefore have higher readmission rates. Do we really want to penalize the best hospitals because they take difficult cases?

Will Replacing Private Health Insurance with Government Insurance Lower Costs?

[F]orcing more Medicare recipients away from a system with low administrative costs and strong purchasing power [by implementing Republican policies] to one where there is excessive overhead costs and profits, marketing, and selection of a lower-cost pool is likely to add to our overall national health care costs. [157]

GENE SPERLING, DIRECTOR OF PRESIDENT OBAMA'S NATIONAL ECONOMIC COUNCIL, APRIL 17, 2012

President Obama has argued that private insurance is more expensive than government insurance because private insurers have to make a profit.[158] In the real world, however, the profit motive drives down costs, including administrative costs. That's why non-profit companies, despite huge tax subsidies, sell very few goods or services. Profits motivate companies to produce better products at a lower cost. But Obama thinks that the experts in Washington can figure out better ways to run things.

What about Obama's frequent claim that Medicare had lower administrative costs than private insurance plans?[159] According to both the CBO and various discussions in the media, Medicare's administrative costs—all the money spent on everything other than patient care—amount to less than 2 percent of total expenditures.[160] By contrast, administrative costs for private insurance companies—including advertising and profits—are about 12 percent.[161] Few experts, however, consider this a valid comparison, since much of Medicare's work is handled through other government agencies.[162]

For example, the IRS collects Medicare premiums. The 2-percent figure also does not include Medicare's billing costs, which (ironically enough) are contracted out to private insurers, who handle the paperwork less expensively than the government could do. Other basic costs are left out of the calculation. Medicare's overhead, for example, does not include the costs of the government buildings from which it operates.[163]

And then there's fraud. It is estimated that one out of every ten dollars of Medicare benefits involves fraud, several times the estimates for the private sector.[164] Medicare does not scrutinize providers' bills or raise questions about discrepancies.[165] In many cases, Medicare is charged for services that are never provided. The system simply pays the claims as they come in. The Inspector General of the Department of Health and Human Services polices cases of "massive fraud."[166] It's true that not spending money on fraud prevention is a savings of some sort, but it's more than offset by the cost of fraud.[167]

Several studies show that when all costs are included, Medicare costs more, not less, to administer. Ben Zycher of the Manhattan Institute estimates Medicare's true administrative costs are "about double the net cost of private health insurance."[168]

Conclusion

Under Obamacare, the type of insurance you have, where you will get it, and what you will pay will be determined not by you and your employer but by the government. Obama's promise that you could keep your health care plan and doctor if you wanted to turned out to be like so many of his other promises. Without that promise, it is unlikely that his health care law would have passed. The ability to be treated by the doctor of your choice is just one of the fundamental freedoms that Americans will lose if Obamacare is not repealed.

But Americans will lose much more than choice. People will die sooner. The innovation that makes the American health care system the envy of the world will be strangled. History gives us no reason to think that government bureaucrats will be any better at running our health care system than they have been at running any other business.

The outright repeal of Obamacare may now be out of reach, but we will have opportunities to mitigate its damage.

CHAPTER TWO

MORE STIMULUS, FEWER JOBS AND LOWER WAGES

What Was Promised

Governor Romney: *Government does not create jobs.*
Government does not create jobs.

President Obama: *I think a lot of this campaign,*
maybe over the last four years, has been devoted to this
notion that I think government creates jobs, that that
somehow is the answer. That's not what I believe.
I believe that the free enterprise system is the greatest
engine of prosperity the world's ever known.

<small>SECOND PRESIDENTIAL DEBATE, OCTOBER 16, 2012[1]</small>

Obama's praise of the free market may have pleased voters, but it disguised what he genuinely believes. Over and over again, in other contexts, he has denigrated the free market, blaming it for virtually everything that goes wrong. Speaking in Osawatomie, Kansas, a year before his reelection, he said,

> "The market will take care of everything," they tell us. If we just cut more regulations and cut more taxes—especially for the wealthy—our economy will grow stronger. Sure, they say, there will be winners and losers. But if the winners do really well, then jobs and prosperity will eventually trickle down to everybody else....
>
> But here's the problem: It doesn't work. It has never worked. (Applause.) It didn't work when it was tried in the decade before the Great Depression. It's not what led to the incredible postwar booms of the '50s and '60s. And it didn't work when we tried it during the last decade. (Applause.) I mean, understand, it's not as if we haven't tried this theory.[2]

President Obama's reluctance to embrace big government in the weeks before the last election was understandable. The gap between what he promised Americans in 2008 and what he delivered in his first term could hardly be bigger. Americans have also grown more skeptical about what government can do. At the time of the 2008 election, voters said by a margin of 51 to 43 percent, "Government should do more to solve problems," but by the 2012 election, those figures had flipped.[3] Instead of confessing that his original policies were mistaken, however, Obama simply denied that his policies relied on government intervention.

As a candidate in 2008, Obama expressed alarm at how much the federal government was spending. In the third presidential debate, less than three weeks before the election, he insisted,

"[T]here is no doubt that we've been living beyond our means and we're going to have to make some adjustments. Now, what I've done throughout this campaign is to propose a net spending cut."[4]

Obama had indeed been promising spending cuts. He assured voters in his second debate with John McCain, "[W]e're going to have to make some investments, but we've also got to make spending cuts. And what I've proposed, you'll hear Senator McCain say, well, he's proposing a whole bunch of new spending, but actually I'm cutting more than I'm spending so that it will be a net spending cut."[5]

We all know what those promises were worth. Obama racked up the largest increases in government spending (even adjusted for inflation) and the largest deficits (including those during World War II) in history. So much for his "net spending cut."[6]

Obama's concern about spending evaporated just a week after he won the presidency, when he started talking about a $500 billion stimulus.[7] Two weeks after the election, Lawrence Summers, his chief economic advisor, told the Associated Press that the amount should be between $500 and $700 billion.[8] The stimulus act that was eventually passed in February 2009 came to $825 billion.[9]

There was no economic news in the week or two after the election to justify Obama's radical change in fiscal policy. The unemployment rate for October, announced three days after the election, was 6.5 percent—not great, but not particularly bad if the country was, as Obama constantly insisted, suffering "the worst economic crisis since the Great Depression."[10]

Misreading the Economy

With the help of Democratic supermajorities in both houses of Congress, Obama pushed through five major "jobs" bills in his first two years. The centerpiece was the $825 billion "stimulus," which was supposed to "create or save" 4.1 million jobs.[11] A string of smaller measures followed: the $38 billion "Hiring Incentives to Restore Employment (HIRE) Act of 2010," which was estimated to create 300,000 jobs, and the $26 billion "Public Sector Jobs Bill of 2010," which was promised to create or save another 300,000 jobs.[12] In addition there was the $42 billion "Small Business Jobs Act of 2010," which was supposed to create or save an additional 500,000 jobs.[13] Finally, the "Disaster Relief and Summer Jobs Act of 2010," a hodge-podge of items, such as $24 billion to help keep teachers, police, and firefighters employed during the recession and $600 million to create 300,000 jobs for youth ages sixteen to twenty-four.[14] The fruit of all this spending, Obama promised, would be over five and a half million jobs created or saved.[15]

Reality, unfortunately, did not keep up with the president's promises. There were only 194,000 more jobs in the United States in October 2012 than when Obama became president. Simply to keep up with the growth in population, there ought to have been about 5.7 million additional jobs in that period.[16]

The best defense of his record that President Obama can offer is that things could have been worse. Without his heavy spending, we *might* have lost 11.3 million jobs. In Obama's world of hypotheticals, no one can ever prove him wrong. Remarkably, he persuaded enough voters with this argument to win reelection.

Optimism about Obama's stimulus plans abounded even before he was sworn into office. Two high-ranking economists in the incoming administration—Christina Romer, the head of the Council of Economic Advisers, and Jared Bernstein, the chief economic advisor to Joseph Biden—predicted that unemployment would peak in late summer 2009 at 7.9 percent and gradually fall to 5.3 percent by October 2012 (Figure 1). Without the stimulus, they warned, unemployment would stay at 9 percent during most of 2010 and stay above

FIGURE 1

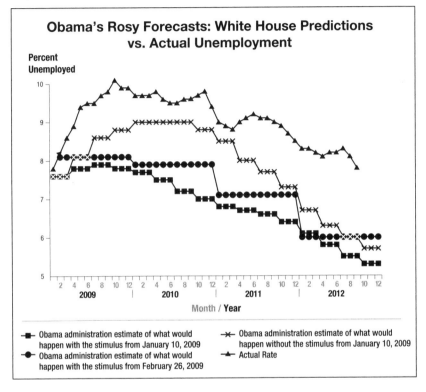

Obama's Rosy Forecasts: White House Predictions vs. Actual Unemployment

- ■ Obama administration estimate of what would happen with the stimulus from January 10, 2009
- ● Obama administration estimate of what would happen with the stimulus from February 26, 2009
- ✕ Obama administration estimate of what would happen without the stimulus from January 10, 2009
- ▲ Actual Rate

6 percent through most of 2012. Obama got his stimulus, and the U.S. unemployment rate on election day 2012 stood at 7.9 percent.

These preposterously inaccurate predictions have been a continual source of embarrassment for the White House.

By July 2009 it was obvious to just about everyone that the White House's initial predictions were way off. Even the mainstream media made the administration defend itself. ABC's George Stephanopoulos asked Vice President Biden how the 9.5-percent unemployment rate in June squared with the administration's forecast of an 8-percent peak.[17] "We and everyone else misread the economy," Biden explained. "The figures we worked off of in January were the consensus figures...."

Biden's answer was an attempt to exonerate his boss of responsibility for the sickness of the economy. The Bush administration,
he wanted us to believe, had left behind a weaker economy than
anyone had realized. The interview sparked a debate over even more
stimulus spending. A day later, a *Wall Street Journal* headline read,
"Calls Grow to Increase Stimulus Spending."[18]

The entire administration joined Biden in the it-was-worse-than-
we-knew chorus. Jared Bernstein contended that the prediction of
an 8-percent peak for unemployment was made "before we had
fourth-quarter results on GDP, which we later found out was contracting on an annual rate of 6 percent, far worse than we expected
at that time."[19] The president himself echoed this claim: "It was only
after the [fourth]-quarter numbers came in, if you recall, that sud-
denly everybody looked and said the economy shrank 6 percent."[20]

The administration's historical narrative, however, is at odds with
the facts. Even after the gloomy numbers for the fourth quarter of
2008 were released on February 28, the administration continued
to paint an upbeat picture of the post-stimulus economy, predicting
unemployment of 8.1 percent for 2009 and 7.9 percent for 2010.[21]
In any case, there were strong indications of a very bad fourth quarter well before the official release of the GDP figures. With a headline
"Fourth-Quarter GDP: Worse and Worse," the *Wall Street Journal* on
December 11, 2008, estimated a drop of 6.2 percent.[22]

"In My Wildest Dreams"

The most prominent advocate for the stimulus outside the administration was Paul Krugman, a professor at Princeton, a columnist for
the *New York Times*, and a winner of the Nobel Prize in Economics.
A staunch advocate of Keynesian policies, Krugman wanted stimulus
spending far beyond the nearly trillion dollars the Democrats gave

him. The day that President Obama signed the original stimulus bill into law, Krugman stated, "I am still guessing that we will peak out at around 9 percent [unemployment], and that would be late this year."[23]

Instead, unemployment peaked at 10 percent and remained above 9 percent for two more years.

Relying on the imagined benefits of its spending, the Obama administration projected a mild decline in GDP early in 2009 and strong economic growth thereafter (see Figure 2). Specifically, the economy would shrink by 1.2 percent in 2009 but grow by 3.2 percent in 2010, 4.0 percent in 2011, 4.6 percent in 2012, and 4.2 percent in 2013.[24] A recovery like that would have been on par with other recoveries since 1970. But the economy did not live up to Obama's expectations. Instead of robust 4-percent growth in 2011, we got an anemic 1.4 percent.[25] The sluggishness continued through the first term of the Obama administration, and the economy grew by less than 3 percent over those four years—a far cry from the 11 percent that was predicted.

FIGURE 2

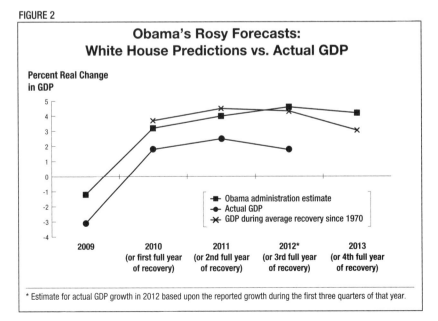

* Estimate for actual GDP growth in 2012 based upon the reported growth during the first three quarters of that year.

It is hard to tell whether President Obama and his advisors were as surprised about the economy as they seemed. Though Obama insisted that he inherited an economy that was worse than anyone thought, he himself had repeatedly warned about an economic apocalypse during the 2008 campaign. In each of the three debates with John McCain, he asserted we were in the "worst financial crisis since the Great Depression."[26] And right after the election he declared, "We've got an unprecedented crisis, or at least something that we have not seen since the Great Depression."[27]

The doom-and-gloom continued after he took office. On January 24, Obama opened his first radio address to the nation, "We begin this year and this Administration in the midst of an unprecedented crisis that calls for unprecedented action."[28] Two weeks later, in his first national press conference, he referred to economic crisis twelve times.[29] On February 18, the day after he signed his stimulus bill into law, the president rehashed the "crisis" line twenty-four times, warning that the entire economy was in peril.[30] And in his address to a joint session of Congress on February 24, he depicted a trembling nation beset by an "economic crisis, a "credit crisis," a "housing crisis," and a "financial crisis."[31]

Why are these details important? Because the Obama administration managed to have it both ways. At the outset, they cried that the sky was falling so as to pass huge spending packages. ("Never let a serious crisis go to waste.") Later, when the spending failed to turn the economy around—and actually, as I will argue, made things worse—they had the audacity to claim that they hadn't realized how bad the economy really was.

Curiously enough, the administration didn't revise its optimistic forecasts after the numbers for the fourth quarter of 2008 had come in. Instead, they kept insisting that prosperity was just around the corner.

Lawrence Summers was one of the early optimists. On January 25, 2009, he promised that the economy would start improving "within weeks" of the stimulus bill's passage.[32] Indeed, Summers touted the "shovel-ready" nature of the projects in which taxpayers were investing.[33] A large number of the unemployed would be hired within ninety days.[34] Vice President Biden bragged that the stimulus would "drop kick" the U.S. out of recession.[35]

"We're beginning to see signs of progress," Obama announced a mere five weeks after Congress passed the stimulus:

> This plan's already saved the jobs of teachers and police officers. It's creating construction jobs to rebuild roads and bridges. And yesterday, I met with a man whose company is reopening a factory outside of Pittsburgh that's rehiring workers to build some of the most energy-efficient windows in the world....[36]

In May he announced that the country was "already seeing results" from the massive spending program, which had created or saved almost 150,000 jobs.[37] In September, a giddy Joe Biden declared, "In my wildest dreams, I never thought it would work this well."[38]

But in April 2010, the unemployment rate was 9.8 percent. Unabashed, the vice president predicted a coming boom: "Some time in the next couple of months we're going to be creating between 250,000 jobs a month and 500,000 jobs a month." The recession-weary United States was going to enjoy a "Summer of Recovery."[39] Each time they turned out to be wrong.

A year later, with unemployment at a painful 9.1 percent, Austan Goolsbee, the chairman of the president's Council of Economic Advisers, boasted about "the solid pace of employment growth in recent months." "The overall trajectory of the economy has improved dramatically over the past two years," he insisted.[40] The mainstream media obediently joined the administration in its denial of reality. The *Los Angeles Times* and the *New York Times*, for example, reported dismal new unemployment figures under headlines trumpeting "solid growth" and "strong growth."[41]

By the end of the summer of 2011, however, unemployment was still at 9.1 percent, and it was no longer possible to pretend that the stimulus had worked. Two and a half years into Obama's presidency, it was a bit late to blame President Bush for the sick economy. In August, Obama lamented,[42]

> In the last few months, the economy has already had to absorb an earthquake in Japan, the economic headwinds coming from Europe, the Arab Spring and the [rise] in oil prices—all of which have been very challenging for the recovery. But these are things we couldn't control.

Blaming the March 2011 earthquake in Japan was silly. The Japanese economy itself had not been severely damaged. Indeed, Japanese unemployment fell while ours rose in the five months following the earthquake.[43] How could Obama blame "headwinds" from Europe when Europe as a whole did not fare so poorly from January to August 2011? While some southern European countries were in considerable economic pain, unemployment fell in Germany, Italy, and Sweden and remained unchanged in France and many European Union countries.[44]

By the autumn of 2011, it was obvious that the stimulus not only hadn't helped the economy but had made things worse. This is exactly what I had predicted in an article two weeks before the stimulus was passed: "President Obama and the Democrats' 'stimulus' package will increase the unemployment rate."[45] As I explained then, the money government spends has to come out of someone's pocket. Throwing a trillion dollars at politically favored projects requires moving a lot of resources from the private sector, eliminating the jobs many people currently hold.

How Bad Was the Economy?

The private sector is doing fine. Where we're seeing weaknesses in our economy have to do with state and local government.

PRESIDENT OBAMA, JUNE 8, 2012[46]

Governor Romney's argument is "we're not fixed, so fire him and put me in." It is true, we're not fixed. When President Obama looked into the eyes of that man who said in the debate, "I had so much hope four years ago and I don't now," I thought he was going to cry because he knows that it's not fixed.

BILL CLINTON, OCTOBER 18, 2012[47]

The "recovery" from the Great Recession, narrowly defined in terms of gross domestic product, began in July 2009. The economic reality for a typical family, however, has been far gloomier. As late as October 2012, just 28 percent of Americans thought their finances were getting better, while 43 percent thought they were getting worse.[48] The difficulty of finding work has been the heart of the problem. Eight-percent unemployment persisted for thirty-eight consecutive months after the so-called recovery began, causing many to give up hope altogether or to settle for a temporary or part-time job.

Liberals have tried to see the glass as half full. A week before the election of 2012, Alan Blinder of Princeton, a member of the president's Council of Economic Advisers in the Clinton administration, wrote in the *Wall Street Journal*, "Progress since 2010 has been slow but palpable. The national unemployment rate peaked at 10 percent in October 2009, dropped to 9.4 percent at the end of 2010, fell to 8.5 percent by the end of 2011, and to 7.8 percent in September 2012. . . . [W]e have finally struggled back to the unemployment rate of January 2009."[49]

Obama's Jobless Recovery

Blinder is correct, strictly speaking. Yet the official unemployment rate reflects only a portion of economic reality. People are classified as unemployed only as long as they are actively looking for work. A person may stop being "unemployed" because he has found a job, of course. But he may also cease to be classified as unemployed because he has dropped out of the labor market alto-

FIGURE 3

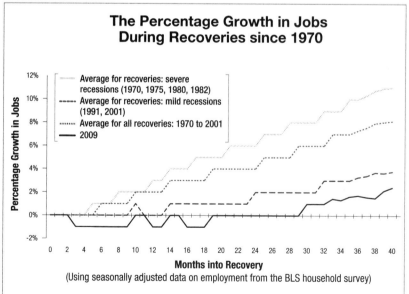

The Percentage Growth in Jobs During Recoveries since 1970

Average for recoveries: severe recessions (1970, 1975, 1980, 1982)
Average for recoveries: mild recessions (1991, 2001)
Average for all recoveries: 1970 to 2001
2009

Months into Recovery
(Using seasonally adjusted data on employment from the BLS household survey)

gether. From the end of the recession in June 2009 until October 2012, 3.4 million jobs were created, but the Bureau of Labor Statistics classified an additional 7.6 million people as "not in the labor force."

We can also compare the Obama recovery with previous recoveries (Figure 3). The number of jobs grew by just 2 percent during the first forty months of the Obama recovery. In every previous recovery since 1970, job growth in the first forty months averaged over 8 percent. And severe recessions, like the one Obama faced, have been followed by stronger rebounds. The four worst recessions were followed by job growth of over 11 percent.[50]

The Obama administration shuns such comparisons, however, pointing instead to twenty-four consecutive months of job growth by September 2012. They prefer graphs like Figure 4, with an impressive string of bars representing job growth.

Unfortunately, this graph can be deceiving. From the start of the recovery through October 2012, America's working-age population

FIGURE 4

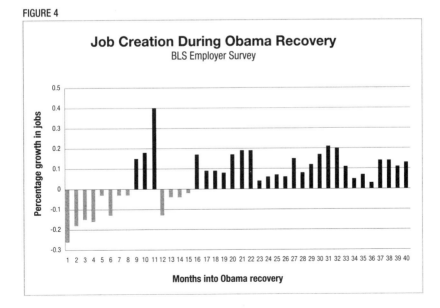

grew by an average of 212,000 persons a month. At the start of the recovery, 66 percent of the working-age population was actually working. (Most of the other third were caring for families or studying.) Thus, it would have been necessary to add about 140,000 jobs each month—5.8 million total—just to keep up with population growth. But we got only 3.4 million new jobs.

Faced with numbers like these, Obama has to cite economic statistics creatively. Commenting on the unemployment figures for July 2012, he boasted, "[W]e've now created 4.5 million new jobs over the last twenty-nine months—and 1.1 million new jobs so far this year." To arrive at these figures, however, the president ignores the jobs that were lost through February 2010, more than a year into his presidency and a year after the stimulus was passed. The 4.5 million jobs he refers to, moreover, include only private-sector non-farm jobs. If public-sector jobs are taken into account, the number drops to four million.

Even if we attribute all the job losses before March 2010 to President Bush, Obama's numbers are nothing to be proud of. Over that twenty-nine-month period, 4.1 million new jobs were needed just to keep up with population growth. The number of jobs really added to the economy, then, was only four hundred thousand. However Obama manipulates it, that's a paltry sum in an economy with over 140 million workers.

The next chart (Figure 5) takes Obama's numbers, as given in Figure 4, and adjusts them for the growth of the working-age population (and the labor-force-participation rate). Now we get a very different picture. Job growth is not consistent at all. After the awful six months from July through December 2009, there is no clear pattern—gains in some months, losses in others. Of the twenty-five months with "growth," only fifteen produced enough jobs to keep up with the increase in population, and even then the growth was usually quite small.

FIGURE 5

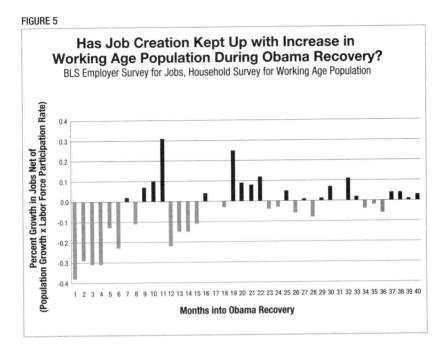

Has Job Creation Kept Up with Increase in Working Age Population During Obama Recovery?

BLS Employer Survey for Jobs, Household Survey for Working Age Population

Not Your Father's Recovery

How does Obama's recovery compare with previous recoveries? Figure 6 on page 76 displays the average job-creation figures for the five recoveries between 1975 and 2001.[51] The Obama recovery looks pathetically stagnant by comparison.

Under Obama, job growth kept up with population growth in only about half as many months as in the previous recoveries. Worse, under Obama, after accounting for population growth, employment shrank an average of 0.03 percent each month. In the previous rebounds, monthly jobs net of population growth *grew* an average 0.07% each month.

The Troubling Tale of New Hires

The picture becomes even bleaker when we consider the small number of new hires (Figure 7 on page 77). This term refers to how many people are newly hired in a given month. It is not the same

FIGURE 6

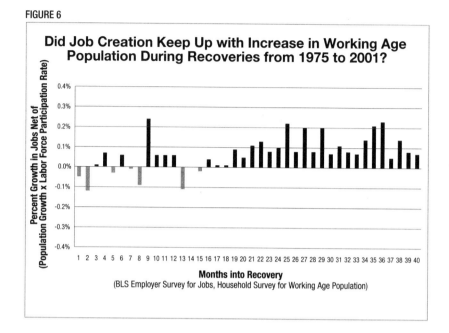

Did Job Creation Keep Up with Increase in Working Age Population During Recoveries from 1975 to 2001?

concept as "jobs added," as it includes people leaving one job and taking another.

In the year and a half before the recession (from May 2006 to November 2007), new hires averaged 5.25 million per month. As you would expect, during the recession (December 2007 to June 2009), new hires fell dramatically, bottoming out at 4.2 million per month in December 2008, right before Obama became president. Yet instead of rising as they normally would in a recovery, new hires fell further. In October 2012 they stood at 4.19 million—a number below the average *during the recession* and virtually unchanged from the day Obama became president.

So how can we have been gaining jobs—albeit at a very slow pace—when new hires have fallen? The answer is simple: an unusually large number of people are staying in the jobs they already have.

Think of it as the level of water in a pool. If the flow of water into the pool (the hires) is decreasing, the level in the pool can rise only if the rate at which water is draining from the pool decreases even more.

A drop in total job separations *can* be a good thing—if, for example, the cause is a decline in layoffs. But that has not been the case in Obama's economy. Rather, there's been a sharp drop in workers quitting—presumably because they fear not being able to get a new job. An astonishing 94 percent of the drop in job separations has been the result of a drop in quits. More than a million fewer Americans are quitting their jobs each month than before the recession.

Quits aren't supposed to fall during a recovery. During a recession, people understandably hesitate to leave the jobs they have. But in a recovery, people sense opportunity, and they chase it. The growth of quits should be especially strong after longer recessions, when unhappy workers have delayed walking off the job. Obama has

FIGURE 7

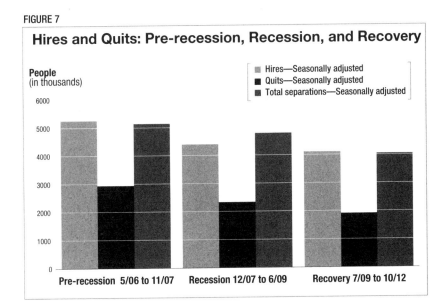

Hires and Quits: Pre-recession, Recession, and Recovery

People (in thousands)

Hires—Seasonally adjusted
Quits—Seasonally adjusted
Total separations—Seasonally adjusted

Pre-recession 5/06 to 11/07   Recession 12/07 to 6/09   Recovery 7/09 to 10/12

overseen a "recovery" in which Americans have grown even *more* fearful about quitting their jobs.

The Hardest Part of a Job Is Finding It

So how hard has it been to land a job? The simplest way to measure the difficulty is to compare the potential workforce with the number of persons being hired (Figure 8). In a normal recovery, people who gave up looking for work during the recession start looking again. The "potential workforce," therefore, includes not only the unemployed but also those classified as "not in the labor force." From the start of the recession in 2007 to October 2009, when the unemployment rate peaked, the ratio of the potential workforce to the number of persons being hired increased by over 50 percent. By the end of 2012, the situation had improved, but it was still considerably more difficult to get a job than when the recession started. As

FIGURE 8

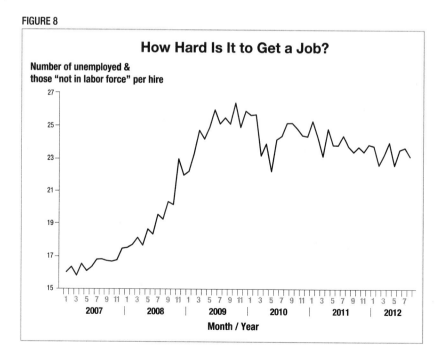

with other measures of the labor market, there was a slight improvement from the bottom of the recession followed by stagnation.

But the gloomiest numbers are for long-term unemployment. More and more people spend an unusually long time looking for work. When Obama became president, 22.5 percent of the unemployed had failed to get a job after twenty-six weeks. That rate peaked in early 2010 at almost 46 percent, a new record and almost twice as bad as the previous record, set in 1983.

It is normal for the job market to decline slightly after a recovery begins. But the extended unemployment under Obama has been anything but normal. In October 2012, 41 percent of the unemployed had been looking for work for at least six months. Long-term unemployment was thus almost as bad as when the labor market bottomed out in early 2010.

Compare Obama's long-term unemployment figures with those of a normal recovery. Had we enjoyed a recovery like the six previous ones, the percentage of the unemployed looking for work for more than twenty-six weeks would have dropped by a quarter from its peak.[52]

The ones really left out in the cold during this jobless recovery have been young people who are entering the job market for the first time. Others may cling to their existing jobs and refuse to quit because of fear that they can't find a new job, but young people don't have that luxury. In 2011, 54 percent of those under age twenty-five with bachelor's degrees were either jobless or underemployed.[53] A 2011 survey of recent college graduates by Rutgers University found that only 20 percent said their first job was on their career path, and starting salaries for those who found employment were 10 percent lower than for those in the same position five years earlier.[54] Since much of the wage gains that people get occurs when they change jobs, this lack of mobility will likely mean that this gap in wages will continue to grow as long as the economy continues on its current path. Even when the overall economy improves, research suggests that the difficulties that young workers are now experiencing in the labor market will haunt them throughout their careers.[55] We may with justification call these young people a "lost generation."[56]

The Messiah vs. the Gipper

Figures 9 and 10 show how Obama's recovery differed profoundly from Reagan's. Both recoveries followed bad recessions. Indeed, Reagan faced even worse unemployment—10.8 percent at its highest—than Obama did. But by two years into the Reagan recovery, the percentage of people unemployed for more than twenty-six weeks had returned to what it was before the recession started. Under Obama, no end was in sight three and a half years into the recovery.

One major difference between the two recoveries is the huge drop in the number of new businesses that are created each year under

FIGURE 9

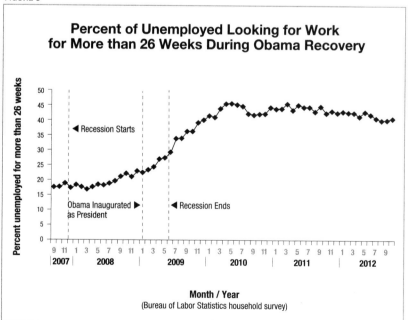

FIGURE 10

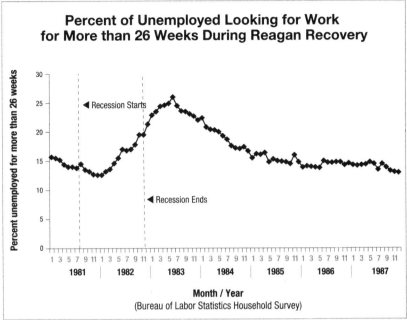

Percent of Unemployed Looking for Work for More than 26 Weeks During Reagan Recovery

◀ Recession Starts

◀ Recession Ends

Month / Year
(Bureau of Labor Statistics Household Survey)

Obama (Figure 11 on page 82). The problem is that newly established businesses are the businesses that create the jobs. From 1994 to 2005, newly established firms had net hires of about 3.1 million per year, but older firms actually had a net loss of a million jobs.[57] If you dramatically cut the number of new firms, you dramatically cut net hires. Data on the establishment of new businesses are available only from 1994 to 2010, but the number of new firms in 2010 was much lower than in any previous year—a 23-percent drop from 2007.

Obama and the Democrats responded to the recession by extending unemployment insurance payments to a record ninety-nine weeks. These payments are a two-edged sword. The benefits were quite generous—unemployment insurance payments plus coverage for health insurance and mortgage payments—and surely helped those in need. But they also discouraged people from taking part-time jobs, as such employment results in the termination of

FIGURE 11

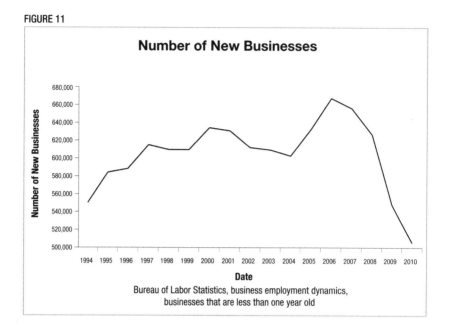

Number of New Businesses

Bureau of Labor Statistics, business employment dynamics,
businesses that are less than one year old

unemployment benefits. Going two years without a job weakens a
worker's skills and affects his attitude, making his reentry into the job
market more difficult.[58] Employers are reluctant to hire such people.

Obama's Recovery and Shrink-to-Fit Incomes

With a smaller fraction of working-age persons holding a job, it
is not surprising that median family income has fallen.[59] From
January 2000 through February 2009, median family income rose
only slightly.[60] But it plunged by 9 percent from February 2009 to
August 2012. Most of that drop took place *after* the recovery started
in June 2009.

The decline in median income is not simply a result of fewer
people working. Wages and salaries have been falling. Low-wage
jobs have replaced mid-wage jobs. Sixty percent of the jobs lost
during the recession were mid-wage, but low-wage jobs account for

58 percent of hiring during the recovery.[61] From the beginning of 2008 through March 2012, truck drivers, administrative assistants, carpenters, and real estate agents suffered the biggest job losses. Those jobs have been replaced by lower-paid jobs in retail sales, food preparation, and food service. Real hourly wages have fallen by about 2.1 percent since the middle of 2010.[62]

Any Way You Slice It

Any way you look at the economy during Obama's first term, it performed miserably. But if we were to pick a single statistic to sum it up, it would have to be gross domestic product. It is abundantly clear that compared with past recoveries, we are doing poorly. Economists since Milton Friedman have understood that economies recover back to trend after economic shocks.[63] Between 1965 and 2007, that trend was an average yearly GDP growth of 3.1 percent.[64]

Figures 12 and 13 on page 84 show GDP growth from 1970 through 1989 and from 1990 through 2012.[65] There were four recessions and recoveries during the period covered by Figure 12, and three more during the time period covered in Figure 13. The most severe recession in each figure is marked with dashed lines, but after all but the most recent recession, a consistent pattern emerges: the bigger the drop in growth, the faster the growth during recovery. In the six recoveries from 1970 through 2001, after the recession ends and GDP stops falling, economic growth exceeds the long-term rate of 3.1 percent and the economy quickly catches up with the trend.

Obama's recovery is strikingly weak in comparison. Not only did the economy fail to bounce back as it did during previous recoveries, growth has actually been slowing. It took three and a half years before GDP even reached its pre-recession level. By contrast, GDP

FIGURE 12

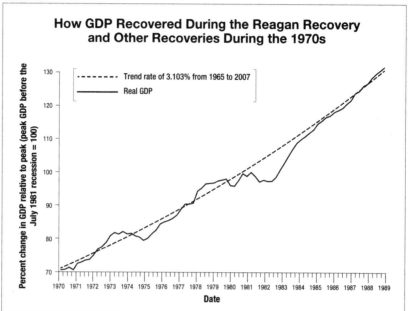

How GDP Recovered During the Reagan Recovery
and Other Recoveries During the 1970s

FIGURE 13

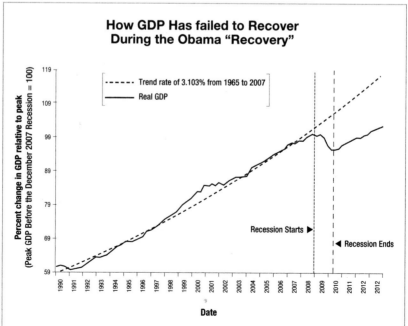

How GDP Has failed to Recover
During the Obama "Recovery"

returned to its pre-recession level in only six months under Reagan. In fact, as of October 2012, GDP had grown only 2.1 percent throughout the Obama recovery, two-thirds of the rate for the entire 1965 to 2007 period. The gap between GDP and the trend has been getting larger with each passing quarter.

The Obama recovery is weak even compared with the recovery from the Great Depression (Figure 14). The drop in GDP during the Great Depression was enormous, almost 27 percent between 1929 and 1933. But the recovery was equally strong, and GDP more than made up for the drop in the following four years. By 1937, GDP was not quite back to the trend line but was growing astonishly fast.[66] Actually, during the first four years of the recovery from the Great Depression, GDP growth averaged about 9.5 percent.[67]

That recovery was interrupted in 1937 and 1938 by what is often referred to as the "Depression within the Depression." Even so, when

FIGURE 14

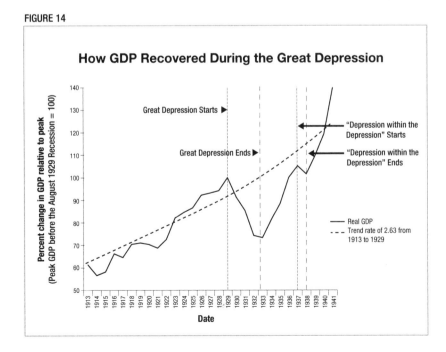

growth resumed the following year it was much faster than the trend rate.

Every way of measuring the performance of the economy points to the same conclusion: Obama has failed to deliver a recovery that matches any of the recoveries of the last forty years. This "recovery gap" is his unique legacy to America.

Putting Keynesianism to the Test

*[I]nequality leads to weak aggregate demand—
or demand that would be weak in the absence of
countervailing actions, say by the Federal Reserve.
The reason is simple: Those at the bottom and middle
consume essentially all of their income; those at the
top save 15 percent, 20 percent, or more. When money
shifts from the bottom to the top—as has occurred in
recent decades in the United States—this low demand
would lead to unemployment
and an anemic economy.*[68]

JOSEPH STIGLITZ, NOBEL PRIZE–WINNING ECONOMIST
AND CHAIRMAN OF PRESIDENT CLINTON'S COUNCIL OF
ECONOMIC ADVISERS, OCTOBER 19, 2012

For a long time, Keynesianism was a highly respected theory. It still is in some quarters, judging from Stiglitz's remarks. Regardless of its possible academic merits, it has a seductive appeal for politicians: it gives a scientific cover for reckless spending. Furthermore, as Keynesian theory calls for immediate spending to get out of a temporary slump, the spending needs to be done quickly. And that translates into less time for debate and careful scrutiny.

In other words, in the name of Keynesian stimulus theory, politicians can come up with a list of urgent pet projects and shower favored groups or industries with money. And that is exactly what happened as soon as Obama became president. His original stimulus and four additional "jobs" packages let Democrats produce all the pork they had been dreaming of.

Keynesian economics is now being used to justify Democratic tax-the-rich schemes, though such measures have little support in Keynesian theory itself. Keynesian theory is all about controlling the business cycle, not about generating growth over the long run.

The Keynesian idea is pretty simple, even if it is fundamentally flawed. It starts with the simple and uncontroversial observation that people spend a portion of their incomes and save the rest. But somehow the savings part is "bad," as though the money disappeared. While most Americans view saving as a virtue, extreme Keynesians see it as an enemy of a flourishing economy. Keynesians even refer to the "paradox of thrift"—what everyone thinks is good is really harmful. But how can savings possibly be "bad"? This question is at the heart of the debate and reveals why Keynesian theory is so unsound.

Let's consider the notion that money saved somehow disappears from the economy. If your work produces more than you consume during one year, what happens to what you don't consume? Take the simplest case of a primitive farming economy. If a family does not eat all the grain it has harvested one year, then (in the absence of mice, mold, etc.) more grain is available the next spring for seeding and for food. Saving one year is an investment for the future.

In a more advanced economy, the "extra" income likewise does not just disappear, no matter what sophisticated mathematical models might be concocted to suggest such a result. It might be difficult to understand precisely where the saved money goes. After all, it does not pile up like grain in a shed. With so many individuals, firms, and financial intermediaries, even an accountant would find it difficult to trace the resources. Nevertheless, it is "real" somewhere out there.

Let's consider a modern example. You get a paycheck and deposit it in your bank. Say you spend half of it on your living expenses. The other half is called "savings." The savings don't just disappear into a bank vault. The bank lends the savings to others—individuals or firms—who spend it or invest it. For instance, the savings may wind its way to help finance a neighbor's house renovation. Some of the money may be used to purchase bonds.

You might think that Keynesians see savings as the equivalent of simply burying money in your backyard. The idea is that saving takes money out of circulation. But that's not what happens, even if the money *is* buried in your backyard. For the economy as a whole, nothing productive has been taken away. The bills cost almost nothing to print. Although burying your money means that you don't get whatever you would have spent the money on, there is no loss to society as a whole.

Even if the money is burned up, the destruction of the bills simply results in an invisible, unintended donation to others. We cannot say to whom the resources would go, though it is easy to picture the government's ending up with them. Suppose the federal government replaces the bills that went up in smoke by printing more money, with which the Federal Reserve then purchases bonds issued by the Treasury Department. The government thus manages to finance a portion of its expenditures equal to the money that was burned. In the end, that might have benefited each taxpayer by a fraction of a penny.

If the government doesn't print more money, there is still a transfer to others. If you take money out of circulation, you increase the value of the money held by others.

In sum, barring true, concrete destruction, resources in the economy do not just disappear. Savings is not a black hole but always corresponds to real resources, somewhere in the economy, in some form or other.

The Myth of the Multiplier

So what does all this imply about the Obama administration's policies?

Those policies rely on the crazy notion that saving is bad. The Keynesian theory focuses strictly on the short term and ignores the consequences for economic growth in the long term, which is when the value of savings is experienced. Keynesians look at savings and see idle capital and workers, resources waiting for something to trigger their use, such as government action.

If you accept the Keynesian premise about savings, then other notions follow—all of them classically left wing. You can understand Stiglitz's claim that taking money from the rich to give to the poor is not only nice for the poor but is good for the economy as a whole. It's true that the rich tend not to consume as large of a fraction of their income as the poor, who need to spend whatever additional resources they get. But does it follow that if we take away from the rich and give to the poor, the economy as a whole will grow because we have stimulated "aggregate demand"?

This Keynesian theory of the "marginal propensity to consume" is the basis for a number of Obama's policies. It was explicitly cited as a reason for expanding the earned income tax credit. It was also the basis of limiting the college tuition tax credit to lower-income families. Even the "Cash for Clunkers" program, though motivated in part by an environmental agenda, was thought to stimulate the economy because the poor own all the gas-guzzling clunkers.[69]

Keynesian theory looks beyond the first level of handouts. The spending is said to have a "multiplier effect," the size of which depends on how much of the money given out is spent. New spending increases the income of still more people, who then increase their spending, and so on. Keynesians encourage government spending in general on the same grounds. It's not surprising that spending on food stamps was calculated to have a particularly high multiplier.

But because of the flaw in the Keynesians' understanding of savings, the theory of the multiplier also falls apart. Taking money from wealthy people and giving it to poor people doesn't create more spending. It just changes who chooses where the resources go. Redistribution doesn't *create* a multiplier effect, it just changes who starts the multiplier process.

Keynesians conveniently forget that the resources used to finance the additional government spending have to come from somewhere, either through taxes or through borrowing. If through taxes, taxpayers have less to spend. If through borrowing, the government absorbs resources that could have been invested in private firms.[70] Of course, the politicians who dole out the money get credit for creating jobs but are not held accountable for jobs that are lost because of the diversion of resources away from other sectors of the economy.

Practical Problems

Another serious problem with Keynesian theory is that it focuses only on the "demand side"—how, supposedly, to increase spending. That means ignoring the "supply-side," which encompasses incentives, capital formation, willingness to work, and so on.

Keynesianism is beset not only by all kinds of theoretical problems but by practical difficulties as well. Keynesian economics is preoccupied with the short term, so its stimulative spending needs projects that can be undertaken quickly—"shovel-ready" as Obama famously put it. In the 1930s, perhaps the government could simply round up some unemployed workers and start digging. In the twenty-first-century economy, however, it's not that simple. Anything more substantial than an Eagle Scout project requires extensive planning, assessment of alternatives, permits, and competing bids before the work begins. Furthermore, most projects require people with skill and experience, as well as specialized equipment. Practically speaking, there's no such thing as a "shovel-ready" project.

Stimulus projects are often artificial. They exist only to put people to "work," even if the work is basically worthless. The classic example is hiring men to dig a ditch and then hiring them to fill it in. The spending goes toward the tally of GDP, but nothing is accomplished. Meanwhile, the workers' time could have been spent on something better—if not another job, at least on training in a new skill.

Many of the new jobs only last as long as the government continues with heavy subsidies. The business of "green" energy—ethanol, wind, solar—is a good example. Few consumers would buy these products in a free market, as the price would be too high without a massive subsidy. Since investors have realized that subsidies might not continue indefinitely, they have been reluctant to hire permanent employees.

So does it make sense to hire people for temporary, low-skill work? Some of these workers will have to move. Some of them, especially the more skilled, might be drawn from existing jobs or might have found a job on their own. This displacement can itself create unemployment, the so called "frictional unemployment" associated with job changes. The problem is often compounded because a spouse may have to quit a job and try to find another one at the new location.

The Keynesian discussion focuses too much on increasing spending for its own sake and on making "jobs" no matter what kind.

Old-fashioned Keynesian stimulus projects are increasingly out of place in a high-tech economy in which two-income families are the norm.

Paul Krugman illustrated the absurd conclusions to which Keynesian theory can lead in a television interview in 2011. Fareed Zakaria of CNN asked Krugman what's wrong with paying people to dig a ditch and then fill it in. These workers are "productively employed [and] they'll pay taxes," right? Krugman agreed:

> Think about World War II, right? That was actually negative social product spending, and yet it brought us out [of the Great Depression]. . . .
>
> If we discovered that space aliens were planning to attack and we needed a massive buildup to counter the space alien threat and really inflation and budget deficits took secondary place to that, this slump would be over in eighteen months. And then if we discovered, oops, we made a mistake, there aren't any aliens, we'd be better off.[71]

Krugman's answer defies common sense. Of course it matters how we spend our resources. In the "Cash for Clunkers" program, for instance, new-car buyers got $3,500 or $4,500, while perfectly good cars, sometimes only five years old, were destroyed.[72] That program made the country poorer. Stimulus spending on alternative energy was equally senseless. Gasoline costs half as much as ethanol yet produces more energy per gallon. It is hardly surprising, then, that consumers had to be forced to use ethanol, despite the already heavy subsidies.[73]

A final problem with the kind of redistributive spending that Stiglitz and his fellow Keynesians favor is that eliminating inequality is not what makes an economy grow. Risk-taking and hard work make it grow. And you get more of that behavior when you let people keep more of the money they earn.[74] As we'll see in more detail below, the countries with the lowest tax rates have experienced the greatest growth rates. Does anyone prefer being poorer but more equal?[75]

"Austerity" Works, Keynesianism Doesn't

"Austerity measures" refers to a government policy of keeping the fiscal reins tight, of controlling spending, of keeping the debt burden down. It is the opposite of spendthrift Keynesian stimulus measures.

Of course, Keynesians argue that austerity only makes the economic situation worse during a downturn. In the words of Paul Krugman:

> We have actually had a massive unethical human experiment in austerity doctrine. Here we have had this view that cutting government spending is going to be good for the economy even when the economy is deeply depressed and we have put it into effect in large parts of Europe and we have put it into effect to a significant effect in the US . . . . And the results have been exactly what someone like me said that they would be, which is there has been a very depressing effect on the economy. Where is the evidence that this other view is at all right?[76]

Actually, there is quite a bit of evidence for us to study. Much of the world is facing a choice between austerity and stimulus, and we can see how different countries have fared. It may be argued that from the standpoint of *ideal* Keynesianism, the stimulus programs that have been implemented in various economies have been flawed. We simply have to do the best we can with the available evidence.

The results of the last few years seem quite clear: deficit spending has not helped countries get out of recession. Indeed, austerity measures seem to have worked better. Ireland, Iceland, Greece, and Spain can readily attest to this—running large deficits hurts a country in the long run. One problem is that large-scale deficits are hard to reverse, as recipients quickly take programs for granted. The debate over deficit spending versus fiscal discipline remains heated, especially in Europe. In July 2012, European Union finance ministers gave Spain permission to delay cutting some government spending and reducing its deficit, though many experts expressed fear that even the relatively limited cuts were too severe.[77]

Greece's EU partners agreed to a bailout on the condition that Greece cut its spending sharply. With its citizen rioting in the streets, however, Greece has been pleading for time to put its budget in order less abruptly.

In the United States, meanwhile, the spending spree has continued. President Obama has even pressed other nations, such as Germany, to abandon fiscal discipline. Austerity, he insists, is the cause of Europe's economic problems. The German finance minister, Wolfgang Schäuble, found Obama's scolding difficult to take. "Herr Obama," he said in June 2012, "should above all deal with the reduction of the American deficit. That is higher than that in the euro zone."[78]

So what does the evidence tell us? Have the countries with the biggest stimulus programs weathered the storm better than countries that reined in spending? We can compare changes in the percentage of the working-age population employed and in per capita GDP in the thirty-two OECD countries between 2007, the last full year before the worldwide recession hit and before governments started their massive government spending programs, and 2010, the latest year for which OECD data are available but which covers the bottom of the downturn and the beginning of the recovery. These numbers tell us that the countries with austerity measures fared better than countries that tried to spend their way out of the recession.

A slightly different way of looking at the same data is to focus on the change in unemployment rates. The results are similar: austerity works, Keynesian policies do not. One caveat, though. Unlike GDP, unemployment is measured differently in different countries. It is difficult to recalculate the rates of different countries to make them comparable. But if we look instead at *changes* in the unemployment rates of different countries, we can make a more useful comparison.

Unfortunately, a comparison of stimulus policies and austerity is more complicated than noting how government expenditures are associated with GDP or employment. For example, government spending as a share of GDP might rise simply because GDP is declining, even though government policy has not changed.[79]

There are a couple ways to approach this problem. There is usually a lag between a change in policy and its discernible effect on the economy. Keynesian stimulus spending does not achieve its full effect on the economy until some time after implementation, so we want to examine *prior* changes in government spending.[80] If increased spending occurs while the economy is doing poorly but *then* the economy soon picks up, it could be a sign that stimulus works after all.

Precision in these calculations is not possible, but it is reasonable to use a one-year lag between spending levels and the date as of which we measure the economy's performance. The resulting calculations are not flawless, but they are a step in the right direction; more complicated calculations that break down the changes on a year-by-year basis show essentially the same result.[81] So, using this analysis, is there any sign that Keynesian stimulus worked?

No. There is no suggestion whatsoever of improvement in GDP or employment. Figures 15 and 16 compare the cumulative change in government spending as a share of GDP from 2006 to 2009 with the change in the percentage employed and the change in per capita GDP over 2007 to 2010. To get the "cumulative change in government spending," we add up the the increases in spending for each year; it is not simply the difference between spending in 2006 and 2009. If we look only at the beginning and end points, we might miss some big government spending in the middle years. (More sophisticated regression analysis will be discussed later, but these figures provide a simple way of illustrating the basic relationship.)

The countries with the largest spending increases suffered the most during the recessions. The more they increased spending or their deficits, the worse they fared.

FIGURE 15

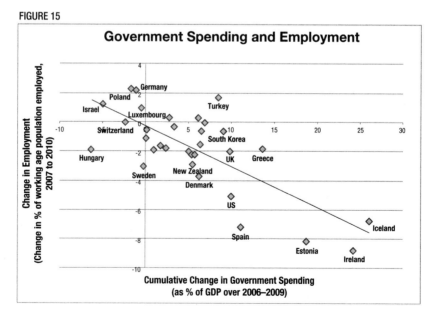

FIGURE 16

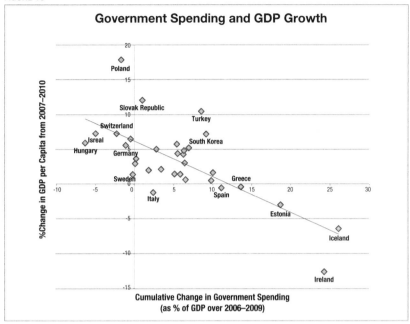

Government Spending and GDP Growth

Ireland, Iceland, Estonia, Spain, and Greece are the most dramatic examples. The increases in per capita government spending in these countries ranged from 11.1 percent to 26.1 percent. These countries also suffered the biggest drops in GDP, contracting on average by 4.4 percent between 2007 and 2010. The share of working-age population that was employed fell in these countries by an average of 6.6 percent.

At the other end of the spectrum, we find the most frugal countries: the Czech Republic, Hungary, Israel, Poland, Sweden, and Switzerland. In these countries, per capita government spending shrank by a range of 6.3 percent to 0.2 percent. The result? Per capita GDP actually grew in these countries by an average of 7 percent over the three-year period. These countries also saw the share of their working-age populations with jobs grow. (These results are not dependent on the inclusion of Ireland and Iceland, whose increases in government spending were comparatively large.)

Contrast the performance of these frugal countries to that of the U.S., where the percentage of the working-age population employed has fallen well below the 2007 level. During this period, per capita GDP growth in the United States was only a quarter of that of the six most frugal countries.

Keynesians differentiate between increases in government spending that are funded through increased tax revenue and those that are funded by deficits. Both kinds of spending increases are supposed to increase total spending in the economy, but spending financed through taxes is believed to be less stimulative than deficit spending.

The process by which tax-financed spending supposedly increases GDP is called the "balanced budget multiplier." Net spending is said to increase if the government takes money from people via taxes and then spends it. Remember our earlier discussion about people not spending all their money. Taking away their money reduces their spending by less than the amount of money taken away. On the other hand, Keynesians assume that government spends all the money that it gets. That difference—the "saving" that individuals would have committed with their money—is the net increase in total spending.

Keynesians say that deficit spending produces a greater increase in total spending because, unlike taxing, borrowing supposedly doesn't reduce people's spending. Of course, the Keynesian model is nonsensical. It assumes that people are too stupid to realize that (a) more government borrowing today means less money for people to borrow for other activities tomorrow and (b) there will be higher taxes tomorrow to pay off this debt. The results in Figure 17 show that larger deficits, like increased government spending, retard economic growth.

As Milton Friedman once observed, "I would rather have govern-ment spend $500 billion and run a deficit of $100 billion than have it spend $800 billion with a balanced budget."[82] It is the level of government spending that determines the level of taxes. Financing government spending by borrowing doesn't eliminate taxes, it only means higher taxes in the future. Taxes today and taxes next year both discourage investment and work. Despite the Keynesians' happy theories, government spending is a drag on the economy.

Not everyone agrees with this analysis, of course. There are still Keynesians among us. But they can offer no evidence that their policies actually work. Paul Krugman tries, so let's consider his argument and the assumptions and data he uses to make it.[83] First, he assumes that normal economic growth, without government stimulus or austerity, will produce annual increases of 2 percent in government revenues. This is a reasonable effort to distinguish the effects of a given policy from what the economy would have done on its own, and I am not going to quibble about his precise adjustment.

FIGURE 17

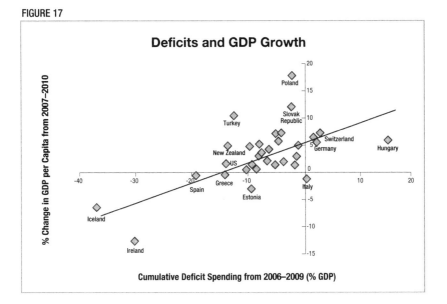

Having established how he will measure the effects of a policy, he compares how "austerity" correlates to the change in GDP—the same exercise that we just went through. Krugman, however, arrives at results that are weakly in favor of Keynesian theory. Why the difference? His analysis is based on a smaller data set, which covers only European countries, though my results hold even if I also use only European data. The real difference is that he does not consider any data before 2009, even though the spike in government growth and deficits in many European nations occurred between 2007 and 2009. According to Krugman's data, the debt of European Union nations went from 0.8 percent of GDP in 2007 to 6.9 percent in 2009.[84] Indeed, deficits reached their peaks in 2009 and declined slightly after that. The effect of stimulus measures is measured by the *change* in deficits, but by starting in 2009, Krugman misses the large changes in the deficits that had already occurred. He never explains why he excludes these earlier data.

FIGURE 18

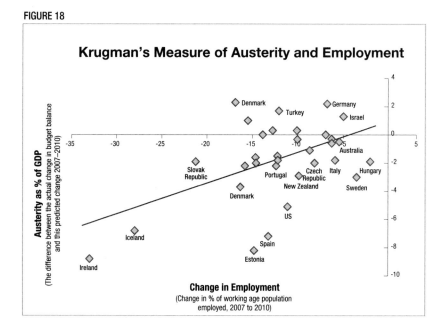

FIGURE 19

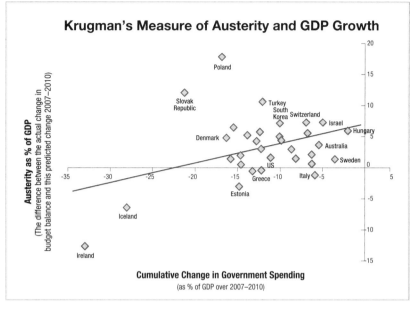

So what results do you get with a larger data set, like the OECD data set we have just analyzed, and over a somewhat longer period? The results are reversed: austerity works, Keynesian stimulus does not (Figures 18 and 19). This is true using Krugman's own 2-percent adjustment. The effects are quite large as well as statistically significant: each 1-percent increase in a country's deficit was associated with about a 0.3-percent decrease in the growth of per capita income between 2007 and 2010.[85]

Krugman has not tried to measure the effect stimulus and austerity have on the labor market. But again, we can use his 2-percent adjustment approach to do so. As before, we find that stimulus has a detrimental effect on employment.[86]

We can apply a more sophisticated, and more difficult, approach, which tracks the year-to-year changes in government spending with GDP growth and employment. This involves more complex regressions with more variables. Nevertheless it allows us to account for the differences across countries and, at the same time, to account for other factors that might explain changes in per capita GDP growth and employment over time.

My regressions find that increasing last year's government expenditures (as a percentage of GDP) by 1 percent reduces per capita GDP by $184.[87] Such an increase in spending reduces the figure for working-age population employed by about 0.5 percent.[88]

The bottom line should be clear. Governments were unable to spend their way out of their problems. "If you look at the experiences of OECD countries over the past five years, there's no evidence that countries that reduced government spending relative to GDP had slower economic growth," said Steve Bronars, an adjunct professor in economics at Georgetown University. "If anything, countries that showed greater fiscal restraint had faster growth in GDP and employment over the past few years."[89]

"Austerity" may be a dirty word to some politicians, but the countries that followed Keynesian policy have assumed a triad of woes: poor GDP growth, poor job growth, and massive debt.

So Would Things Have Been Worse without the Stimulus?

If Keynesian policies work so well, the American economy should have performed well compared with countries that followed other policies. That turns out not to be the case.

Our next-door neighbor Canada provides an interesting contrast. Our economies are closely interconnected. Canada is our largest trading partner, and when American consumers cut down on buying products many of those products are Canadian-made.

Before proceeding, we should note that Canada treats people as "unemployed" if they have engaged in "any" job search during the previous month, no matter how superficial. The United States, on the other hand, deems someone "unemployed" if he is out of work and is "actively" searching—that is, applying for jobs and going through the necessary interviews.[90]

Fortunately, the U.S. Bureau of Labor Statistics has recalculated Canadian unemployment rates so that their measure is reasonably comparable with the U.S. rate. It turns out that Canadian and U.S. unemployment rates were remarkably similar from 1976 until the beginning of 2009, never differing by more than 1.3 percent and usually by much less than 1 percent.[91]

In 2008, the recession hit Canada hard, just as it did the United States. In December, Canadians viewed their economy as gloomily as Americans did theirs, and they were at least as pessimistic about the future.[92] Canadian and U.S. unemployment rates increased in lockstep from August 2008 to February 2009, when the United States passed Obama's stimulus. Figure 20 on page 104 illustrates how the two countries' unemployment rates shot up together.

But the picture changed when the stimulus passed. Canada began substantially to outperform the U.S. in job creation, supposedly the point of the stimulus. In the U.S., unemployment rose to 10.1 percent by October 2009 and remained at least at 9.5 percent for the next fourteen months. In sharp contrast, Canadian unemployment peaked at 7.7 percent in July and August 2009 and has been falling ever since. When the American unemployment rate in September 2011 was stuck at 9.1 percent, Canada's had fallen to 6.3 percent. The U.S. rate had increased by 1.3 percentage points since Obama became president, while Canadian unemployment had already fallen below its January 2009 level.

In January 2009, before the stimulus was passed, American economic forecasters surveyed by the *Wall Street Journal* had predicted

FIGURE 20

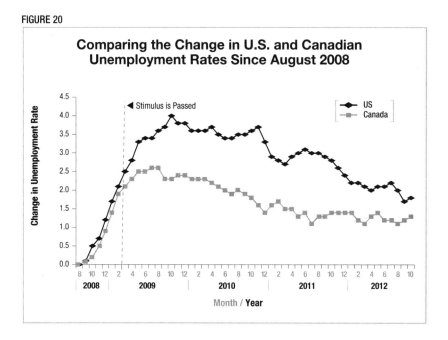

Comparing the Change in U.S. and Canadian
Unemployment Rates Since August 2008

that the U.S. unemployment rate would increase by 0.8 percent by December 2009. Instead, it climbed by 2.1 percent. In Canada, it went up by 1 percent.

Obama's expensive Keynesian policies contrasted sharply with the Canadian approach. Tax revenues fell in Canada because of the recession, and the deficit grew, but the conservative Canadian government chose not to introduce any new big government programs. The U.S. federal government's net debt rose as a share of GDP from 2008 to 2012 by 33 percentage points, from 48 to 81 percent. Canada's net debt rose by just over 13 percentage points, from 22.4 to 35.8 percent.[93]

Canada's stimulus differed radically not just in its size but also in what it did. Obama's stimulus raised the effective marginal tax rates on individuals, discouraging work. While he insisted on keeping the total U.S. corporate tax rate at 40 percent, Canadians gradually cut their total corporate income tax rate from 34 percent in 2007 to 26 percent in 2012.

A few years have made an enormous difference in Canadian and American perceptions about their economies. From July to September 2011, fewer than 10 percent of Americans viewed their economic conditions as "good or excellent," and 53 percent viewed it as "poor."[94] Over that same period, Canadians were fairly happy with their lot. Over 60 percent of them thought their economy was in "good or very good shape."[95]

The gap between the U.S. and Canadian unemployment rates began to close shortly after the stimulus funding ended. Almost 99 percent of the money had been awarded by the third quarter of 2011.[96] Meanwhile, the unemployment gap between the two countries reached its maximum, 2.1 percentage points, at the end of 2010, but it was still 1.9 percentage points in July 2011. After that point, the gap consistently fell, reaching just a half a percentage point in October 2012.

Ironically, Republican success at forestalling more stimulus spending after the 2010 elections allowed the U.S. unemployment rate to fall and helped Obama to win reelection. And their continued opposition to the new stimulus proposals that Obama was pushing after the election will only continue to keep him from doing further harm.

There are other differences between the Canadian and U.S. economies, of course. In particular, the U.S. was burdened by regulations that forced mortgage companies to make loans on which they expected to lose money. But it is hard to see how those other differences would cause the sudden change in fortunes at the very moment the stimulus was passed.

Countries in other parts of the world are also faring better—even in Europe. Despite strong political pressure from Obama to spend about $225 billion more on fiscal stimulus, many European countries decided against such a measure.[97] In March 2009, with German Chancellor Angela Merkel nodding in agreement, President

Nicolas Sarkozy of France declared, "the problem is not about spending more." Even the British Labor party rejected Obama's call for more spending. Later that month, the president of the European Council, Prime Minister Mirek Topolanek of the Czech Republic, said European leaders were "quite alarmed" at the Obama administration's deficit spending and bank bailouts and described them as "a road to hell."[98]

The *Washington Post* concluded that the European resistance to Obama's pressure revealed a "fundamental divide that persists between the United States and many European countries over the best way to respond to the global financial crisis. U.S. officials have pressed their European counterparts to spend substantially more public money in an attempt to revive economic growth and global trade. Some countries, led by Germany, have strongly resisted, predicting that such a path could lead to unsustainable debts. . . ."[99]

These European nations chose the better path, as is clearly revealed by their unemployment numbers. The U.S. Bureau of Labor Statistics has recalculated the unemployment rates for eight foreign countries in addition to Canada—Australia, Japan, France, Germany, Italy, the Netherlands, Sweden, and the United Kingdom—so that we have rates to compare with our own. The United States passed a much more extensive stimulus, measured as a percentage of our GDP, than did any of those countries. Indeed, it was almost three times as large.[100] During the U.S. spending spree, none of these other countries performed as consistently poorly as the U.S. Their unemployment rates, like Canada's, diverged from ours right after the American stimulus was passed.

We have identified several countries that practiced "austerity." Four European countries in particular are consistently classified as having restrained spending and deficit policies: Hungary, Sweden, and, to a lesser extent, Germany and Switzerland.

To compare these countries' economic record with the United States', most economists look at the percentage of the working-age population that is working. There are many reasons why this percentage differs across countries, such as whether women stay home to raise children, but sudden changes in this number indicate whether it is easier or harder to get a job.

EuroStat provides detailed data on both employment and the number of working-age people.[101] Similar numbers for the U.S. are available from the Bureau of Labor Statistics.[102] Since the beginning of 2009, the labor force participation rate in the U.S. has fallen by 3 percent. In the seventeen countries of the eurozone, it has fallen by only half as much (Figure 21 on page 108). Considering these figures, it is strange that President Obama frequently cites Europe as an explanation for our slow job growth. During the summer of 2012, Obama complained, "slower growth in Europe means slower growth in American jobs."[103] If Obama were right, then Europe should have had an even slower rate of job creation than the United States. Instead Europe's labor force participation rate remained fairly constant from 2009 through 2012; the U.S. rate plunged.

Contrast the labor force participation rates with the dramatically different picture that emerges in a graph of unemployment rates for Europe and the U.S. (Figure 22). It was quite common in the months before the 2012 election to see headlines such as this from July in the *Los Angeles Times*: "Think 8.2% unemployment is bad? It's a record 11.1% in Europe."[104] So is this evidence that the United States is much better off than Europe in 2012?[105] Sorry, no.

As mentioned, there are some complications in comparing American and European unemployment figures. Europe measures unemployment in much the same way Canada does. That is, a person is counted as "unemployed" if he says he desires a job, whether or not he is actively seeking. And because of Europe's heavy

FIGURE 21

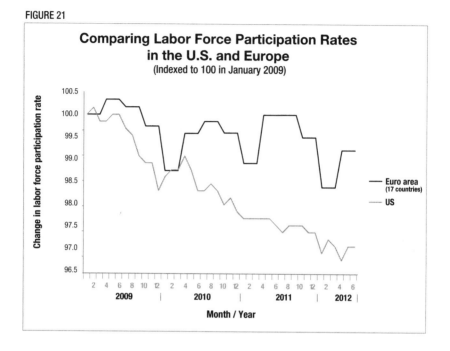

**Comparing Labor Force Participation Rates
in the U.S. and Europe**
(Indexed to 100 in January 2009)

unionization, part-time employment is rare. People who are unable to find a full-time job don't take a part-time job to make ends meet.

The so-called "U6" unemployment rate for the U.S. is a better figure for comparing with the European rate. It includes those who are no longer actively looking for work but would take a job if it were offered as well as those who were looking for a full-time job but were forced to take a part-time position. The U6 rate has fallen from its peak of 17 percent in late 2009 and early 2010, but the October 2012 rate of 14.6 percent was hardly desirable.

American unemployment rates actually compare less favorably with Europe's than the U6 rate suggests (Figure 22). Those who are willing to work but who have given up looking are counted as unemployed for the U6 calculation for only twelve months.[106] Europe places no such time limit. If the U6 measurement of unemployment

FIGURE 22

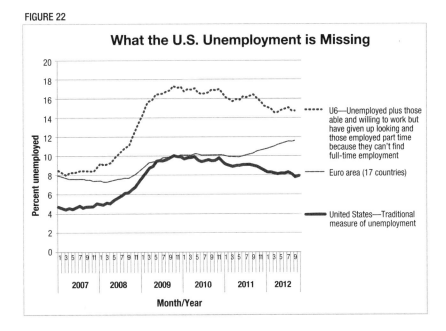

were adjusted to be more comparable to Europe's, it would go up another 1.2 percent, reaching 15.8 percent in October 2012.

The four million Americans who have taken part-time jobs because they couldn't find full-time employment further disguise the seriousness of U.S. unemployment. The portion of workers in this frustrated category rose from 3 percent in late 2007 to 6 percent in October 2012 (Figure 23 on page 110). During the recovery, these new part-time jobs were never replaced with permanent ones.[107]

We have to be careful, of course, in talking about the "European" economy or "European" unemployment rates. Different parts of Europe have fared quite differently from each other. If we look at the four countries that have most clearly rejected Obama-style stimulus spending, the failure of the U.S. economy is even more dismaying. As Figure 24 on page 111 shows, Germany, Sweden, Hungary, and Switzerland have all seen their labor force participation rates improve.

FIGURE 23

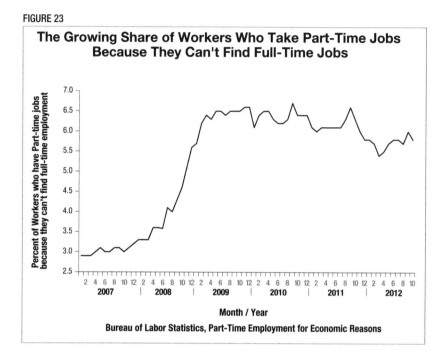

The Growing Share of Workers Who Take Part-Time Jobs Because They Can't Find Full-Time Jobs

Month / Year

Bureau of Labor Statistics, Part-Time Employment for Economic Reasons

Europe has lots of economic problems, but it is hard to see how we can take Obama seriously when he blames Europe for America's poor job market. The European job market is somehow outperforming our own.

Germany—the special target of Obama's ire—really stands out. While America's labor force participation rate has declined under Obama, Germany's has increased. The stimulus partisans have been urging Germany to pull the rest of the world out of recession by spending more money, but they obviously have done a better job by ignoring that advice.

Paul Krugman might want to forget his predictions about Germany. He called the reduction in German government spending in June 2010 a "huge mistake," warning, "budget cuts will hurt your economy and reduce revenues [by reducing economic growth]."[108] He continued his attack on German austerity in August, but hedged

FIGURE 24

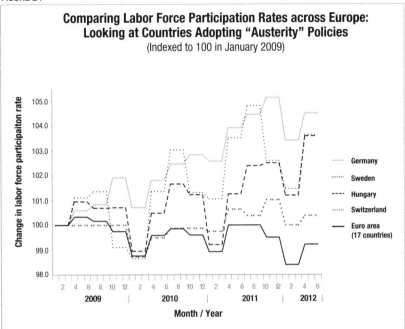

Comparing Labor Force Participation Rates across Europe: Looking at Countries Adopting "Austerity" Policies
(Indexed to 100 in January 2009)

that it was still too early to evaluate the policy.[109] More than a year later, Germany's labor force participation rate was still growing, having risen by another 2 percent between June 2010 and August 2011. Since then Germany's rate has stabilized while America's has continued its fall.

When the evidence became too obvious to ignore, Krugman claimed that Germany had never really adopted a conservative spending policy. Dodging his record as a prognosticator, he wrote in 2012 that "tales of German austerity are greatly exaggerated; the Germans haven't actually done much real austerity, just as we here haven't done much real stimulus."[110]

The economic news from Britain has also been unkind to Krugman. In June 2010, just weeks after an election that brought the Conservatives and Liberal Democrats to power in a coalition, the government promised to cut the budgets of almost all government

FIGURE 25

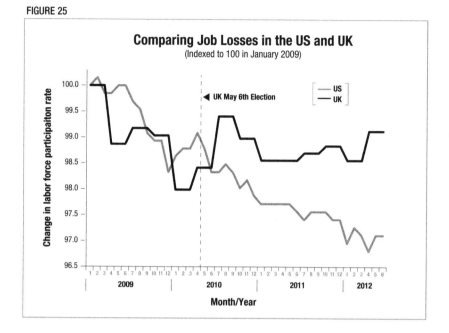

Comparing Job Losses in the US and UK
(Indexed to 100 in January 2009)

departments by an average of 25 percent over the next five years.[111] Paul Krugman, of course, predicted disaster: "Trying to balance budgets in the face of high unemployment and falling inflation is still a really bad idea. . . . There have been widespread claims that deficit-cutting actually reduces unemployment because it reassures consumers and businesses; but . . . this claim has no basis in reality."[112] He was still berating British politicians in 2012 when he noted, "Cameron and Osborne insist that they will not change course, which means that Britain will continue on a death spiral of self-defeating austerity."[113]

Britain has had a hard time, but its job market has outperformed America's (Figure 25). The labor force participation rate in the U.S. and the U.K. dropped by the same amount between January 2009 and June 2010, but after the British announced their spending cuts, a greater share of their labor force found work. The "stimulated" U.S. job market kept on shrinking.

Are Recoveries from Financial Crises Really That Slow?

Recoveries that follow financial crises are slower and more protracted, as Carmen Reinhart and Ken Rogoff have famously written. They are slower.

Treasury Secretary Timothy Geithner speaking to the Economic Club of New York on March 15, 2012[114]

Carmen Reinhart's and Kenneth Rogoff's book *This Time Is Different* has become the bible of the Obama administration. That's hardly surprising, since it supports one of the president's favorite economic excuses: he can't be held responsible for the lame recovery because recoveries are always slow after financial crises.[115] The economy "is not growing quite as fast as we would like," Obama explained in April 2010, "because after a financial crisis, typically there's a bigger drag on the economy for a longer period of time."[116] Shortly before the 2012 election, former President Bill Clinton, with characteristic hyperbole, proclaimed, "If you go back 500 years, whenever a country's financial system collapses, it takes between 5 and 10 years to get back to full employment."[117]

Reinhart's and Rogoff's thesis has been repeated so often and is such an important prop for Obama's economic policy that it has achieved the status of a truism in the media. Economists, however, are more critical.[118]

The United States certainly experienced a major financial crisis in late 2008. But that crisis does not explain the weakness of the recovery that began in June 2009.[119] Neither historical data nor recent international comparisons support Reinhart's and Rogoff's claim about the weakness of recoveries after financial crises. Indeed, their findings are at odds with two well-known facts:

1. As Milton Friedman observed, "A large contraction in output tends to be followed on the average by a large business expansion; a mild contraction, by a mild expansion."[120]
2. Most severe recessions are accompanied by financial crises.

Because of these two facts, economists have long believed that financial recessions lead to faster growth. Michael Bordo and Joseph Haubrich have recently found that "since the 1880s, the average annual growth rate of real GDP during recoveries from financial-crisis recessions was 8 percent, while the growth rate from non-financial-crisis recessions was 6.9 percent."[121] Other economists—Jerry Dwyer and James Lothian, for example, as well as John Taylor—have reached similar conclusions through independent research.[122]

Comparisons across different countries tell a similar story, though this is tricky work. Whether a particular economic disruption was a "financial crisis" is a subjective call and subject to debate, as Reinhart and Rogoff acknowledge.[123] In 2009, they identified eleven countries that had suffered a financial crisis in 2007 and 2008: Austria, Belgium, Germany, Hungary, Iceland, Ireland, the Netherlands, Spain, the United Kingdom, Japan, and the United States. They classified thirty-one other countries (including Canada) as not having suffered a financial crisis. They came up with these classifications before any subsequent data on GDP and jobs were available. Thus nobody can suspect that there was arbitrary picking and choosing of the two groups so as to get the "right" results.

Though Reinhart and Rogoff put the United States and Canada into different classifications, the two countries' unemployment rates rose in lock step from August 2008 until February 2009, when the stimulus was passed in the United States. If financial crises make recessions deeper, why did the U.S. not suffer more than Canada in the midst of its financial meltdown?[124] It was only after the United States enacted the stimulus that the two countries' economic fortunes began to diverge, and it is sensible to assume that the stimulus had something to do with it. There was no sudden change in the U.S. financial markets at that time that could be blamed.

In another book, *Debacle,* I have compared American unemployment data with data (adjusted by the BLS) from eight other countries plus Canada. Reinhart and Rogoff identify four of these nine countries as suffering from a financial crisis (Germany, Japan, the Netherlands and the United Kingdom) and five as not (Australia, Canada, France, Italy, and Sweden). I found that countries hit by a financial crisis did not fare worse than others. Indeed, from January 2009 to December 2011, unemployment rates went up *less*, not more, in the countries suffering a financial crisis (0.66 percentage points versus 0.86 percentage points).[125]

My comparison, however, is not completely satisfying. I studied only nine countries, and despite the BLS's efforts, the unemployment rates are still not calculated in exactly the same way. It is better to use a different measure—the percentage of the working-age population that is working.[126] Data are available for all ten foreign countries that Reinhart and Rogoff classify as having had a financial crisis[127] and for eighteen countries that had no financial crisis.[128]

These labor force participation rates allow us to draw two striking conclusions. Figure 26 on page 116 shows virtually identical drops in labor force participation rates between the two sets of countries; the differences are so small as to be statistically insignificant.[129]

Figure 27 on page 117 shows that individual countries suffering financial crises fared very differently. The drop in labor force participation for countries suffering financial crises is almost entirely due to the severe problems suffered by just two of the ten

FIGURE 26

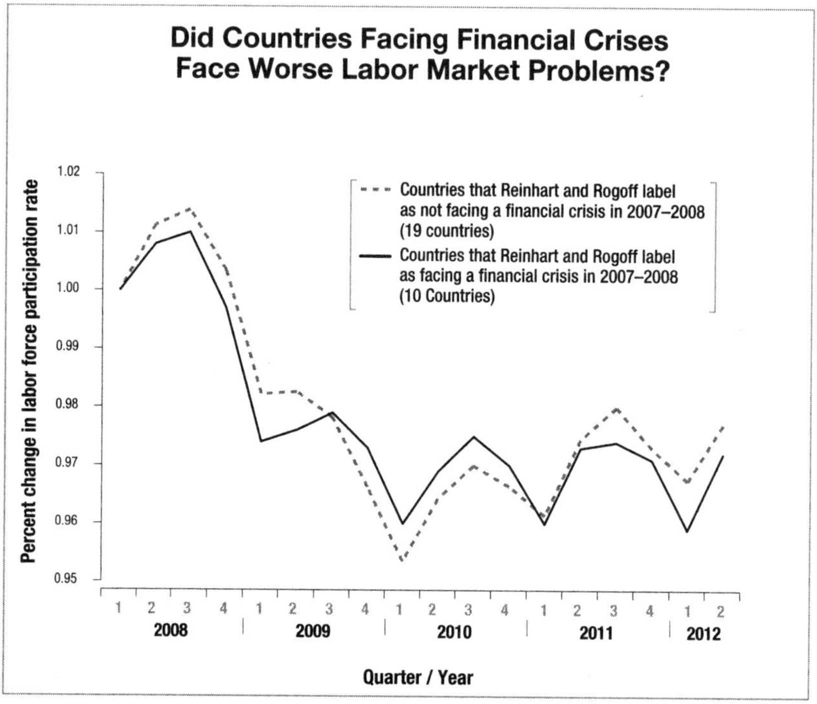
Did Countries Facing Financial Crises
Face Worse Labor Market Problems?
Countries that Reinhart and Rogoff label as not facing a financial crisis in 2007–2008 (19 countries)
Countries that Reinhart and Rogoff label as facing a financial crisis in 2007–2008 (10 Countries)
Percent change in labor force participation rate
1.02
1.01
1.00
0.99
0.98
0.97
0.96
0.95
1 2 3 4 1 2 3 4 1 2 3 4 1 2 3 4 1 2
2008
2009
2010
2011
2012
Quarter / Year

countries (Ireland and Spain). The dashed line in the middle of the figure shows the change in labor force participation rates for all ten countries as a group. The line at the bottom of the graph shows how the Irish and Spanish economies collapsed, with their labor force participation rates plummeting by 15 percentage points in four years. The solid line at the top of the figure shows how labor force participation rates changed for the other eight countries with financial crises. Surprisingly, despite their financial crises, these eight countries did quite well and had completely recovered by the summer of 2012. These eight, despite suffering financial crises, performed better than the countries without such crises. Indeed, all eight countries were better off by the summer of 2012 than the average country that didn't have a financial crisis.[130] The difference

FIGURE 27

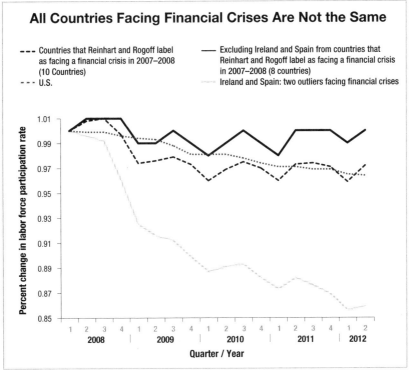

All Countries Facing Financial Crises Are Not the Same

--- Countries that Reinhart and Rogoff label
    as facing a financial crisis in 2007–2008
    (10 Countries)
--- U.S.

—— Excluding Ireland and Spain from countries that
    Reinhart and Rogoff label as facing a financial crisis
    in 2007–2008 (8 countries)
⋯⋯ Ireland and Spain: two outliers facing financial crises

is statistically significant and completely at odds with Reinhart's and Rogoff's predictions.[131]

Who Got the Stimulus Money?

President Obama promised that his stimulus "include[d] help for those hardest hit by our economic crisis" and that, "[a]s a whole, this plan will help poor and working Americans."[132] The facts, however, tell a different story. The states hardest hit by the recession received the least money, and the states with the highest incomes received the most. Rather than helping those in the toughest shape, the Democrats helped their supporters, including unions and many wealthy contributors.

According to the Obama administration's Recovery.gov website, a total of $512 billion in federal contracts, grants, and loans was awarded to states and territories between February 17, 2009, and June 30, 2012. The amounts varied from state to state, Virginia received the least ($1,005 per capita) and Alaska the highest ($2,500 per capita). The District of Columbia was the real winner, at a whopping $7,631.

The transfers to the states with the least economic problems were large. My regression analysis reveals some interesting relationships, including:

- Each additional thousand dollars of per capita income is correlated, on average, with $150 more per capita in stimulus funds (Figure 28).

FIGURE 28

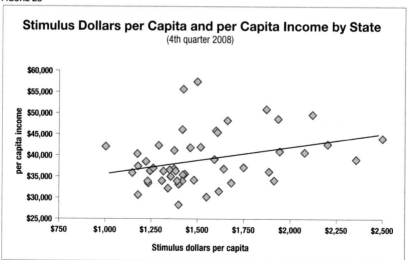

FIGURE 29

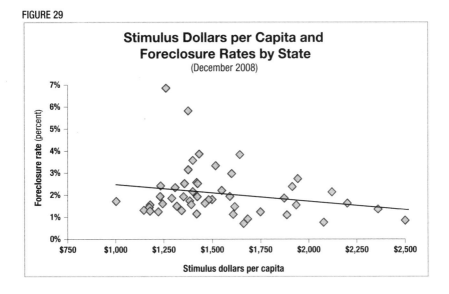

- States with higher bankruptcy rates got less money, not more—roughly $68 less per person for each percentage point increase in the state's bankruptcy rate (Figure 30 on page 120).
- For each 1-percent drop in the rate of foreclosures, the state gained $59 more per person (Figure 29).

States with higher unemployment rates, on the other hand, got almost the same amount of money as states with lower rates (Figure 31 on page 120).

The group that benefitted the most was unions. The ten states receiving the most stimulus money got over 70 percent more money per person than the ten states that received the least money. At the same time, those states had more than twice the share of their workers represented by unions. No previous president ever produced such a prodigious transfer of wealth to unions.

Obama's $825 billion stimulus particularly benefitted union workers. There was the $26 billion Public Sector Jobs Bill of 2010

FIGURE 30

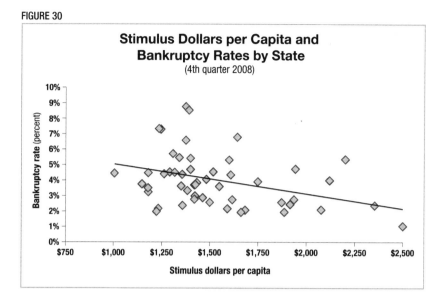

as well as the Disaster Relief and the Summer Jobs Act, providing $24 billion to teachers, policemen, and firefighters.

The Davis-Bacon Act's "prevailing wages and benefits" rules were required for contracts receiving any stimulus money.[133] These rules

FIGURE 31

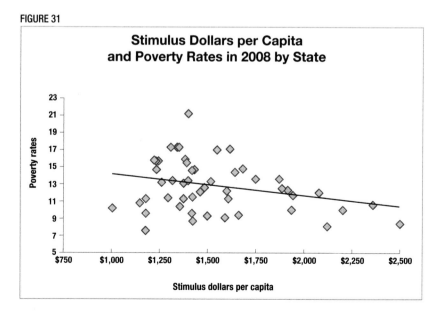

FIGURE 32

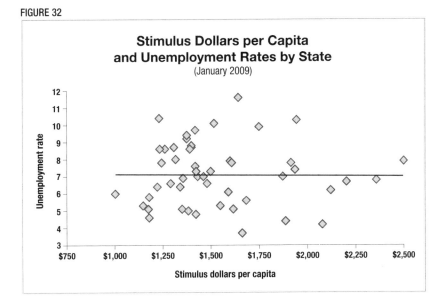

typically forced companies to pay union wages. In addition, Obama issued executive orders that forced some contractors bidding for government contracts to recognize unions and adopt existing collective bargaining agreements.[134] Obama even went so far as to impose a gag order on what firms could tell employees about unions and collective bargaining when union organizing efforts were undertaken.

The receipt of stimulus money was highly correlated to Democratic control of a state (Figure 33). Having an entirely Democratic congressional delegation in 2009, when the bill passed, increased per capita stimulus dollars by $515. In addition, the states that Obama won by the largest margin in 2008 benefitted the most. This isn't surprising, given that Congressional Democrats wrote the stimulus legislation without any Republican cooperation. But the money didn't go to the poorest states or the ones with the highest poverty, bankruptcy, or foreclosure rates. Wealthy, heavily unionized states that support Democrats were the ones receiving it.

FIGURE 33

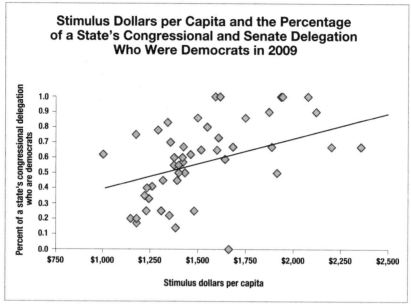

Stimulus Dollars per Capita and the Percentage
of a State's Congressional and Senate Delegation
Who Were Democrats in 2009

Conclusion

Keynesianism may never die for one simple reason: it gives politicians an excuse to spend money. Even though Keynesian policies reduce growth and employment, politicians still get praise for handing out the money. Voters see the jobs created by the money being given out, but what is never as clear are the jobs that will never exist. When politicians are giving out money, it is easy for them to be declared as caring even as their policies leave the country much poorer.

The lessons to be drawn are: (1) If you want a wealthier country, restrain government growth. (2) The stimulus was a giant slush fund that didn't go to the states that were hurting the most from the recession. The money went to Democrats and President Obama's supporters. It is hard to think of any justification for Democrats to be taking money from poorer states and giving it to wealthier ones simply because that is where the Democrats are.

CHAPTER THREE

BEWITCHED, BOTHERED, AND BEWILDERED

That's just a complete lie. It's a complete lie. . . .
You need to stop repeating a blatant lie, about what
happens in other countries. . . . No, you're not going to
get away with this. You lied about it the other day. . . .
Stop lying, because what you say drives Americans to
defend themselves.

PIERS MORGAN, CNN *PIERS MORGAN TONIGHT*,
DECEMBER 21, 2012[1]

The emotions couldn't have been more raw. People's hearts were torn by the horrible murder of twenty children and six staff members at Sandy Hook Elementary School in Newtown, Connecticut.

It is natural to think that these crimes wouldn't occur if guns were banned. Piers Morgan's outburst was directed at me when I tried to explain, "Every place that guns have been banned, murder rates have gone up." Morgan exploded. Working with him as a tag team, Christiane Amanpour claimed, "After [the 1996 school massacre at] Dunblane [Scotland], they put in these bans, they put in these punishments, fines, jail sentences, etc., and it's true that straight afterwards there wasn't a huge change, but 2002–2003 until 2011 the rate plummeted by 44 percent."

Most Americans are probably familiar with the explosion of murder and violent crime that Washington, D.C., and Chicago suffered after they imposed gun bans. Yet this is not just a U.S. phenomenon. It has been observed worldwide. When guns are banned, even in island nations such as the United Kingdom, Ireland, and Jamaica, the pattern has been the same. The problem is that gun bans disarm law-abiding people, not criminals. If your victim has been disarmed, it's easier to commit a crime.

Let's look more closely at the country Christiane Amanpour cited, the United Kingdom. Was she right? Did the murder rate go down after Britain banned handguns?

In only one (2010) of the fifteen years following the ban was the homicide rate lower than it had been before the ban. The average homicide rate over those years was 13 percent higher than it was from 1990 to 1996. Island nations are supposed to be the ideal setting for successful gun control. But in Ireland and Jamaica, there were even more dramatic increases in murders after guns were banned.

My point here is that people's emotions and preconceptions about guns blind them to the facts about what gun control actually achieves.

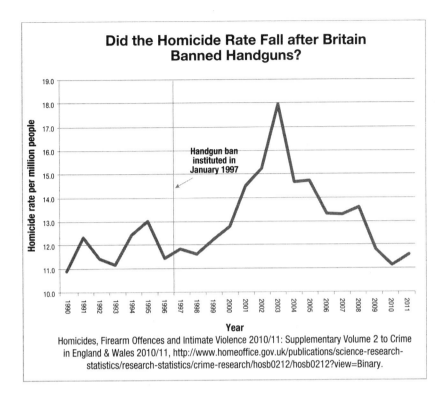

Did the Homicide Rate Fall after Britain Banned Handguns?

Handgun ban
instituted in
January 1997

Homicide rate per million people

Year

Homicides, Firearm Offences and Intimate Violence 2010/11: Supplementary Volume 2 to Crime in England & Wales 2010/11, http://www.homeoffice.gov.uk/publications/science-research-statistics/research-statistics/crime-research/hosb0212/hosb0212?view=Binary.

Your position just completely boggles me.
Honestly, I just do not understand it.

Soledad O'Brien, CNN *Starting Point*, December 17, 2012[2]

The police simply can't be everywhere. But for many, it is difficult to accept the notion that letting people defend themselves with guns can deter crime. Soledad O'Brien, for example, could not wrap her head around that idea when she interviewed me after Sandy Hook. I tried to explain that research into gun crimes indicates that establishing "gun-free zones" (at schools, for example) actually makes mass shootings more likely, and I offered facts and figures to back this up. Ms. O'Brien would have none of it. She kept repeating exclamations of bewilderment at my observations, as though any argument other than "We've got to take away the guns!" were unworthy of even momentary engagement.

Piers Morgan's, Christiane Amanpour's, and Soledad O'Brien's performances were fairly typical of the media's incomprehension of the realities of guns and crime. The Sandy Hook shooting sparked a new outcry for gun-control laws in spite of the powerful evidence that such laws are counter-productive. Leading the chorus is the number-one enemy of gun rights in America, President Obama.

What Is at Stake

Leon Harris: *"You support the D.C. handgun ban?"*
Barack Obama: *"Right. . . . We also have violence on the streets that is a result of illegal handgun use. And so, there is nothing wrong, I think, with a community saying we are going to take those illegal handguns off the streets."*

FORUM SPONSORED BY WJLA-TV AND POLITICO, FEBRUARY 12, 2008[3]

I got to know Barack Obama when we both worked at the University of Chicago Law School. He did not come across as a moderate who wanted to bring people together. I first met him in 1996, shortly after my research on concealed handgun laws and crime had come to national attention. I introduced myself, and he responded, "Oh, you are the gun guy."

"Yes, I guess so," I answered.

"I don't believe that people should be able to own guns," Obama replied. I then suggested that it might be fun to have lunch and talk about that sometime. He simply grimaced and turned away, ending the conversation. That was the way numerous interactions with Obama went.

At a faculty seminar that we both attended, he asked a question, but the speaker seemed to misunderstand his point. Afterwards, I told Obama that I thought he had an interesting point but that it might have been clearer if he phrased it differently. Obama's response was to turn his back.

Obama not only disagreed with me about gun control, he acted as if my views were evil. The University of Chicago Law School was famous for the openness of its faculty, conservative and liberal, to intense but friendly engagement with colleagues of differing views. Obama, however, preferred silent, scowling disdain to collegiality. "[I]f teaching alongside some of the most formidable conservative minds in the country had any impact on Mr. Obama, no one can quite point to it," observed Jodi Kantor in a *New York Times* article about his time there.[4]

In the years since those encounters in Chicago, Obama has gotten better at giving lip service to intellectual openness, if only because it facilitates his political slipperiness. Just four months after the interview with Leon Harris quoted above, and after the U.S. Supreme Court had struck down the District of Columbia's handgun ban and gunlock laws, Obama described his views quite differently in an interview with Fox News: "I have said consistently that I believe that the Second Amendment is an individual right, and that was the essential decision that the Supreme Court came down on. . . . The D.C. law, according the Supreme Court, went too far."[5]

Despite his assurance to Fox News that he understands the Second Amendment, it's a good bet that the positions Obama took on guns during his time at Chicago reveal his true convictions. They certainly explain his infamous remarks to supporters in San Francisco during the 2008 campaign that Americans in "small towns . . .

cling to guns or religion,"[6] and his private reassurances to Sarah Brady about his "under the radar" efforts at gun control.[7]

Obama told a university audience in 1998, "The vast majority of Americans would like to see serious gun control. It does not pass because there is this huge disconnect between what people think and what legislators think and are willing to act upon."[8] So what does Obama think "serious gun control" involves? In 1996, Obama supported a ban on handguns.[9] In 1998, he supported a ban on the sale of all semiautomatic guns (a ban that would have encompassed the vast majority of guns sold in the United States).[10] In 2004, he advocated banning gun sales within five miles of a school or park, which would have shut down nearly all gun stores.[11]

Obama has been deeply involved in the gun debate for years, even before he held political office. He spent eight years on the board of directors of the Joyce Foundation, the largest private funder of anti-gun research in the country.[12] He knows the difference between semiautomatic and machine guns, yet at various times he has made inflammatory statements that are obviously false. After the mass murder in an Aurora, Colorado, cinema in 2012, Obama declared, "I also believe that a lot of gun owners would agree that AK-47s belong in the hands of soldiers, not in the hands of criminals, that they belong on the battlefield of war, not on the streets of our cities."[13] During the second presidential debate in 2012, the president brought up Aurora and insisted that it's important to "get automatic weapons that kill folks in amazing numbers out of the hands of criminals and the mentally ill."[14]

That charge is powerful. But it is also wrong. The Smith & Wesson M&P 15 used in the Aurora shootings and the Bushmaster .223 used at Newtown are "military-style" weapons—emphasis on "style." They bear a cosmetic resemblance to the M-16, which has been used by the U.S. military since the Vietnam War. The civilian versions of

the M&P and Bushmaster use the same sort of bullet as small-game hunting rifles, fire with the same rapidity (one bullet per trigger-pull), and inflict the same damage. The AK-47 is similar, though it fires a much larger bullet—.30 inches in diameter, as opposed to the .223-inch rounds used by the M&P and Bushmaster. There's not an army in the world that would use the civilian version of these guns.

A couple of days after Sandy Hook, Wolf Blitzer asked me a question that many people were asking: "Why do people need a semiautomatic Bushmaster to go out and kill deer?" The answer is simple: It's a hunting rifle made to look like a military weapon.

The real issue here, however, isn't the usefulness of semiautomatic weapons to hunters. It's that semiautomatic weapons protect people and save lives. A single-shot rifle is of limited use when you face multiple criminals or when your first shot misses or fails to stop your attacker.

In their push to regulate semiautomatic guns, some politicians try to frighten the public by conjuring up the image of machine guns on America's streets. Yet not a single multiple-victim public shooting has involved a machine gun.

Indeed, banning guns on the basis of how they look and not how they operate will make no difference in crime. That's what the original federal assault-weapons ban did. There are no published academic studies by economists or criminologists that find that the assault-weapons ban, which was in effect from 1994 until it expired in September 2004, reduced murder or violent crime generally. Even research done for the Clinton administration did not find that it reduced crime. Nor is there any evidence that state assault-weapons bans reduce murder or violent-crime rates.

Since the federal ban expired, murder and overall violent-crime rates have actually fallen. In 2003, the last full year of the ban, the U.S. murder rate was 5.7 per 100,000 people. By 2011, the murder rate had fallen to 4.7 per 100,000 people. In fact, murder rates fell immediately after September 2004, and they fell more in the states without assault-weapons bans than in the states with them.

The large-capacity ammunition magazines used by some of these killers are also misunderstood. The common perception that so-called "assault weapons" can hold larger magazines than hunting rifles is simply wrong. A gun that can hold a magazine can hold one of any size. That is true for handguns as well as rifles. A magazine, which is basically a metal box with a spring, is also easy to make, and it is virtually impossible to stop criminals from obtaining one. The assault-weapons ban covered larger magazines but with no effect.

Obama's comments about guns that "belong on the battlefield of war, not on the streets of our cities" isn't his only inflammatory remarks about guns. Recall how he inserted himself into the controversy over George Zimmerman's shooting of Trayvon Martin in Florida. When a reporter asked about the "allegations of lingering racism within our society" and the "Stand Your Ground" law, Obama said we need to "examine the laws."[15] He then tried to personalize the tragedy, saying, "If I had a son, he'd look like Trayvon."

Vice President Joe Biden also jumped into the controversy: "The idea that there's this overwhelming additional security in the owner-ship and carrying concealed and deadly weapons . . . but the prem-ise that it makes people safer is one that I'm not so sure of. . . . You know, the bulk of the people who are shot with a weapon . . . end up being shot with their own weapon."[16]

In fact, the "Stand Your Ground" law had nothing to do with the shooting and nothing to do with George Zimmerman's legal defense. The law requires a would-be victim of serious bodily harm to retreat as far as possible before defending himself. If Martin was on top of Zimmerman, pounding his head against the pavement, there was no possibility of retreat. But Obama and Biden didn't let the facts get in the way of attacking gun rights.

Biden's assertion that most people who are shot get shot with their own guns is absurd. When guns have been banned in the District of Columbia, Chicago, and other places around the world, murder rates have gone up not down.[17] None of the criminologists or economists who have studied concealed-carry handgun laws has found an increase in murder, suicide, or accidental death.[18] Indeed, the vast majority of studies have found the opposite.

Never bashful about pushing the limits of the president's personal power, Obama has unilaterally tried to change federal gun policies. In signing statements attached to two parts of the 2012 Omnibus Spending bill,[19] he denied Congress's authority to restrict funding for gun-control lobbying and for National Institutes of Health studies of gun control.[20]

The administration has skillfully implemented gun-control regulations in many less visible ways, such as a ban on the importation of "historic" semiautomatic rifles[21] and restrictions on selling "high-powered" rifles, defined as greater than .22 caliber.[22] They also tried to slash funding for the Armed Pilots program by over 50 percent, but the Republican-controlled House stopped the proposal.[23]

Sometimes public opposition has prevented Obama from reaching his goals. In November 2011, his administration moved to ban target practice on public lands, but the opposition was so swift and strong they immediately backtracked.[24] Nevertheless, a number of shooting sites have been closed down.[25] Federal park rangers now stop and search vehicles and interrogate visitors about their legal use of guns.[26]

Obama has appointed to office people who habitually demonize gun ownership. Jon Wellinghoff, his chairman of the Federal Energy Regulatory Commission, claims that .22-caliber rifles are "among the greatest threats to the reliability of the nation's power system."[27] Obama nominated Andrew Traver, a vocal advocate of Chicago's gun ban, as head of the Bureau of Alcohol, Tobacco, Firearms, and

Explosives (ATF), which enforces federal gun regulations. Traver's nomination was stalled for over two years because of his views on guns. The president, however, has refused to withdraw the nomination leaving the agency under the supervision of an acting director.[28]

The administration has taken to seizing guns from citizens who have never been charged with a crime by abusing civil forfeiture rules.[29] Designed for seizing the assets of organized crime, these rules are being applied in situations for which they were never intended. A recent example of civil forfeiture involved a New York businessman who had hired an armored car company that, unbeknownst to him, was under investigation for fraud by the FBI.[30] The man's assets were seized as part of the government investigation, and he had to wage a costly legal battle to get his property back.

Obama's most lasting influence on gun policy, however, is likely to be through the federal judges he appoints. His most visible appointments to the Supreme Court have been strong advocates of gun control. Justice Elena Kagan led President Clinton's push for gun control in the 1990s.[31] And Justice Sonia Sotomayor has signed on to a Supreme Court opinion stating that there is no individual right to "private self-defense" with guns.[32]

The gun-control views of Obama's nominees have occasionally impeded their confirmation by the Senate despite Democratic control. Caitlin Joan Halligan, nominated for the court of appeals for the D.C. circuit, was particularly controversial. She opposes an individual's right to self-defense and has sued gun makers on the grounds that they are liable for the criminal acts of gun owners.[33] Goodwin Liu was a law professor at the University of California at Berkeley when he was nominated for the Ninth Circuit. In a law review article co-authored with then Senator Hillary Clinton, he attacked two Supreme Court decisions that struck down gun control laws.[34]

By the end of his second term, especially with a Democratic-controlled Senate, Obama will have appointed over half the federal judges. Even more important, the Supreme Court is only one vote away from reversing the five-to-four decisions that struck down the handgun bans in Chicago and the District of Columbia.

Despite the overwhelming evidence of Obama's anti-gun agenda, the media have consistently portrayed him as pro-gun and depicted his opponents on gun policy as lunatics.[35] During the 2008 presidential campaign, for example, ABC News assured voters that "President Obama will not push for more gun control."[36] In November 2012, Charles Blow attacked the NRA in a *New York Times* column, asserting, "Here is the reality. The president has done almost nothing in his first term to restrict gun ownership."[37] The media appear to be determined to mask Obama's antipathy to Americans' Second-Amendment rights.[38]

Mass Shootings and Gun Control

[There is a] Wild West, Dirty Harry mentality, people who actually believe that if a number of people were armed at the theater in Aurora, they would have been able to take down this nut job in body armor and military-style artillery. In fact, almost every policeman in the country would tell you that would have only increased the tragedy and added to the carnage.[39]

BOB COSTAS ON LAWRENCE O'DONNELL'S *THE LAST WORD*,
MSNBC, DECEMBER 4, 2012

In his speech at the prayer vigil in Newtown after the Sandy Hook shooting, Obama vowed to "use whatever power this office holds to engage my fellow citizens—from law enforcement to mental health professionals to parents and educators—in an effort aimed at preventing more tragedies like this."[40] And what form is that effort taking? Just as he did half a year earlier after the Aurora shooting, Obama called for a ban on so-called assault weapons, erroneously suggesting that these massacres are usually committed with the same types of guns that are used in the military. The president has missed the real common feature of these attacks.

Let's start with this question: Why did the killer in Aurora pick the Cinemark's Century 16 Theater on July 20, 2012, to commit mass murder?

You might assume that it was the closest one to the killer's home or that it was the one with the largest audience. Neither explanation is right. Of all the movie theaters near the killer's home showing the new Batman movie that night, the Century 16 was the only one that banned guns. In Colorado, individuals with permits may carry concealed handguns in most malls, stores, theaters, and restaurants. But private businesses may determine whether permit holders can carry guns on their premises.[41]

Most movie theaters allow permit-holders with guns. But the Century 16 posted a sign at its entrance forbidding guns. One more theater in the area has banned guns since the shootings.

With a simple web search and some telephone calls, one can easily find out how the Century 16 compared with other theaters as a target.[42] Seven theaters within twenty minutes of the killer's home were showing *The Dark Knight Rises* on July 20. At four miles' distance and an eight-minute car ride, the Century 16 was not the closest. The film was showing only 1.2 miles from the killer's home. Another theater was slightly farther than the Century 16, 5.1 miles (ten minutes). It is the self-proclaimed "home of Colorado's largest auditorium." The potentially huge audience would have been attractive to someone trying to kill as many people as possible. He could also have chosen from four other theaters that were between ten and thirteen miles from his apartment. But all of these alternatives permitted concealed handguns.

Only at the Cinemark Century 16, which banned concealed guns, could the murderer be confident of a disarmed audience of sitting ducks.

Carrying a concealed gun is more common than many people would think. Over 4 percent of the adult population in Colorado have concealed handgun permits, so it's quite likely that in a movie audience of two hundred adults at least one would have a permit.

The recent shootings in Newtown and Aurora, at the Sikh temple in Wisconsin, and at the Azana Salon and Spa (also in Wisconsin), are by no means the only times that killers have targeted gun-free zones.[43] We have witnessed mass public shootings in such places as the Westroads Mall in Omaha and the Trolley Square Mall in Salt Lake City. Both malls banned guns, but similar settings nearby allowed guns and were spared. With just one exception (the shooting of Congressman Gabrielle Giffords and others in Tucson), every public shooting in the United States since 1950 in which more than three people were killed has taken place where citizens were not allowed to carry guns.

It is especially chilling to consider that Dylan Klebold, one of the two Columbine High School killers, was following the progress of legislation in Colorado that would have let citizens carry a concealed handgun.[44] Presumably, he feared being thwarted during his attack by someone with a weapon. In fact, the Columbine attack occurred the very day that final passage was scheduled.

Opponents of concealed-carry laws, such as Mayor Michael Bloomberg of New York, insist that the presence of armed citizens at mass shootings would result in even more deaths because of crossfire. But armed civilians prevented mass shootings on many occasions—in schools, a mall, and other public places—and there is no instance on record of a permit holder's accidentally shooting a bystander.[45]

One such incident took place at the New Life Church in Colorado Springs in December 2007.[46] Seven thousand people were in the church when an armed man entered and began firing. He had killed two people and wounded others when a female churchgoer with a concealed-carry permit stopped him.

On the same August day in 2012 as the Sikh temple shooting, a gunman opened fire in a trailer park in Early, Texas.[47] Almost no one heard of the Texas case, however, because an armed citizen shot the gunman when he had killed only two persons.

As for what policemen think about concealed carry, the 2010 annual survey by the National Association of Chiefs of Police found 78 percent of its members believed that concealed-handgun permits issued in one state should be honored by other states "in the way that drivers' licenses are recognized through the country" and that making citizens' permits portable would "facilitate the violent crime-fighting potential of the professional law enforcement community."[48] Street officers are even more supportive.[49]

Aggressive gun control hasn't prevented multiple-victim public shootings in Europe. In 2011, a gunman slaughtered sixty-nine people in Norway and injured an additional 110. Germany, despite having some of the strictest gun-control laws anywhere, has been the scene of two of the three worst school shootings in the world.[50] There are more examples of attacks in countries with strict gun control, such as Austria, Britain, France, Finland, and Italy. The per capita rate of shootings in Europe and the United States are similar.

The problem with gun control is that it's law-abiding citizens, not those intent on mass murder, who comply. The guns used for the attacks in Germany and Norway were obtained illegally. When individuals plan these attacks months or even years in advance, it is virtually impossible to stop them from getting the weapons they want.

Switzerland has permissive concealed-carry laws, but the mass shootings there—the worst was in the cantonal parliament building in Zug—have occurred in the few places where guns are forbidden. Gun-free zones are a magnet for those who want to kill many people quickly. Even the most ardent gun-control advocate would never post a "Gun-Free Zone" sign at his home. If we want to get serious about preventing mass shootings, we should stop posting them where the public gathers.

Assault Weapons Bans and Crime Rates

Obama's gun strategy is to scare Americans about machine guns on their streets. In his second debate with Mitt Romney in 2012, he argued that banning assault weapons was part of "how we reduce the violence generally."[51] But it is hardly obvious why banning guns based on how they *look* rather than how they *operate* would have any effect on crime rates.

Research funded by the Justice Department under President Clinton found that the effect of banning so-called assault weapons "has been uncertain."[52] When the same researchers released an updated report in 2004, looking at crime data through 2000—the first six full years of the federal law assault-weapons ban—they stated:

We cannot clearly credit the ban with any of the nation's recent drop in gun violence. And, indeed, there has been no discernible reduction in the lethality and injuriousness of gun violence, based on indicators like the percentage of gun crimes resulting in death or the share of gunfire incidents resulting in injury, as we might have expected had the ban reduced crimes with both [assault weapons] and [large-capacity clips].[53]

Murder and violent crime rates started falling in the United States in 1991, three years before the federal ban on assault weapons went into effect. They continued to fall after the ban, but the states that had the biggest drops were the ones that already had their own bans. If the ban were effective, we should have seen the opposite result: the states that were previously unprotected by a ban should have seen their crime rates fall the most.

Despite all the dire predictions, murder and overall violent-crime rates have fallen since the federal ban expired in September 2004. In 2003, the last full year before the law expired, the U.S. murder rate was 5.7 per 100,000 people. By 2011 it had fallen to 4.7 per 100,000 people, and in no year after the ban was it higher than it was in 2003.[54]

My own research in my books *More Guns, Less Crime* and *The Bias Against Guns* found no benefits from either state or federal assault-weapon bans when they were adopted or when they expired.[55] This result held even after an array of other factors were accounted for, such as law enforcement (e.g., arrest rates, percentage of the population in prison, the number of police officers), income, poverty, unemployment, other gun-control laws, and extensive demographics on age, race, and sex.

UN Arms Control Treaty

Hours after U.S. President Barack Obama was re-elected, the United States backed a U.N. committee's call on Wednesday to renew debate over a draft international treaty to regulate the $70 billion global conventional arms trade.

REUTERS, NOVEMBER 7, 2012[56]

When the UN Arms Trade Treaty talks collapsed on July 27, 2012, many were relieved and attributed the treaty's failure to the power of the NRA. But their relief proved premature. Some speculated that the negotiations had been temporarily scuttled to save President Obama from having to deal with gun control during an election year. And on November 7, 2012, the day after Obama won reelection, he announced his support for renewing the negotiations.

The optimism in the summer of 2012 about the treaty's demise now looks unfounded. The negotiations broke down when the United States, China, and Russia asked for more time, but the idea of the treaty itself was never rejected.[57] Indeed, when the negotiations stalled, Argentina's ambassador predicted that the treaty would be approved in 2013.[58]

The UN Arms Trade Treaty negotiations were to resume, behind closed doors, in the spring of 2013.[59] The countries negotiating the treaty—Russia, China, France, Britain, and the Obama-led United States—should worry supporters of American gun rights. Russia and Britain ban handguns and many other types of weapons. China completely bans the possession of guns for self-defense. France has long made private ownership of guns difficult, though not impossible. There is no gun-friendly party to the negotiations.

While it seems unlikely that the treaty could receive the support of two-thirds of the Senate, it could nevertheless spell trouble for Americans.[60] The restriction of private gun ownership around the world will increase the pressure for gun control in our own country.

The treaty is purportedly aimed at preventing rebels and terrorist groups from acquiring weapons. The treaty's advocates claim that at least 250,000 people die each year in armed conflicts and that the vast majority of these deaths are caused by so-called "small arms"—machine guns, rifles, and handguns.[61] But governments, not private individuals, are the sources for these weapons. For example, the FARC fighting in Colombia get their guns from the Venezuelan government.[62]

The regulations most likely to be imposed by the UN treaty are the same ones American gun-control advocates have pursued for years: registration and licensing, micro-stamping ammunition, and restrictions on the private transfer of guns. Unfortunately, these measures have a long history of failure. They inconvenience or disarm law-abiding gun owners and do nothing to prevent crime.

Gun registration and licensing supposedly enable authorities to track down the suppliers of illicit weapons, yet they have been ineffective. Canada recently closed its long-gun registry because it was a colossal waste of money and manpower. Between 1998 and February 2012, Canadians spent $2.7 billion on creating and running a registry for long guns. (The equivalent cost in the United States, based on the number of gun owners, would be $67 billion.)

Gun-control advocates claim that registration is a safety issue. Their reasoning is straightforward: if a gun is left at a crime scene and has been registered to the person who committed the crime, the registry will link it to the criminal. Unfortunately, it rarely works out this way. Criminals are seldom stupid enough to leave behind guns that are registered to themselves.

From 2003 to 2009, there were 4,257 homicides in Canada, 1,314 of which were committed with firearms. Data provided last fall by the Library of Parliament reveal that murder weapons were recovered in less than a third of the homicides with firearms.[63] About three-quarters of the identified weapons were unregistered. Of the weapons that were registered, about half were registered to someone other than the person accused of the homicide.

In only sixty-two cases—nine per year, or about 1 percent of all homicides in Canada—was the gun registered to the accused. Even in these cases, the registry did not appear to have played an important role in finding the killer. The Royal Canadian Mounted Police and the Chiefs of Police have not provided a single example in which tracing was of more than peripheral importance in solving a case.

The Canadian data, it should be noted, cover *all* guns, including handguns. There is no evidence that Canada's handgun registry, started in 1934, has *ever* been important in solving a homicide.

Micro-stamping places a unique code on a bullet. The most commonly discussed method is a special etching on the tip of the firing pin, the piece of metal that strikes the bullet and sets off the explosion, which leaves a mark on the bullet casing. If the casing is left at a crime scene, the thinking goes, the bullet can be traced to the owner of the gun. The problem is that firing pins can easily be replaced or altered.[64]

The most common type of restriction on the private transfer of guns is the background check. Yet economists and criminologists who have studied the Brady Law and the so-called gun-show loophole don't find evidence that such regulations reduce crime. They might even increase it.[65] Indeed, as the surges in murder rates after gun bans in the U.S. and around the world show, such regulations don't stop criminals from getting guns. A huge percentage of violent crime in the United States is related to drug gangs. Just as those gangs can bring in their illegal drugs, they can bring in the weapons that they use to protect that valuable property.

Fast and Furious: the Government Lied, People Died

It was quite a strange set up. The Obama administration ordered gun dealers—over the dealers' objections—to sell guns to persons the dealers feared were criminals.[66] The program, which started in October 2009, was supposedly intended to study how Mexican drug gangs obtained their guns. Yet that explanation never made sense. Despite desperate warnings from Bureau of Alcohol, Tobacco, Firearms, and Explosives (ATF) agents, the guns sold to criminals were never traced, and Mexican officials were never informed of the sales. So guns were shipped to Mexican drug gangs with no effort to trace them in either the United States or in Mexico. This was Operation Fast and Furious.

Sharyl Attkisson of CBS News reported that gun dealers who cooperated with the ATF "only went through with suspicious sales because ATF asked them to. Sometimes it was against the dealer's own best judgment."[67] One gun dealer wrote in an email to officials on April 13, 2010, "we were hoping to put together something like a letter of understanding to alleviate concerns of some type of recourse against us down the road for selling these items."[68] The government's response:

> I understand that the frequency with which some indi-
> viduals under investigation by our office have been pur-
> chasing firearms from your business has caused concerns
> for you. . . . However, if it helps put you at ease we (ATF)
> are continually working in conjunction with the United
> States Attorney's Office (Federal Prosecutors) to secure

the most comprehensive case involving the different facets of this organization. If it puts you at ease I can schedule a meeting with the Attorney handling the case and myself to further discuss this issue.[69]

After extensive denials that the program even existed and numerous inaccurate claims about who knew what and when, the Obama administration now describes the program as a mistake. Yet no one has explained why the government would set up a tracing program but never try to trace the guns.

Unlike other government scandals, this one involved deaths. On December 14, 2010, Brian Terry, a Border Patrol agent, was shot and killed by one of the guns about eighteen miles inside the Arizona border near Rio Rico.[70] By September 2012, three hundred Mexicans had also been killed.[71]

The Mexican drug gangs undoubtedly would have gotten guns from other sources without the Fast and Furious program, so the murders they committed would have occurred anyway. But that argument would invalidate their entire gun-control argument involving Mexico. Anyone who did what the Obama administration did would have been prosecuted for any murders committed with the guns that they had supplied to the drug gangs.

A series of Department of Justice emails has emerged discussing how to use Fast and Furious to push for more gun control. As Fox News reported in July 2011, "Fox has obtained a number of internal ATF emails that seem to suggest that ATF agents were counseled to highlight a link between criminals and certain semiautomatic weapons in order to bolster a case for a rule like the one the DOJ announced yesterday [Monday, July 11]."[72] Another email—dated July 14, 2010, before the scandal broke—from ATF headquarters in Washington to a special agent in Phoenix expresses the desire to use the guns supplied in the operation to justify more gun control: "[C]an you see if these guns were all purchased from the same [licensed gun dealer] and at one time. We are looking at anecdotal cases to support a demand letter on long gun multiple sales. Thanks."[73]

Was this scheme as crazy as it sounds? The U.S. government used murders committed with guns that it arranged to be sold to criminals as an argument for gun control? Welcome to Obama's America.

Besides dead bodies, the scandal has offered everything that might attract media attention. Whistleblowers have been fired or threatened with retaliation.[74] An official who approved Fast and Furious was given permission to receive paychecks simultaneously from both the ATF and a private firm.[75] Relations with the Mexican government have been damaged.[76] Subpoenas from Congress have sat unanswered for over eight months, forcing Congress to go to court to get the information it wants.[77]

In 2008, Obama promised "the most transparent administration ever" and berated those who "try to hide behind executive privilege."[78] Now that he's president, what has he done? He has tried to expand executive privilege to cover government decision-making that didn't involve the president.[79]

The Fast and Furious story hit the mainstream media in early February 2011 with reports from the *Washington Post* and Fox News.[80] Attention was quickly focused on a letter of February 4, 2011, from Assistant Attorney General Ronald Weich to Senator Charles Grassley, a Republican from Iowa, asserting that concern "that ATF 'sanctioned' or otherwise knowingly allowed the sale of assault weapons to a straw purchaser who then transported them to Mexico—is false. ATF makes every effort to interdict weapons that have been purchased illegally and prevent their transportation to Mexico."

A squirming Attorney General Eric Holder claimed in May 2011, "I probably heard about Fast and Furious for the first time over the last few weeks."[81] Somehow he had missed the news coverage in February. It was then revealed that "weekly reports" summarizing activity in the Justice Department began mentioning the operation as early as July 2010.[82] Holder responded that he and his staff simply didn't have the time to read even the departmental status summaries.[83]

Holder demonstrated how uncooperative he could be under questioning by Representative Jason Chaffetz, a Republican from Utah.[84] After Holder reiterated that senior political appointees at Justice had not seen the wiretap applications, Chaffetz read from an email exchange between Deputy Assistant Attorney General Jason Weinstein and James Trusty, the chief of Justice's Organized Crime and Gang Section, dated October 17, 2010[85]—well before the February 4, 2011, letter denying any "gun walking," the term used to describe letting guns be taken illegally into Mexico.

> *Weinstein*: Do you think we should have [Assistant Attorney General] Lanny [Breuer] participate in press when Fast and Furious and Laura's Tucson case [Wide Receiver] are unsealed? It's a tricky case, given the number of guns that have walked, but it is a significant set of prosecutions.

> *Trusty wrote back*: I think so, but the timing will be tricky, too. Looks like we'll be able to unseal the Tucson case sooner than the Fast and Furious (although this may be just the difference between Nov. and Dec).... It's not any big surprise that a bunch of US guns are being used in

MX [Mexico], so I'm not sure how much grief we get for "guns walking."

Holder's response? He insisted that the emails referred *only* to the Bush administration's "Wide Receiver" operation, an earlier attempt to trace weapons into Mexico.[86] The attorney general persisted in denying the obvious—that the email exchange also dealt with Fast and Furious. This was not his first attempt to mislead Congress. He told Congress that the wiretap applications he reviewed offered no hint of any gun walking.[87] But as the Capitol Hill newspaper *Roll Call* noted, "the wiretap applications contained a startling amount of detail about the operation, which would have tipped off anyone who read them closely about what tactics were being used. Holder and Cummings have both maintained that the wiretap applications did not contain such details...."[88]

Some Democrats dismissed the investigation of Holder's role as a Republican plot to disrupt the attorney general's defense of voting rights.[89] Holder himself suggested that the Republicans' scrutiny was racially motivated.[90] The White House offered the slightly more serious defense that Fast and Furious originated in the Bush administration's Operation Wide Receiver in 2006 and 2007. The Democratic chairman of the Senate Judiciary Committee, Patrick Leahy, tried to pursue this blame-Bush strategy as well.[91]

The two programs, however, were different in one crucial respect: Wide Receiver involved the Mexican authorities. The operation might have been misconceived—the Mexican police were not up to tracing the guns—but the Bush administration had the sense to end the program when it became clear that it wasn't working. The Obama administration, by contrast, obstinately ignored complaints from the field that no one was tracing the guns.[92]

The press adopted the fiction that Wide Receiver and Fast and Furious were equivalent "gun-walking" operations.[93] Nevertheless, Holder was soon forced to concede that Wide Receiver and Fast and Furious were quite different. In a later Senate hearing, Senator John Cornyn, a Republican from Texas, and Holder had the following exchange:

> *Cornyn*: Do you know that Wide Receiver was done in conjunction with the government of Mexico, and the intention of the plan was to follow the weapons, and neither was there the intention to follow the weapons on Fast and Furious, nor did Mexico know that the United States government was allowing guns to walk into the hands of the cartels. Did you know that?
>
> *Holder*: Senator, I have not tried to equate the two. I have not tried to equate Wide Receiver with Fast and Furious.
>
> *Cornyn*: I was just asking if you know the differences between the two.
>
> *Holder*: Sure, what I know about Wide Receiver, what you have said is in fact correct.[94]

Many months after Holder's admission, however, President Obama was still denying any responsibility for Fast and Furious. In an interview on Univision in September 2012, he claimed, "I think it's important for us to understand that the Fast and Furious program was a field-initiated program begun under the previous administration."[95]

Thirty-four months after Operation Fast and Furious began supplying guns to Mexican drug gangs in October 2009, twenty-two months after one of those guns killed a U.S. Border Patrol agent, Brian Terry, and twenty months after Senator Grassley demanded answers, the Department of Justice's inspector general finally released a 512-page report on Fast and Furious.[96] Unfortunately, the inspector general took Obama administration officials at their word, failing to pursue inconsistencies within and among the officials' statements. Many crucial questions are left unanswered.[97]

The report continually states, "We found no evidence that the agents responsible for the cases had improper motives."[98] That conclusion, however, is difficult to reconcile with the circumstances in which Fast and Furious operated. We know that no one was tracing the guns sold to Mexican criminals. We know that the Mexican authorities were not informed of the operation. And we know that important officials in the ATF knew these things. Was the incompetence really that shocking, or might there have been another reason to move those guns into Mexico?

Fast and Furious was initiated, coincidentally, just when the Obama administration was asserting that 90 percent of the guns used in crimes in Mexico come from the United States. Everyone from President Obama to Secretary of State Hillary Clinton to administrators at the ATF was making that claim in 2009.[99] That statistic, however, is preposterous. Not all of the guns confiscated at crime scenes in Mexico are traced. The Mexican police trace only those guns that they have reason to think might come from the United States—about 19 percent of the confiscated guns. About 17 percent of the confiscated guns turn out, after tracing, to be from the United States. The correct figure, then, is that 90 percent *of 19 percent* of the guns taken from Mexican crime scenes came from the United States.

If guns were being sold into Mexico but not traced once they turned up there, could it be that someone wanted the number of American guns used in Mexican crimes to increase? Is it too outlandish to speculate that an administration only too eager to depict Mexico as awash in American guns might have concocted Fast and Furious to build pressure in the United States for gun control? The inspector general's report never addresses or even acknowledges this concern. Given that prominent news outlets, such as CBS News and Fox News, as well as senators and congressmen were raising this question, one might expect the report to address it.[100]

Three ATF managers, Phoenix agent in charge Bill Newell, supervisor Dave Voth, and case agent Hope MacAllister, receive much of the blame in the inspector general's report, but they "contend that the report's conclusion that the strategy for Fast and Furious was hatched in Phoenix is not true."[101] MacAllister says that the policy was part of an overall ATF strategy, implying that it came directly out of Washington. The report never explains why it accepts the word of scandal-wary political appointees and administrators in Washington over the word of these agents. You can argue about whom to believe, but the report should have considered these conflicting accounts.

If Fast and Furious wasn't intended to trace guns, why would anyone order reluctant merchants to sell guns to drug cartels? It would be easy to write off Fast and Furious simply as incompetence. Yet an administration that pledged transparency has offered no explanation for this otherwise inexplicable operation and it has stonewalled attempts to obtain the documents that might shed light on the mystery.

I'm afraid that, for all the political fireworks, the most important lesson of Fast and Furious (and Wide Receiver) has been obscured. That lesson is that *gun-tracing programs don't work*. Regardless of whether Fast and Furious was a scheme to build support for gun control, gun-control advocates should feel embarrassed.

Conclusion

Barack Obama is the most anti-gun president ever. That claim is based not on my own interactions with him back in the 1990s but on his public record over many years. He will inflict lasting damage on the rights and safety of Americans through his regulatory power and through shadier machinations like Fast and Furious. But the greatest threat is in his power to reshape the federal courts. Supporters of the citizen's right to self-defense will have to be particularly vigilant when Obama nominates new judges. Each appointment to the Supreme Court could determine whether the people are allowed to keep their guns.

CHAPTER FOUR

THE WAR ON BUSINESS

Making It Hard to Fly

A merican businesses are facing an explosion of new regulations. Much of the blame for the huge drop in business startups that I described in chapter two—a drop that accelerated during the Obama "recovery"—can be placed on new regulations and on fear of future ones.

Health care, financial, and environmental regulations have all been fiercely debated. But we should not forget how Obama is transforming the country through a multitude of smaller regulations that for the most part have passed unseen. All in all, Obama's regulatory regime makes running a business more costly and will make markets more rigid.

Take a seemingly minor example, one among a thousand. When Obama took office, pilots were required to have 250 hours of flight experience to be licensed to fly U.S. passenger and cargo airplanes.[1] But the Airline Safety and Federal Aviation Administration Extension Act of 2010, quietly enacted when Democrats enjoyed massive majorities in the House and Senate, raised the requisite number of hours by a factor of *six*, to 1,500 hours.[2] It applies even to pilots who have been trained in the military.[3]

The impetus for the new rule was the crash of Colgan Air Flight 3407 near Buffalo, New York, in February 2009. All forty-nine passengers and crew members were killed. Although commercial airplane crashes are exceedingly rare—the last one had occurred in August 2006, and as I write there has been none since—the accident provoked cries for more safety regulations.[4]

Like gun-control laws, the regulations eventually enacted were unrelated to the causes of the problem they were supposed to address. Had the 1,500-hour rule been in place in February 2009, Flight 3407 still would have crashed. The pilot, Marvin Renslow, had 3,379 hours of flight experience. The co-pilot, Rebecca Lynne Shaw, had over 2,200 hours, including 772 hours flying the type of plane that crashed.

Competence, not training, was the real problem in this case. When a stall warning went off in the cockpit, Captain Renslow raised the plane's nose, the opposite of what pilots are trained to do and a fundamental error. Renslow had failed five "check rides," proficiency tests conducted in a cockpit or a simulator.[5] One safety expert at the National Transportation Safety Board observed, "It does raise a flag when you see five."[6] Renslow apparently failed to tell Colgan about the three check rides he had failed before they hired him, and the Federal Aviation Administration does not make such failures public. Those three failures probably would have kept him from being hired. After he failed two more tests, Colgan had to know that Renslow was one of their weaker pilots, but he would have enjoyed the powerful protection of the pilots' union.[7]

The costs of the new training requirements are huge. Traditionally, prospective pilots have paid for their training themselves. The first 250 hours involve a flight instructor and cost about $200 per hour. The next 1,250 hours of training in a single-engine plane don't require an instructor, but they still cost about $150 per hour. The total cost, then, for single-engine training is about $237,500. The cost of training in a multi-engine aircraft—the training that is required to become an airline pilot—is higher still. That training itself will take a couple of years to complete, so it is difficult to hold down a normal job at the same time. The number of hours one can train in a single week has not yet been restricted, but fatigue limits how long you can fly. How flight students will finance this additional training is anyone's guess. Airlines are reluctant to pick up the tab, because once a pilot is trained, there's nothing to keep him from taking a job with another airline.

This new rule, along with new regulations that substantially limit the number of hours that licensed pilots can fly,[8] promises little improvement in safety and a reduction in the supply of pilots—just as thousands of Baby Boomer pilots are starting to reach the mandatory retirement age of sixty-five.[9] Roger Cohen, president of the Regional Airline Association, warned in a talk in Wichita, Kansas, in July 2012, "Absent a game-changing shift in the supply of trained aviation professionals, particularly pilots, communities even larger than Wichita—and certainly those smaller—are in jeopardy of losing some, if not all, of their scheduled flights. This could cut off communities from today's global economy where airline service is as important as an Internet connection."[10]

Ironically, while the Obama administration imposed rules that will curtail air service to small and medium-size cities, it was generously giving out stimulus money to small airports around the country to expand. In Alaska, $15 million went to build a bigger airport for Ouzinkie, a village of 165 people, and $13.9 million went to Akiachak with 660 residents.[11] Tiny Murtha Airport in Johnstown, Pennsylvania (named after its late Congressman John Murtha), which offers only three commercial flights a day, received $800,000 for a new runway.[12] Standing Rock Airport in Fort Yates, North Dakota, got $1 million even though it handles only two hundred takeoffs a year.[13] A third of the stimulus dollars for airports went to "little-used airports" or those catering to private planes. By contrast, Hartsfield-Jackson Atlanta International Airport, the busiest in the world, and many other large airports received no stimulus money.[14]

So why massively reduce the number of pilots? Why make it so difficult for even well-trained military pilots to fly commercial passenger planes? Why not make it easier to fire incompetent union pilots? Why jeopardize the economy of many small towns around the country?

Who are the obvious beneficiaries of these new training requirements? Airline pilots. This sudden cutback in the supply of new pilots will dramatically drive up the salaries of pilots. The regulation was simply a means to please a union, as the administration has done so many other times.

Businessmen as Bad Guys

I've created about 250,000 direct and indirect jobs according to the state of Nevada's measurement. If the number is 250,000, that's exactly 250,000 more than this president, who I'll be damned if I want to have him lecture me about small business and jobs. I'm a job

*creator. Guys like me are job creators and we don't like
having a bulls-eye painted on our back.*[15]

DEMOCRATIC BUSINESSMAN STEVE WYNN, CEO
OF WYNN RESORTS, OCTOBER 9, 2012

Even before he first ran for president, Mr. Obama's attitude toward business was clear: the problems that the country faces were due to unbridled capitalism and greed, and the federal government needed to step in to fix it. According to Obama, deregulation—even under his Democratic predecessor Bill Clinton—produced an "'anything goes' environment that helped foster devastating dislocations in our economy."[16] The proper government regulations can compensate for the "chaotic, unforgiving" nature of capitalism.[17] In the telecommunications, electricity, banking, and accounting businesses, he blamed every failure on out-of-control markets and government regulations too weak to rein in "an ethic of greed, corner cutting, insider dealing, things that have always threatened the long-term stability of our economic system."[18]

Perhaps it isn't surprising that the late Steve Jobs told his biographer, Walter Isaacson, "the administration needed to be a lot more business-friendly.... [I]t was almost impossible [to build a factory] these days in America, largely because of regulations and unnecessary costs."[19]

A year and a half after winning the White House, the Democrats realized that their heavy-handed rhetoric was going to cost them in the midterm elections, so they would occasionally try to convince voters that President Obama wasn't really anti-business. "[I]t's very hard to find evidence of anything that we've done that is designed to squash business as opposed to promote business."[20] His administration's economists, primarily Austan Goolsbee, argued that

Obama was actually *pro-business*.[21] Other Democrats joined in. For instance, the former Clinton labor secretary Robert Reich insisted that the Obama administration "has been one of the most business friendly in history."[22]

It was difficult, however, to keep up this new pro-business rhetoric. Obama regularly calls Wall Street executives "fat cats" and bondholders "speculators."[23] Even New York's liberal mayor, Michael Bloomberg, has warned, "[Obama's] bashing of Wall Street is something that should worry everybody."[24] The president accuses doctors who zealously test their patients of being "driven from a business mentality" that actually harms patients' health.[25] He blames business rather than the government for the financial crisis of 2008.[26] Indeed, the only offense for which Obama blames the federal government is not regulating enough.

By late 2011, Obama was back in full cry. Despite a report by a former pollster for Bill Clinton that "Occupy Wall Street" demonstrators showed "deep commitment to radical left-wing policies" and "support for radical redistribution of wealth,"[27] Obama expressed his sympathy for the protestors.[28] A White House spokesman even claimed that Occupy Wall Street represented the "interests of 99 percent of Americans."[29]

Obama has held well-publicized meetings with businessmen to demonstrate his openness and understanding. The media obediently report these staged events as though they were serious encounters between the president and representatives of American business, though the *National Journal* revealed the true agenda of one such meeting—a gathering in November 2012 with fifteen small business owners. "White House lines up stalwart supporters to counter anti-business image," ran the headline.[30]

In its zeal to blame businesses for the financial crisis, the Obama administration has brought numerous legal actions—civil and criminal—against the financiers supposedly responsible. Time after time, however, these cases have been thrown out of court.

Take the high-profile case of Edward Steffelin, a financier for JPMorgan Chase, who created one of those derivatives that, as Obama tells it, are the root of all evil. Steffelin devised a way for investors to bet on whether the housing boom would continue. Many investors obviously lost their bets, and the administration accused Steffelin of securities fraud.[31] The case was framed as a civil action, requiring the government to prove his guilt only by the "preponderance of the evidence," not by the higher criminal standard of "beyond a reasonable doubt." Even so, the federal district court threw out the fraud charges, calling them a "big stretch."[32] The administration eventually gave up and dropped its negligence action as well.[33]

Obama poses as the scourge of speculators, but he clearly doesn't understand what markets do. In April 2012, with gasoline a whisker under four dollars per gallon, the president explained the high price this way:[34]

> [W]e still need to work extra hard to protect consumers from factors that should not affect the price of a barrel of oil. That includes doing everything we can to ensure that an irresponsible few aren't able to hurt consumers by illegally manipulating or rigging the energy markets for their own gain. We can't afford a situation where speculators artificially manipulate markets by buying up oil, creating the perception of a shortage, and driving prices higher—only to flip the oil for a quick profit. We can't afford a situation where some speculators can reap millions, while millions of American families get the short end of the stick. That's not the way the market should work. And for anyone who thinks this cannot happen, just

think back to how Enron traders manipulated the price
of electricity to reap huge profits at everybody else's
expense....[35]

What Obama identified as "rigging" prices actually represents the
way markets are *supposed* to work. Oil prices spiked in April 2012
when Iran threatened to close the Strait of Hormuz, through which
a fifth of the world's oil passes.[36] Tensions were particularly high as
the UN Security Council pressured Iran to give the UN nuclear
watchdog fuller access to its facilities.[37]

With those facts in mind, here's a simple economics lesson.
Speculators make profits by buying oil when the price is low and
selling it when the price is high. Buying oil now to set aside in case
supplies are interrupted protects consumers. If disaster strikes, the
stockpiled oil will be released, and the reduced supply will be partially alleviated. Without those stockpiles, prices would go even
higher. Higher prices today also encourage more conservation, so
more oil will be available if supplies are cut off. Had there been no
speculators and had the Strait of Hormuz been closed, there would
have been a much greater increase in oil prices, with disastrous
economic consequences. Speculators make money by smoothing
out price changes over time.

Speculators risk their own money. In this case, nothing happened
and Iran didn't carry through its threats. The speculators who had
bet on oil prices going up were out of luck, paying a lot for the oil
they stored and ending up selling it for less. Obama didn't shed tears
over the money those speculators lost. Indeed, President Obama still
called for the Department of Justice and the Federal Trade Commission "to make sure that acts of manipulation, fraud, or other illegal
activity are not behind increases in the price that consumers pay at
the pump."[38] Yet if the supply of oil *had* been cut and the stockpiled

oil kept prices from skyrocketing, would the president have thanked the speculators for a job well done? Absolutely not.

At other times, Obama has blamed greedy oil companies for high prices.[39] Sure, with oil prices high, energy companies were making a lot of money. In 2011, just a couple of weeks before one of Obama's verbal attacks, ExxonMobil, the largest company in the United States, reported quarterly profits of $10 billion, earning about nine cents per dollar of revenue. Royal Dutch Shell, Europe's biggest oil company, earned eight cents, and ConocoPhillips pulled in five cents. But what's wrong with that? The prospect of high profits is precisely the lure needed to encourage further investments in producing energy. That is how oil supplies are increased and future prices held down.

Understanding Obama's Dislike of Businessmen

Look, if you've been successful, you didn't get there on your own. You didn't get there on your own. I'm always struck by people who think, well, it must be because I was just so smart. There are a lot of smart people out there. It must be because I worked harder than everybody else. Let me tell you something—there are a whole bunch of hardworking people out there. (Applause.) If you were successful, somebody along the line gave you some help. There was a great teacher somewhere in your life. Somebody helped to create this unbelievable American system that we have that allowed you to thrive. Somebody invested in roads and bridges. If you've got a business—you didn't build that. Somebody else made that happen.[40]

PRESIDENT BARACK OBAMA, ROANOKE, VIRGINIA, JULY 13, 2012
(EMPHASIS ADDED)

If harder work doesn't explain a businessman's success, then higher taxes, which depress the incentive to work more, must be economically harmless. Hard work, after all, isn't the cause of success. But Obama's "you didn't build that" comment seems to go further. If success is the result of luck or help from others, then businessmen haven't earned it and they don't deserve it. Obama's belief that government should "spread the wealth around" becomes more understandable.[41]

When pressed, Obama has seemed to acknowledge that higher taxes might reduce tax revenue. Yet, he apparently believes that "fairness" outweighs that cost. In 2008, for example, when confronted in a debate with the fact that higher capital gains taxes consistently reduce tax revenue, Obama was undeterred: "What I've said is that I would look at raising the capital gains tax for purposes of fairness."[42] He prefers a smaller economic pie as long as it is cut into equal pieces.

Obama's smug insistence that American businessmen haven't succeeded without help from the government is simply false as a matter of history. American businesses were successful and growing long before the government did much of anything. There was little public education in many states until about 1870, and yet the literacy rate averaged 93 percent in those states.[43] Public universities were started long after private universities, and well into the twentieth century the vast majority of our colleges were still private and operating without government subsidies.

Even the subways in New York City were originally privately built and operated. The city gradually forced the transit companies into bankruptcy by imposing a five-cent limit on fares in 1904. "Mayor La Guardia has said that the city will use all means within its power to prevent an increase in fare," the *New York Times* reported in 1938.[44] The private transit companies were all out of business by the following year, and the city had taken over their operations.[45] Fares quickly doubled. There were also many private highways in the United States until 1916—even a few in the last half-century.[46]

A variety of services that people now assume only the government can provide in fact used to be privately provided. From 1750 to around 1900, fire departments were either owned or paid for by insurance companies.[47] New York City's public fire department was not established until 1865, when the population was over 726,000.[48] Philadelphia didn't have a public fire department until 1870 when its population reached 674,000 people.[49]

Police services in colonial America and for some time after the American Revolution were often handled privately.[50] The system relied almost exclusively on volunteer night watchmen and citizens who were responsible for the identification and pursuit of criminals. When a criminal was identified, citizens would band together in a posse to track him down. Police departments weren't established until 1807 in Richmond, 1838 in Boston, and 1845 in New York. In the West, the law was privately enforced until much later.[51] Cattlemen's associations, land clubs, and merchant groups would hire their own law enforcement to protect property rights and catch criminals.

Despite the shocking lack of government services, the United States somehow developed into a prosperous industrial power. Perhaps hard work and brains are related to success after all.

Ever More Regulations and Their Burden

When he was asked at a press conference in June 2011 if regulations might "chill job growth," Obama reprimanded businesses for complaining:

Keep in mind that the business community is always complaining about regulations. When unemployment is at 3 percent and they're making record profits, they're going to still complain about regulations because, frankly, they want to be able to do whatever they think is going to maximize their profits.... But what I have done—and this is unprecedented, by the way, no administration has done this before—is I've said to each agency, don't just look at current regulations—or don't just look at future regulations, regulations that we're proposing, let's go backwards and look at regulations that are already on the books, and if they don't make sense, let's get rid of them....[52]

Even the liberal PolitiFact rated Obama's assertion that his administration was doing an "unprecedented" review of existing regulations as a complete lie: "We rate Obama's statement Pants On Fire." To soften the blow, they added, "Lots of presidents have done that."

Paul Krugman echoes Obama's claim that businessmen are whiners: "But aren't business people complaining about the burden of taxes and regulations? Yes, but no more than usual."[53] Krugman's evidence? A survey of small businesses by the National Federation of Independent Business, which represents hundreds of thousands of small businesses, asked, "What is the single most important problem your business faces?" The top answer was "poor sales," not "regulation." But it's silly to conclude that businesses therefore aren't concerned about taxes and regulations. The economic downturn was so sharp that it would have been surprising if businesses hadn't complained about "poor sales." Krugman neglects to mention that government policy, "taxes," and "regulations" collectively are the biggest concern for 35 percent of businesses, while "poor sales" are the biggest for 30 percent. Surely that says something about how bad taxes and regulations are.

There is a simpler way to find out what the members of the National Federation of Independent Business think of Obama's regulations: ask them. The week before Krugman's column was published, the association released a survey showing that 90 percent of its members thought that "federal overregulation hampers their ability to function and grow as a business," and about half found it "extremely challenging" to keep up with new federal regulations.[54] Indeed, two days before Krugman's column ran, the association's executive director, Roger Geiger, wrote a column of his own, observing, "Small businesses across America are being caught under a deluge of federal regulations, which are not only expensive to comply with but hinder job growth and raise prices for consumers."[55] His piece went on to note that as of September 2011, there were a record "4,226 federal regulations in the pipeline," and that since 2005 there had been a 60 percent increase in regulations "defined as 'major' or 'economically significant'—each costing the economy $100 million or more."

The U.S. Chamber of Commerce survey of CEOs of small and medium-size businesses found only 13 percent wanted "a helping hand" from the government, while 80 percent wanted government to "get out of the way."[56] Among the top challenges facing small businesses, "loss of revenue" came in fifth—well behind over-regulation, the Obama health care bill, and even behind America's growing debt.

The average annual number of regulations imposed during Obama's first three years in office has been higher than during either George W. Bush's or Bill Clinton's administrations, but the dramatic increase has occurred in what are called "economically significant" regulations, those which the government thinks will

FIGURE 1

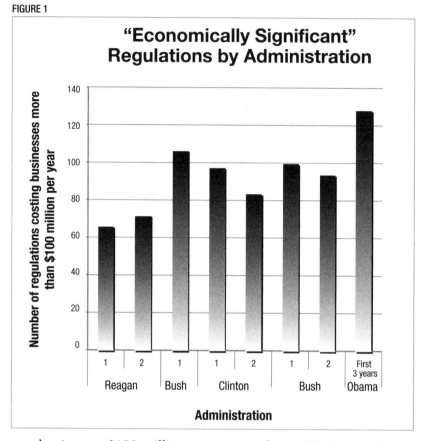

cost businesses $100 million or more each year.[57] The number of economically significant regulations issued in Obama's first three years was 37 percent higher than the total for Bush's second term and 54 percent higher than the total for Clinton's second term. Just seventy-five of those new regulations under Obama will cost companies an average of $38 billion a year over the coming decade.[58]

In July 2012, Politico reported that Cass Sunstein, a long-time friend of Obama's from Chicago who was in charge of reviewing new regulations in Obama's first term,[59] "imposed what is essentially a soft freeze on new regulations" during the election year.[60] New regulations weren't rejected, just delayed until after the 2012 election.

The Obama administration has done all it can to conceal the tidal wave of new regulations that has been building up. The White House budget office's "unified agenda" reports how many regulations are in the pipeline. Publication of this document is mandated by law, but it hasn't been published since the fall of 2011.[61]

So how many regulations have been on hold? We can make a rough guess. There was a huge drop in the number of new regulations issued in the first ten months of 2012. From Reagan through George W. Bush, presidents have usually tried to rush more regulations out the door during the last year of their term (about 10 percent more than the rate that they put out regulations during the first three years of their administrations). The pattern is so well known that it is called the "Cinderella Effect," and it is particularly pronounced before another political party is taking over the presidency.[62] Outgoing administrations issue a spate of new regulations to leave their mark before the other party takes over.

But Obama didn't follow the normal pattern. While he averaged 128 "economically significant" regulations a year during his first three years in office, "only" sixty-eight were issued from January through October in 2012. There has been no such drop since Reagan, and it is statistically significant.[63]

It is understandable that the National Federation of Independent Businesses has been warning of "Obama's Regulatory Tidal Wave."[64] We know that the administration, with the help of Cass Sunstein, has been hiding new regulations.[65] Perhaps they have been hiding the economic impact of their regulations in other ways. The estimated cost of a regulation is not an objectively derived number with which everyone will agree. The so-called "behavioral economics" that Sunstein advocates gives him even more flexibility in downplaying the economic costs of regulations. Susan Dudley, who held

Sunstein's position in George W. Bush's administration, points out how Sunstein has worked to exaggerate the benefits of regulations. New "particulate matter" regulations do save lives, for example, but they are the lives of already sick eighty-year-olds, who will live a few more months.[66] That's great, but such a benefit is not the equivalent of saving the life of a teenager who will live another seventy years. This sleight of hand, Dudley warns, is allowing Obama to get away with regulations that will put a large portion of U.S. coal-burning plants out of business.

The costs of regulations are real, not just figments of greedy shareholders' imaginations. Americans will feel them in the pocketbook. For cars, even Obama's National Highway Traffic Safety Administration and the Environmental Protection Agency estimate that his regulations will add an average of $2,000 to the price of the typical car.[67]

Many organizations have tried to measure the effect of these regulations. Since 1995, the *Wall Street Journal* and the Heritage Foundation have tracked protection of property rights, regulations on investments, financial market regulations, regulation of business, and business and individual tax rates in different countries. Does the government encourage investment by protecting private property rights, not only by having the laws on the books but also vigorously enforcing them?[68] And how onerous are regulations on investments and financial markets?[69] For general business, do regulations make it harder to start, operate, and close a business?[70]

While the U.S. ranking has slipped across the board, some areas have deteriorated dramatically over the last few years. America's rank in terms of business regulations has slipped only a little, falling from tenth in 2008 to fourteenth in 2012. But the other changes have been dramatic, particularly when considering how short the time involved. Over the same four years, the U.S. rankings on investment and financial regulations have plummeted from ninth to thirty-sixth and from eighth to seventeenth, respectively. Property rights in the United States have also become much less secure compared with other countries. The United States has fallen from a first place (tied with Hong Kong, Singapore, and Ireland) to nineteenth. These changes will surely make the United States a much less attractive place to invest.

The U.S. tax system in particular has become dysfunctional, falling from a rank of forty-eight in 1995 to 113 in 2001, 117 in 2008, and 133 in 2012. The decline was mitigated briefly during the George W. Bush administration, leaving the U.S. ranking at the end of his term only a little worse than when he came into office, but the decline has resumed under Obama.

The left-leaning World Economic Forum also ranks the business environments of countries. Though the WEF disagrees with the Heritage Foundation on most policy issues, it does agree that the United States has become less competitive. After the current index began in 2004, the United States was ranked for five years as the world's most competitive economy, slipping to second in 2009. The drop continued to fourth in 2010, fifth in 2011, and seventh in 2012.[71]

The libertarian Cato Institute has published the Economic Freedom of the World Index since 1980. The U.S. ranking plunged from sixth in 2008 to eighteenth in 2010 (the last year for which Cato's rankings are available).[72] The United States suffered similar declines in connection with regulation of credit, labor, and business (going from sixteenth to thirty-first), and the U.S. ranking for protecting property rights fell from twenty-first to twenty-eighth.[73]

The future of American competitiveness looks bleak. In October 2011, Michael Porter and Jan Rivkin, both of the Harvard Business School, surveyed ten thousand of the school's alumni from around the world.[74] The verdict was devastating: 71 percent expected U.S. competitiveness to decline over the next three years. Only 16 percent of those responding were optimistic about the future. And a large majority, 64 percent, believed that U.S. firms would be less able to keep paying high wages and benefits over the next three years. The outlook differed somewhat according to perspective. Those working for the government were among the most optimistic about American competitiveness, while those in manufacturing were the most pessimistic. Of the alumni surveyed, 1,159 had personally helped reach decisions to locate business activities and jobs in the United States or elsewhere. Over seven times more of the alumni were planning on moving jobs *out* of the country than moving jobs *into* the United States. Even worse, job transfers out of the United States averaged much larger numbers of employees than transfers into the country.

The thankless task of contradicting the charge that Obama is anti-business used to fall to Austan Goolsbee, who told the *Wall Street Journal* in late 2010 that Obama had "pushed through 16 tax cuts to assist small businesses and proposed additional incentives."[75] The comment about "small business" is revealing. Obama obviously considers it to be government's job, not the private sector's, to decide what size of businesses should invest the most. But even for small business, the tax deductions and government loans in the bill were targeted at firms that behaved in ways that Obama approves of.

The "bonus depreciation" in Obama's Small Business Jobs Act,[76] for instance, provided a 50 percent first-year depreciation. Among the lucky assets that were eligible: "Single purpose agricultural (livestock) or horticultural structures," "storage facilities (except buildings and their structural components) used in connection with distributing petroleum or any primary product of petroleum,""sewage disposal services," and "off-the-shelf computer software."

Omniscient Democratic regulators have somehow determined that an agricultural building serving a single purpose deserves a deduction, but if it serves two or more purposes, it should not be subsidized. So, a farmer who would have built one building will now build two so that he can get a huge depreciation on both. Why should larger farms, where it may make more sense to have several buildings with separate functions, be the ones that benefit? This regulatory scheme is nonsensical, of course. And so is the quick write-off for certain types of computer software but not others. And why do "sewage disposal services" deserve special treatment?

Some people point to these breaks as evidence that Obama is actually pro-business, and surely the firms that successfully lobbied for these treats have benefited. But favoring a few politically well-connected companies is not being "pro-business."

Goolsbee explained away the anger of businessmen toward Obama by blaming the bad economy: "When the unemployment rate is 9.6 percent, and when you're coming out of the deepest hole in anybody's lifetime, you knew that there were going to be a lot of people generally upset and not feeling good about where they are...." Nevertheless, despite an unemployment rate that hit 10.8 percent in the early 1980s, no one viewed Ronald Reagan as anti-business. President Obama has earned this label.

It will be years before we see the full economic effect of all the laws passed during Obama's first two years in office. It takes time for government agencies to draft the regulations that accompany a new law. One six-page section of Obamacare has produced 429 pages of dense regulations, released in 2011 by the Department of Health and Human Services.[77] In other cases, a single paragraph of the bill will eventually produce hundreds or more pages of rules. Obamacare created 159 new agencies, commissions, panels, and other bodies.

The Dodd-Frank financial regulatory act comes with 447 new rules that are either required or suggested.[78] The other new regulatory laws include "sweeping restrictions on credit-card issuers" and the Helping Families Save Their Homes Act, which makes foreclosures more difficult and prevents so-called "predatory lending practices."[79]

Many of the new Obama-era regulations are based on already existing laws. During the summer of 2009, the Food and Drug Administration (FDA) threatened to ban the sale of Cheerios[80] because of two claims printed on the box: "Cheerios is clinically proven to reduce cholesterol 4 percent in 6 weeks" and "Cheerios can help reduce the risk of coronary heart disease, by lowering the 'bad' cholesterol."[81] The FDA explained, "This is a food product and they do have a health claim.... [General Mills] could say 'heart disease,' but they are being specific and saying 'coronary heart disease.'" Indeed. Unless the claims were removed, Obama's FDA would classify Cheerios as a new drug and proscribe its sale until it had passed FDA safety testing.

After the 2012 election, the Obama administration targeted Intrade,[82] a betting exchange based in Ireland that provides strikingly accurate predictions on everything from elections to the Oscars. These trades, says the administration, are "commodity options," and Intrade isn't licensed under Dodd-Frank to trade commodity options. Yet the administration has turned down Intrade and similar American companies that have applied for a license.[83] It is easy to see why Obama waited until after the election to make public his regulations for Intrade.

All kinds of bizarre regulations are already scheduled to go into effect in 2013. The Department of Energy, for instance, will add thousands of dollars to the cost of replacing a home furnace by requiring that it be vented through a wall rather than a chimney.[84]

The new rules might also require many homes to put a new furnace in a different location and thus require expensive reworking of the duct system.

Beginning in 2013, Obamacare will require restaurants with twenty or more locations to list calorie counts on their menus.[85] The Office of Management and Budget estimates that U.S. restaurants will spend a total of 14.5 million hours each year complying with this rule. The FDA has even stipulated the size of type to be used on menus and signs. The regulations cover everything from convenience stores to pizza delivery outlets. New York—Obama's city of the future—already imposes a similar regulation on its restaurants. Researchers at New York University have found no change in the amount of calories consumed.[86] Apparently, people already had a pretty good idea of what they were buying.

Occasionally, one of Obama's regulations proves too absurd to withstand public outrage. The administration tried to ban many children under eighteen from doing chores on their family's or neighbors' farms.[87] On a bigger scale, the EPA unleashed an "unprecedented wave of rules" that even internal administration critics warned would threaten the security and reliability of the U.S. electric power supply. The Federal Energy Regulatory Commission's chairman, Jon Wellinghoff, revealed in Senate testimony that the administration's air quality regulations would reduce the generation of electricity by as much as 8 percent.[88] Under pressure from Democrats and the EPA, Wellinghoff later backtracked, but he was unwilling to supply any new estimates.

Socialist Takeovers

On September 29, 2010, the very day that the government announced it was taking a 92 percent ownership stake in AIG,

Austan Goolsbee declared it "totally bogus" to say that the president "is a socialist."[89] The government's ownership of General Motors was supposed to be temporary, but by September 2012, over three years after the original takeover, the government was still by far GM's largest shareholder, with 32 percent of the company's stock.[90] It still owns 74 percent of what used to be known as General Motors Acceptance Corporation, now Ally Financial, which primarily handles auto financing and insurance.

Even when there isn't government ownership, President Obama thinks that government, not consumers and private businesses, should ultimately run the economy.

But Obama's animosity toward the private sector goes beyond disapproving of profits. He has little respect for property rights. When he can't get his way with businesses, he does not hesitate to threaten them with financial destruction. What Obama fails to recognize is that these threats scare not only the firms he threatens, but also investors around the world, to whom investments in the United States no longer seem so safe. America's decline in economic competitiveness is the predictable result.

Cliff Asness, the co-founder of the $20 billion hedge fund AQR Capital Management, reacted to the president's aggression in a May 2009 interview:

> The President screaming that the hedge funds are looking for an unjustified taxpayer-funded bailout is the big lie writ large. Find me a hedge fund that has been bailed out. Find me a hedge fund, even a failed one, that has asked for one. In fact, it was only because hedge funds have not taken government funds that they could stand up to this bullying. The TARP recipients had no choice but to go along.[91]

American businesses have been the target of a string of intimidation tactics by the White House. The bullying started with threats of costly public audits to get firms to comply with Obama's wishes and moved on to threats of firing recalcitrant CEOs. The investment firm Perella Weinberg Partners, one of Chrysler's debt holders, got a taste of White House thuggery when Steven Rattner, Obama's car czar, threatened to apply "the full force of the White House press corps [to] destroy [the firm's] reputation" if it resisted the government's reorganization plans for the failed auto maker.[92]

The White House had pushed hard to nationalize the automobile companies. While bondholders and the government had loaned similar amounts to GM and Chrysler, the White House felt that the government should get a 70 percent stake in GM and leave only 10 percent for the creditors. If a company were worth less than what creditors had lent it, the creditors would normally get 100 percent, not 10 percent. The White House made sure that the unions also got stock and other benefits that should have gone to creditors.[93] The United Auto Workers ended up owning 63.5 percent of Chrysler.[94] The *Wall Street Journal* quoted an anonymous Chrysler debt holder calling the government's proposal "ugly" and promising to fight it.[95]

Quite a deal for the unions, seeing that normal bankruptcy proceedings would not have showered them with goodies and in fact would have invalidated their contracts.[96] The Chrysler deal was just one of Obama's many wealth transfers to unions. As the *Washington Post* noted, for workers already at GM, "Union concessions were 'painful' only by the peculiar standards of Big Three labor relations: At a time when some American workers are facing stiff pay cuts, UAW workers gave up their customary paid holiday on Easter Monday and their right to overtime pay after less than forty hours per week. They still get health benefits that are far better than those received by many American families upon whose tax money GM jobs now depend. Ditto for UAW hourly wages.... Cumbersome UAW work rules have only been tweaked."[97]

Austan Goolsbee, who also served on Obama's Auto Task Force, saw the matter differently. It was the greedy bondholders who were demanding special treatment, he insisted. "I think there has been an element, especially on the part of the bondholders, of feeling like, well, ultimately the government will just keep bailing us out, so we don't actually have to bite the bullet and make these sacrifices. And the president made clear that's not going to be the case."[98] Goolsbee later talked of shared sacrifice—"bondholders are going to have to take some haircut," he said.[99]

Most of the financial institutions holding GM and Chrysler bonds went along with Obama's nationalization of the companies for a simple reason—they themselves had been partially nationalized, so they did the government's bidding. JPMorgan Chase, Citigroup, Morgan Stanley, and Goldman Sachs have been given up to $100 billion by the government.[100] The irony is that the same government that bailed them out because they were hemorrhaging money now orders them to throw away money, taking losses that no private company would voluntarily endure.[101]

The financial institutions that avoided government bailouts and thus government control fought the nationalizations. But Obama had ways to bend these pesky bankers to his will. The standard method was threats.

When they did not cave in over the auto bailouts, the president made good on his threats against these creditors. In his announcement of Chrysler's bankruptcy, he warned, "While many stakeholders made sacrifices and worked constructively, I have to tell you some did not."[102] Despite the financial institutions' offer to give up 50 percent of their bonds' value, Obama claimed, "They were hoping that everybody else would make sacrifices, and they would have to make none." The *New York Times* and other media have joined in on this attack.[103] The administration denies having threatened Chrysler's creditors, but there is no other plausible explanation for their having agreed to take pennies on the dollar when they were entitled to so much more.

Some creditors, such as Perella Weinberg, gave in to the president. But breaking contracts through thuggish threats makes investment riskier and increases the costs as much as a big tax increase. Driving investment overseas is not the way to make America wealthier.[104]

Steven Rattner was in many ways the perfect person to handle the political payoffs and serve as the enforcer of the auto bailouts. In April 2009, he was implicated in a long-running pay-to-play investigation.[105] His former partners at the private equity firm Quadrangle Group denounced his "unethical behavior" in paying bribes to get government contracts.[106] Rattner was eventually forced to pay $10 million in restitution and to repay $6.2 million to the Securities and Exchange Commission. He was barred from the securities business for two years.[107]

To Obama, "haircuts" for bondholders at the expense of unions and the government might be a matter of "fairness." But making bonds riskier makes it more difficult in the long term for companies to borrow money, and that means fewer jobs and less tax revenue for the government.

So how did Obama's "investment" in the automobile industry turn out? More than $100 billion in taxpayer money was spent to bail out General Motors. Yet at the end of November 2012, the entire company, not just the government's share, was worth only $39 billion. By anyone's definition, that investment is a glaring failure.

Obama's campaign assured voters in 2012 that "all loans have been repaid to the federal government," that the bailout saved "more than one million American jobs," that "U.S. automakers are hiring hundreds of thousands of new workers," and that GM is again the "number-one automaker." Every one of those assertions is based on creative accounting.[108]

The money the government spent adds up quickly: $50 billion in TARP bailout funds,[109] a special waiver of $45.4 billion in taxes on auto makers' future profits,[110] exemption from all product liability on cars sold before the bailout,[111] $360 million in stimulus funds,[112] and the $7,500 tax credit for those who buy a Chevy Volt.[113] GM's share of other programs is harder to quantify, but it includes some of the $15.2 billion that went to Cash for Clunkers.[114] Those costs are in addition to the billions that the Obama administration took from GM's bondholders.

A look at the accounting shows the trouble with contentions that much of the TARP money is being paid back. The administration compares the $50 billion in direct bailout funds with the price it will eventually be able to get for selling the GM stock it owns. But that assumes that the stock price won't reflect government subsidies, including GM's exemption from paying $45 billion in taxes. By the Obama administration's logic, if the stimulus grants to TARP recipients were simply large enough, all the TARP money could be paid.

The claim that GM paid back its TARP loan is accurate but misleading. Obama wants to create the impression that all the money given to the auto companies has been paid back. But the $6.7 billion loan to GM was just a tiny fraction of the money given to it. As the TARP special inspector general, Neil Barofsky, explained, GM used "other TARP money" to pay off the loan.[115]

What about Obama's boast that the bailout "saved probably a million jobs" and that "GM is now the number-one automaker again in the world"? The "million jobs" contention is quite a stretch.

Before filing for bankruptcy in July 2009, GM had 91,000 employees in the United States.[116] You can argue that 400,000 jobs were at stake in GM's bankruptcy by counting the jobs of its suppliers and dealers as well. In 2011, employment in the entire automotive industry in the United States (including Ford, Toyota, and other companies and their suppliers, in addition to GM and Chrysler) was only 717,000.[117]

The president's hyperbole is more disgraceful because his economic advisors had warned him that these claims were false. They told him during an April 2009 meeting that job losses in the auto industry would be only a fraction—10 to 20 percent—of the numbers he was throwing around, even for the much weaker Chrysler.[118] They pointed out what was obvious: Bankruptcy would not kill every job at GM, and even with cutbacks, suppliers would pick up other work. But Obama has persisted in telling economic fairy tales.

Even if the auto bailout saved 20 percent of 400,000 jobs that were arguably at risk (a generous estimate), they were saved at quite a cost—at least $780,000 per job. How many GM workers would have been willing to quit for a $400,000 severance payment?

The "number-one automaker" assertion is no more accurate. Obama's sales figures include 1.2 million cheap commercial vehicles built by China's Wuling, a company in which GM owns a small stake, and it excludes sales by vehicle makers in which Volkswagen owns a majority share.[119] *Fortune* reports GM's revenue as smaller than Toyota's and Volkswagen's.[120]

The only real winners in the GM bailout were unions, which were protected from pay cuts, from losing extravagant overtime terms, and from cuts to their extremely generous benefits.[121] They faced only minor tweaks to their inefficient work rules. As for "hundreds of thousands of new workers," the truth is closer to a tenth of that.

Having just $39 billion to show for a $100 billion investment would get any chief executive fired. Obama not only wasn't fired, he doesn't even seem to understand how all that money was wasted.

Having "saved" the automakers, Obama muscled his way into other industries. He has tried to resolve the housing crisis by pressuring mortgage lenders to forgive huge portions of the debts their customers imprudently assumed. If homeowners don't owe as much money, he argues, they are less likely to default.[122] But if the reduced risk from default really offset lenders' costs from writing off portions of their loans, no one would need to force lenders to make the write-offs. Obama might make existing borrowers happy by wiping out their debt, but what about anyone who wants a new loan? Why would a lender write a mortgage if a year later it will face government pressure to write off $50,000 or $100,000 of the debt? If potential homeowners can't borrow money to buy houses, fewer houses will be purchased, and the price of houses will fall.

In February 2012, the administration pressured the Bank of America, JPMorgan Chase, Wells Fargo, Citigroup, and Ally Financial to set aside up to $39 billion for mortgage holders, much of it going to reduce principal.[123] The concern was that in handling the deluge of defaults, the forms had not always been signed by the proper person within the mortgage company.

Obama has committed a long list of abuses against the financial industry. In December 2009 he summoned the CEOs of America's twelve largest financial institutions to the White House and threatened them with regulatory retaliation if they persisted in lobbying against the Dodd-Frank financial regulation bill. He then paraded the chastened executives in front of television cameras at a press conference.[124]

While making the thinly veiled threat that he really didn't want "to dictate to them [how to run their companies] or micromanage their compensation practices," the president told the gathered reporters,

> Now, I should note that around the table all the financial industry executives said they supported financial regulatory reform. The problem is there's a big gap between what I'm hearing here in the White House and the activities of lobbyists on behalf of these institutions or associations of which they're a member up on Capitol Hill. I urged them to close that gap, and they assured me that they would make every effort to do so.[125]

One executive after another acknowledged the error of his ways and said he always meant to support Mr. Obama's regulatory takeover. They had all, every single one of them, simply miscommunicated their desires to their lobbyists. The public humiliation of the leaders of American finance was an unprecedented display of presidential power. Regulatory threats stopped financial institutions from lobbying against legislation that directly affected them.

Some companies learn the hard way not to cross the Obama administration. The Justice Department has been investigating Standard & Poor's improper rating of dozens of mortgage securities prior to the financial crisis. But since S&P downgraded the U.S. government's credit rating in August 2011, Democrats have "questioned the agency's secretive process, its credibility and the competence of its analysts, claiming to have found an error in its debt calculations."[126] The government is now investigating the agency for not foreseeing a financial crisis that the government itself did not foresee. If S&P's ratings of bonds and other assets are not reliable, no one will pay them for those ratings. The market will punish S&P for any mistakes that it makes.

The omnipresent Austan Goolsbee joined in the hunt for political scalps. The battle between the Koch bothers and President Obama hasn't received as much coverage as that between George Soros and Republicans, but it is nearly as bitter. In an August 2010 press briefing, Goolsbee revealed that Koch Industries, a multi-billion-dollar energy business run by the libertarian Koch brothers, had paid no income taxes. "[W]e have a series of entities that do not pay corporate income tax. Some of which are really giant firms, you know Koch Industries is a multibillion dollar business," he told reporters.

Since Koch Industries is a privately held company, its tax returns are not a matter of public record. People wanted to know how Goolsbee had obtained this information. At first the White House claimed that it was publicly available, referring to testimony before the president's Economic Recovery Advisory Board and Koch's own website.[127] The claim was false. Information about Koch Industries' taxes was available from neither source. The administration then changed its story: Goolsbee had simply misspoken; he didn't mean to say what he said, and he had merely guessed about Koch's taxes.[128] But it was quite a lucky guess. The IRS Inspector General promised to investigate whether Goolsbee had illegally obtained confidential tax information,[129] but a report was never released. With Democrats in control of both the Senate and the House at the time, there was no congressional pressure on the Obama administration to release the report.[130]

The power to regulate is the power to destroy, and it can be used to pressure companies in areas far outside the activities that are regulated. Ford Motor Company, the one American car maker that didn't take bailout funds, briefly ran an advertisement in 2011 featuring a real customer named "Chris" with a simple message:[131]

I wasn't going to buy another car that was bailed out by our government. I was going to buy from a manufacturer that's standing on their own: win, lose, or draw. That's what America is about is taking the chance to succeed and understanding when you fail that you gotta pick yourself up and go back to work. Ford is that company for me.

The *Detroit News* reported the government's reaction:[132]

> But the Obama administration didn't care for the free market message and ... the White House contacted Ford to discuss the ad and the company has now pulled the popular spot.... [S]uch inquiries from the White House represent coercion.... The most obvious reason [for the White House's concern] relates to the president's re-election bid.

The battle to pass Obamacare was filled with similar stories. When the health care battle heated up in September 2009, Democrats imposed all sorts of regulatory costs on one of their major opponents, the private insurance industry.[133] Private insurance companies were given less than three weeks to supply the government with detailed compensation data for board members and top executives as well as a "table listing all conferences, retreats or other events held outside company facilities from January 1, 2007, to the present that were paid for, reimbursed or subsidized in whole or in part by your company."[134] For employees or officers making more than $500,000 a year, the companies were mandated to provide detailed "salary, bonus, options and pension" information.

These demands were made at the same time that President Obama was attacking insurance companies for "making record profits,"[135] though the profits were hardly record-breaking.[136] The Democratic speaker of the House, Nancy Pelosi, labeled insurance companies as "villains."[137] Similar demands were not made on other parts of the health care industry, such as the pharmaceutical companies, which contributed up to $150 million to passing Obamacare on the promise that their interests would be protected in the final bill.[138]

Regulatory power was clearly abused. The *Wall Street Journal* editorialized about a couple of egregious cases, in which the administration forced the removal of two CEOs at small pharmaceutical companies.[139] The government didn't argue that these CEOs themselves had done anything wrong. Instead, it asserted the "odd" charge that a kind of "marketing to doctors common among drug companies amounted to fraud against Medicare and Medicaid." It was only after the executives agreed to a plea bargain that the government "unearthed a dusty provision in the Social Security Act" that bars health company executives from doing business with the government when the firms are guilty of criminal misconduct. Their real crime seems to have been their opposition to Obamacare.

Regulations can be used not only to punish opponents but to reward supporters. By August 19, 2011, the secretary of Health and Human Services, Kathleen Sebelius, had granted 1,472 waivers from the onerous requirements of Obamacare.[140] Even though unions strongly backed the new law, 50 percent of Sebelius's waivers went to organizations with unionized employees,[141] a figure that is grossly out of proportion to the 6.9 percent of private-sector workers who are unionized.

Let's consider the case of the pharmaceutical firm Siga Technologies, of which the billionaire Democratic donor Ronald Perelman owns a controlling share. In May 2011, the Obama administration granted the company a highly unusual $433 million no-bid contract to supply a smallpox treatment that cannot be tested on humans.[142] The drug was being designed to treat unvaccinated troops who became exposed to a smallpox biological weapon from Russia, the only other country besides the United States that has a sample of the virus. Critics point out that since we already have a vaccine, even if such a biological weapon were developed, there would be little benefit from a drug that can't be tested. The existing vaccine costs only $3 per dose and can successfully treat people when given up to four days after exposure.

Despite the administration's crusade against "greedy" pharmaceutical companies, Siga secured the removal of the government's lead negotiator when he objected to the company's astonishing 180 percent profit margin on the project. Mr. Perelman apparently has learned how to win friends and influence people.

The Future

Barack Obama is remaking the American economy. There is a reason that he delayed the release of hundreds of regulations until after his reelection. Trillions of dollars will be spent on new regulations that will lower wages, cut profits, and in many cases will harm the environment.

Obama's Environmental Protection Agency will be an especially destructive force. Methane-emission regulations now under review will pummel dairy farmers. Besides costing hundreds of billions of dollars, the rules will actually increase methane emissions by driving milk production to countries like Mexico, where it takes several cows to produce as much milk as one American cow.[143] The new greenhouse gas rules will affect churches, schools, restaurants, and hospitals.

During his reelection campaign Obama took credit for the increase in American natural gas production, which is the result of the "fracking" revolution. In his second term he will shut down many of those operations, which have brought the United States in sight of energy independence. Obama's regulations will cost about $254,000 per well and are based on highly questionable evidence.[144]

Strict new regulations are being drawn up for the temperature of nuclear power plant cooling ponds.[145] While the warmer water at one plant in Florida has brought an endangered crocodile species back from the brink of extinction and helped other animals at other places, the EPA is worried that the small areas affected could cause some fish to relocate.[146]

These examples offer only a glimpse of the EPA's agenda for the second Obama administration.[147] When you add the new Dodd-Frank financial regulations and the imposition of Obamacare, the prospects for economic chaos in the coming years are chilling.[148] The best that House Republicans might be able to do is reduce funding for regulatory agencies to temporarily stem the flow of Obama's new regulations.

CHAPTER FIVE

TAXES

Taxes Affect Behavior

D o taxes affect behavior? Yes. And we only need to look at what was happening at the end of 2012 to see how quickly businesses and individuals react.

After the election in November 2012, a long list of companies whose management had apparently been hoping for a different result moved quickly to make dividend payments before the end of the year. Even National Public Radio figured out what was going on: "Companies Rush Dividends To Beat Possible Tax Hike."[1] With Obama determined to tax dividend income at the same rate as ordinary income, many shareholders would face rates as high as 44.7 percent, up from 15 percent. A corporation would be crazy to wait until 2013 to issue a dividend.[2]

Among the 150 major companies that announced dividends by early December were Oracle, Disney, and Wal-Mart.[3] Oracle, a giant business software company that normally pays a dividend every three months, paid nine months' worth of 2013's expected dividends at the end of 2012.[4] The Washington Post Company, whose flagship newspaper endorsed Obama's reelection, accelerated its entire 2013 dividend, enabling its shareholders to delay paying their "fair share" for another year.[5] Progressive Insurance, whose chairman, Peter Lewis, bankrolls such organs of the hard-left as MoveOn.org and the ACLU, also overcame its redistributionist scruples and issued a special one-time end-of-November dividend.[6]

Costco's reaction was even more dramatic. It borrowed $3.5 billion to pay special dividends before the end of the year.[7] That kind of corporate behavior is practically unheard of. Companies usually pay dividends little by little, over time, and only if they are doing well and have sufficient liquid assets.

The timing of dividend payouts is merely one example of how companies react to tax laws. Individuals do the same. Sometimes their motives are explicit, other times we are left to infer them. Many have speculated that George Lucas, the creator of *Star Wars*, sold his film empire to Disney in 2012 to avoid Obama's looming tax hikes. The *Wall Street Journal*'s MarketWatch noted,

> That Lucas struck a deal in 2012 may be no accident either, advisers say. Long-term capital gains tax from the sale of assets held more than one year are taxed at a rate of 15% for investors in the 25% income tax bracket or above (Lucas's level), and zero for investors in the 10% or 15% bracket. Those rates are set to jump to 20% and 10%, respectively in January. . . .[8]

Others sold off their stock so as to avoid being hit by the higher capital gains tax. A typical headline read "Apple execs race to sell stock before reaching the fiscal cliff."[9]

People will go to great length to avoid taxes. We have long known that estate taxes determine where people choose to retire,[10] but they can even influence when people die. Yes, that's right—*when* they die. Some individuals have taken measures to die sooner or to stay alive longer, depending on whether estate tax rates are about to rise or fall.[11] When the estate tax was tentatively scheduled to increase in 2011, one lawyer related how more than a dozen clients had provided that "whoever makes end-of-life medical decisions [should] consider changes in the estate-tax law." These are not isolated incidents. Each 1-percent change in estate taxes raises the probability of people dying in the low-tax period by 1.6 percent.[12]

Even Obama's strongest supporters can be squeamish about handing over their life savings to the government when they die. Warren Buffett has been a conspicuous advocate of higher estate taxes. Yet in December 2012, as a huge increase in the federal estate tax was about to take effect, he helped a long-time friend and Berkshire Hathaway investor avoid hundreds of millions of dollars in estate taxes through a $1.2 billion share buyback.[13] The small businessman whose family, when he dies, will be forced to sell the fruits of his life's labor "to slow the concentration of wealth and power," as the sage of Omaha puts it, apparently needs a friend like Buffett to help him game the system.

Tax law affects decisions about the other end of life as well. One study finds that a $500 change in the child tax credit means that 27 percent of the babies who were expected in the first week of January are born in the last week of December instead.[14]

It isn't just Americans who try to avoid taxes. People all across the world behave similarly. France's richest man, Bernard Arnault, moved to Belgium when the new Socialist government raised its top rate to 75 percent.[15] Fearing an exodus of high-earners—and perhaps recalling Margaret Thatcher's quip about running out of other people's money—the Socialists expressed concern and promised to levy the tax in "an intelligent manner."[16] A Swiss tax consultant observed, "Since the socialists came to power in France, I have been deluged with inquiries from rich French people who would rather pay their tax in Switzerland."[17]

This issue involves much more than where aging rich people choose to retire. It affects firms in general, especially startups with their young founders.[18] Facing the possibility of massive corporate flight, the French budget minister, Jérôme Cahuzac, announced in October 2012 that the recently enacted 60.5-percent capital gains tax on startups was "a mistake" and promised that the government would lower the rate.[19]

There are limits, apparently, to how much social disruption some French leftists will tolerate for the sake of high taxes. There has been talk of exempting sports and entertainment stars from the new confiscatory marginal rates.[20] There are some people a self-respecting country can't afford to lose.

If high taxes drive out businesses and individuals, low taxes attract them. During the 2009–2010 tax year, sixteen thousand people in the United Kingdom declared earned incomes of a million pounds or more.[21] The following tax year was very different, however. After the top tax rate had risen from 40 to 50 percent, the number of such high-earners plummeted to six thousand. But the following year, when the new Conservative government had reduced the rate slightly, to 45 percent, the number of million-pound earners rose to ten thousand.

What Is a "Fair" Tax Rate?

We can either settle for an economy where a few people
do really well and everyone else struggles to get by,
or we can build an economy where hard work pays off
again—where everyone gets a fair shot,
everyone does their fair share. . . .[22]

PRESIDENT OBAMA, MARCH 31, 2012

President Obama is emotionally committed to raising taxes on "the rich." He has spent an entire decade talking about it, and he continues to lash out at those who oppose higher taxes.

For Democrats, tax rates are about "fairness," not their effect on the economy or even their effectiveness in raising revenue for the government. Bill Clinton put it this way: "I think the people that benefit most should pay most. That's always been my position—not for class warfare reasons; for reasons of fairness in rebuilding the middle class in America."[23]

But what is "fair"? Much of the present confusion arises because people don't understand the concept of percentages or rates. Obama and the Democrats often play to ignorance here, implying that the wealthy will pay more taxes than you or I only if they face higher tax *rates*.

If Peter makes five times as much income as Paul, should Peter pay five times more in taxes? Perhaps. That surely meets Clinton's definition of fairness, that higher-income individuals should pay much more in taxes. Even with a flat tax, where everyone pays the same percentage of his income, Peter would pay much more in taxes than Paul. You don't need higher tax *rates* to achieve that result.

Current U.S. tax rates, of course, aren't flat. They increase rather quickly as you make more income, not only because the rates themselves rise but also because high-income taxpayers lose certain deductions and credits.

Let's take a simple example. Compare two married couples with two children and no special deductions. One couple makes $60,000 per year and the other makes five times that, $300,000. The lower-income family would be near the top of the lowest one-fifth of households, while the higher-income family would be in the top 5 percent of households.[24] If you Google "TurboTax TaxCaster," you will see that the $60,000-a-year couple paid $2,194 in federal income tax for 2012.[25] The couple whose income was five times higher faced a tax bill of $70,154. That isn't five times more than the other couple. It isn't ten or even twenty times more. It is *thirty-two* times more.

In this scenario, we haven't even taken into account education and childcare expenses or other credits and deductions that are available only to lower-income taxpayers. With a couple of credits and deductions, the lower-income family isn't paying any income tax at all. For example, $2,200 spent on tuition at a local college would turn a $2,194 tax bill into a $91 refund. The Alternative Minimum Tax also makes it difficult for higher-income taxpayers to benefit from deductions.

Why should a couple that makes five times more money pay thirty-two times more in federal income taxes? Yet to judge from their rhetoric, Democrats think this still isn't fair.

Tax rates have fallen over time, but they have fallen much more for households with the lowest incomes. Adding together the income tax, excise taxes, and corporate income taxes borne by individuals, the average federal tax rate for the bottom 20 percent of households fell by 9.9 percent between 1979 and 2009 (the years for which the Congressional Budget Office has compiled data). For the top 20 percent of households, the rate fell by 5.6 percent.

Table 1: Change in Average Tax Rates by Income Group: Adding Together Income Tax, Excise Taxes, and Corporate Income Taxes					
	Bottom 20% of households	Second 20% of households	Third 20% of households	Fourth 20% of households	Top 20% of households
Percentage change in average tax rates 1979–2009	-9.9	-8.0	-7.7	-7.0	-5.6

Source: CBO distribution of household income and federal taxes, http://cbo.gov/publication/43373.

U.S. tax rates have been structured to make higher-income tax-payers carry more and more of the burden of financing government.

The tax burden borne by the highest-income households has gradually increased (see Figures 1 and 2 on pages 192 and 193). Figure 1 shows the share of federal tax liabilities by income group for the income tax, excise taxes, and corporate income taxes. From 1979 to 2009, the share of federal taxes paid by households in the top 10 percent of incomes rose from slightly less than half (48.3 percent) to almost three-quarters (72.8 percent). By contrast, the share of federal taxes paid by the bottom 60 percent of households fell from 17.1 percent to -0.9 percent—the members of this group got more money back through the tax system than they paid in. Breaking down the bottom 60 percent into thirds shows -4 percent for the bottom 20 percent, -1.2 percent for the next 20 percent, and 4.3 percent for the next 20 percent. To put it differently, the IRS sends a check to the bottom 40 percent of households equal to 5.2 percent of total tax revenue.

The results vary depending on whether Social Security payroll taxes are considered (Figure 2). Including those taxes makes the system look less progressive, but the overall trend is still the same. Since the Social Security program as a whole transfers money from higher-income individuals to lower-income ones, including only the payroll taxes for the program is misleading. In 2012, the program's

FIGURE 1

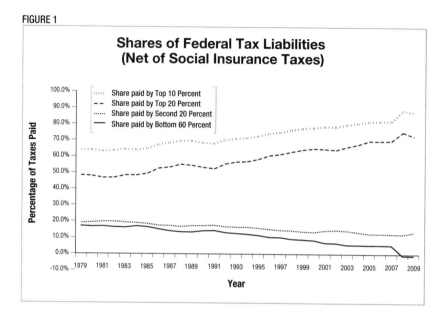

taxes were generally proportional up to $110,100, the maximum income on which Social Security taxes are collected.[26] But Social Security benefits are highly progressive. The lower your average earnings, the higher your benefit relative to your contribution.

How progressive is Social Security? A low-income earner—someone who earns about half the average income—who started working in 1995, enjoys a *negative* tax rate on his Social Security contributions. In other words, each dollar he contributes is matched by an eighteen-cent gift from the federal government.[27] By contrast, for someone earning the maximum income taxable by Social Security, seventy-nine cents of every dollar contributed is a pure tax—money that he will never see again. But the current system is insolvent, and the benefit cuts and tax increases that are being proposed, such as means testing, will likely hit higher-income earners the most. So you can expect Social Security to become even more progressive.

FIGURE 2

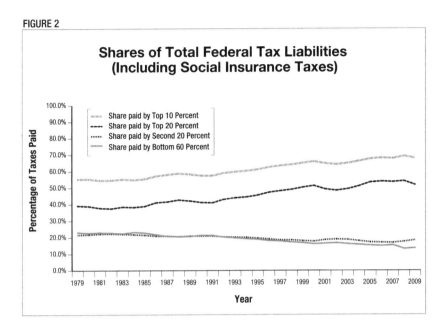

When politicians try to justify higher taxes on the wealthy, they sometimes compare them to someone who won the lottery. The phrasing suggests that the wealthy didn't deserve the money they made. And if the money just came to them without any effort, there is no need to worry about the disincentive effect of taxes. There is a flaw in this logic, though. Even if some people became rich because of good luck, how does that justify taxing all income based upon that premise?

Inheritance is an example of unearned income. True, in the technical sense it is unearned by the recipient. But often the very reason people work hard is to improve the lives of their children and grandchildren—the people they love the most. If you hamper the ability to give to future generations, you discourage work just as surely as increasing income taxes.

The discussion so far has talked only about average tax rates—your total taxes as a share of total income. But a very important concept is your marginal tax rate, how much your taxes go up if you earn an additional dollar. If your income goes up by one hundred dollars and you therefore have to pay thirty-three more dollars in tax, then your marginal rate is 33 percent. When you are trying to decide whether to work more or make more investments, how much you get to keep of the *additional* money can make the difference.

But the tricky part is that your "official" marginal tax rate is not the same as your "effective" marginal tax rate. In 2012 there were officially six marginal income tax rates (10, 15, 25, 28, 33, and 35 percent), but in most cases these rates did not accurately reflect how your total taxes were affected when you earned that additional hundred dollars. That's because you lose certain credits and deductions as your income increases. For example, lower-income individuals can claim the earned income tax credit and the college tuition credit, which are "phased out" at higher incomes.

And the story does not end here. Setting aside state welfare programs, there are a number of federal assistance programs that also phase out rapidly as income increases, ranging from housing subsidies to food stamps. If we include these losses in our calculations, we can end up with ridiculously high rates for people struggling at the bottom of the income scale. There appears to be some awareness of this problem in both political parties but no consensus as to whether something should be done about it.

The liberal-leaning Urban Institute estimates that for a family of two parents and two children, the effective loss of income from earning an additional dollar can be huge.[28] Those earning between $15,000 and $40,000 get to keep at most twenty cents of every additional dollar they earn. To put it another way, the combined effective marginal income tax rate and the lost-benefit rate is between 80 and 100 percent. This is the ultimate irony of government assistance. The more help that's given, the more disincentive there is to work. It's hardly a surprise that many chose not to work if they can keep only a fifth or less of their additional earnings.

The gap between the official and effective marginal income tax rates because of phased-out benefits is a relatively recent problem. In 2010, Katherine Bradley and Robert Rector identified "over 70 different means-tested anti-poverty programs that provide cash, food, housing, medical care, and social services to poor and low-income persons."[29] They showed that such programs had exploded in size even before Obama became president. Between fiscal years 1989 and 2008, means-tested welfare programs almost quadrupled, growing "faster than every other component of the government" and more than twice as fast as spending on either defense or education.

Obama has made the problem much worse, especially with Obamacare, as large health insurance benefits will phase out with higher incomes. For example, individuals and families with incomes between the federal poverty level and four times the poverty level will pay reduced premiums for health insurance.[30] In addition, incomes between the poverty level and 2.5 times the poverty level will receive subsidies for the out-of-pocket costs of co-payments and deductibles. These subsidies are scaled back as income increases and at a certain level are eliminated.

Then there are the tax changes in the stimulus. Obama increased tax credits in an effort to help the poorest, but the credits rapidly phase out as people make more money. He also accelerated the phase-out of existing credits. That hurts the near-poor and encourages welfare dependency.

The stimulus tax cuts created a similar problem. The total tax (and thus the average tax rate) for many low-income earners was lowered, but the effective *marginal* income tax rates went up because of benefit phase-outs. Again, the result is a poverty trap.

Obama expanded various federal assistance programs, including food stamps. Between 2008 and 2011, federal spending on means-tested welfare programs grew by as much as 32 percent. This spending now accounts for 21 percent of the federal budget.[31]

The "Buffett Rule"

President Obama justifies his frequent call for higher taxes on the wealthy on the grounds that millionaires should not pay lower tax rates than middle class workers. Nevertheless, his proposed increase of the capital gains and dividend taxes will raise an already high tax burden for high-income individuals. The higher taxes will drive more capital out of the United States.

The so-called "Buffett Rule"—individuals making more than $250,000 per year should pay an average tax rate of at least 30 percent—is based on Warren Buffett's claim that he pays lower taxes than his secretary:

> The 400 of us [here] pay a lower part of our income in taxes than our receptionists do, or our cleaning ladies, for that matter. If you're in the luckiest 1 per cent of humanity, you owe it to the rest of humanity to think about the other 99 per cent.[32]

There is a grain of truth to this, but not much more. It is correct that at least through 2012, the 15-percent maximum tax on capital gains and on dividends was less than the *marginal* income tax rate for many ordinary workers. But it is extremely unlikely that the *average* tax paid by an ordinary low-income worker would ever amount to 15 percent. In many cases it is far less than that, often even below zero, because of the various personal exemptions, deductions, and credits.

But much more importantly, the Buffet Rule ignores that corporate income is not taxed primarily through the individual income tax but through the corporate income tax. In the United States, the combined federal and state corporate tax rate is 39.2 percent, the highest in the world. It is only after such taxes have been paid that income is handed over to the individual, to be taxed again at the 15-percent rate.

Let's take a simple example. Suppose Warren Buffet invests his money in a company and that company earns one dollar. The company pays thirty-nine cents in income tax. If the remaining sixty-one cents is paid as a dividend, the 15-percent dividend tax leaves the stockholder with fifty-two cents, for a combined effective tax rate of 48 percent. The analysis is the same if the company keeps the money, raising the value of its stock and thus creating a capital gain.

By contrast, Mr. Buffett's secretary in Omaha simply doesn't pay income tax at an average rate of 48 percent. President Obama tries to have it both ways, as he claims that his proposals did not amount to "class warfare,"[33] while at the same time accusing the wealthy of not paying their "fair share."[34]

If you add up the federal personal income taxes, corporate taxes, and excise taxes that Americans pay, you can see how progressive the tax system is. The average tax rate paid by the top 1 percent of taxpayers in 2009 was 26.4 percent. By contrast, individuals in the bottom 20 percent and the next lowest 20 percent on average received tax *rebates* equal to 7.3 and 1.1 percent of their income, respectively (Figure 3 on page 198).

Heavier taxes on the rich would bring in little additional revenue and thus would have only a small effect on federal deficits. According

FIGURE 3

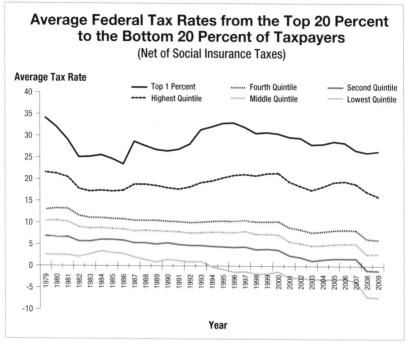

to the Obama administration's own numbers, raising the top income tax rates for the upper-income earners to 36 and 39.6 percent and taxing dividends as ordinary income would raise $44.6 billion in 2013 (see Table 2). That total is only 1.2 percent of the $3.8 trillion that the administration plans to spend in 2013—the equivalent, that is, of four days of federal spending. And that estimate is optimistic: the administration assumes that higher tax rates won't affect how much people work and won't reduce investment.[35]

Even as Democrats bay for higher tax rates, they resist means-testing the programs where the real money is spent—Social Security and Medicare. These two programs are projected to cost a combined $1.34 trillion in 2013, and they face long-term unfunded liabilities of $42.8 trillion and $20.5 trillion, respectively.[36]

Year	Reinstate 36% and 39.6% income tax rates for top brackets	Tax qualified dividends as ordinary income for upper-income taxpayers	Higher earned-income rates plus new treatment of dividends	Projected federal spending	New tax revenue as a percentage of federal spending	No. of days of federal spending for which new tax revenue will pay
2013	$23,101	$21,537	$44,638	$3,803,000	1.17%	4
2014	$32,492	$10,483	$42,975	$3,772,000	1.14%	4
2015	$35,507	$15,624	$51,131	$3,828,000	1.34%	5
2016	$39,133	$20,183	$59,316	$3,962,000	1.50%	5

Table 2: Obama Administration's Expectations of Revenue in Second Term from Taxing High-Income Earners (millions of dollars)

Source: Office of Management and Budget, fiscal year 2013 budget, pp. 210, 219, and 220, http://www.whitehouse.gov/sites/default/files/omb/budget/fy2013/assets/budget.pdf

Why oppose means-testing Social Security and Medicare? Apparently, to maintain political support for the programs. As Congressman Keith Ellison, Minnesota Democrat, said, "I don't see want to see [sic] Medicare turn into a welfare program which is what it would be if wealthier people didn't benefit from it or had a significantly reduced benefit."[37] Max Richtman, the president of the liberal National Committee to Preserve Social Security and Medicare, is even more explicit: "If Medicare turns from an earned benefit into a welfare program, you will see support dissipate."[38] Democrats don't want to spoil the illusion that people are getting benefits that they have "earned" through their "contributions." Admitting the reality that Social Security and Medicare are massive wealth-transfer programs, Democrats fear, could be politically fatal.

Tax Rates in Other Countries

Now let's consider the following statements, both of which downplay the importance of incentives:

The modern American right, and much of the alleged center, is obsessed with the notion that low tax rates at the top are essential to growth. Remember that Erskine Bowles and Alan Simpson, charged with producing a plan to curb deficits, nonetheless somehow ended up listing "lower tax rates" as a "guiding principle."

Yet in the 1950s incomes in the top bracket faced a marginal tax rate of 91, that's right, 91 percent, while taxes on corporate profits were twice as large, relative to national income, as in recent years. The best estimates suggest that circa 1960 the top 0.01 percent of Americans paid an effective federal tax rate of more than 70 percent, twice what they pay today.

PAUL KRUGMAN, *NEW YORK TIMES*, NOVEMBER 18, 2012[39]

[A]s an actually empirical matter, what were the four fastest years, I think, of economic growth in the last thirty years? I think '83 to '86, under Reagan. What were the top marginal tax rates? Fifty percent. Honestly, 35 to 39 percent, by itself, is not going to cripple the economy.

WILLIAM KRISTOL, NOVEMBER 13, 2012[40]

Liberals like Paul Krugman and conservatives like Bill Kristol have convinced themselves that high tax rates don't really matter. They point out that relatively high tax rates and high growth rates have coincided in the past. At the end of November 2012, the *New York Times* ran a major story claiming that the deficits were a result of taxes being too low, because tax rates had fallen since 1980.[41] But the world has changed substantially since the 1950s and even since the 1980s.

One major change has been increased international competition between countries over taxes. For investors with hundreds of trillions of dollars in international capital markets looking for the highest return, even a small difference in tax rates can determine where their money goes. For example, the United States has the highest corporate tax rate in the world at 39.2 percent. Our next-door neighbor Canada's rate is 26 percent, and the average European country's is 21 percent. If you're trying to decide whether to invest in Canada or in the United States, you will notice that you get to keep thirteen cents more of every dollar that you earn in Canada rather than in the United States. That's a big difference, and unless it's offset by lower costs, higher productivity, or some other advantage in the United States, you'll invest in Canada.

FIGURE 4

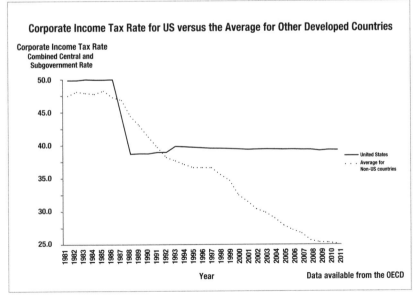

Tax rates have been falling in the United States, but they have been falling even faster for decades in other thirty-four developed countries (Figure 4).[42] Between 1981 and 2011, the U.S. corporate income tax rate fell by 11 percentage points, from 50 to 39 percent. The rate for other developed countries fell twice as much, 22 percentage points, plunging from 47 to 25 percent. There was a brief period starting in the Reagan administration when the U.S. tax rate fell below the average rate for other countries.

The United States had better keep up with the competition. Krugman and Kristol ignore the dramatic change in world tax rates. The tax rates that worked in 1980 are not competitive in today's internationalized market. The gap between the United States and other countries is already large, but if we were to follow Krugman's and Kristol's advice and return our corporate tax rate to where it was in 1980, there would be a massive exodus of capital from the United States. Instead of a corporate tax rate 14 percentage points higher than other developed nations', the United States would have a rate 25 percentage points higher. And that's in a world with much more flexible capital markets, where money can be moved from one place to another with a few mouse clicks.

As for personal income taxes, the top U.S. rate is now just slightly higher than other developed countries'. Kristol is correct that the highest marginal rate for the U.S. personal income tax was still 50 percent from 1982 to 1986. But he commits an error of omission, for he does not consider that even the 50-percent rate was a reduction from the top rate under Carter and was dramatically lower than the rates in other countries. Reagan *lowered* the rates, with happy economic results.

From an international perspective, Reagan's tax cuts changed the United States from a relatively high-tax country to a relatively low-tax country. During those high-growth years 1982 to 1986, America's top personal income tax rate was 10 percentage points lower than the average for other developed countries. Kristol surely wouldn't have said what he said about tax rates in the 1980s if he had examined Figure 5 below.

Reagan and his "Supply-Side Revolution" sparked an era of lower taxes around the globe. After world rates went down and, under Clinton, U.S. rates went up, America's rates were back to "normal" internationally. Subsequent economic history validates the importance of incentives: lowering tax rates spurs growth, especially if rates become lower than in other nations.

Suppose that you owned a share of stock in a company that earned one dollar of profit per share. In 1980, the federal government would immediately take fifty cents of that profit through the corporate income tax. If the company paid out the remaining fifty

FIGURE 5

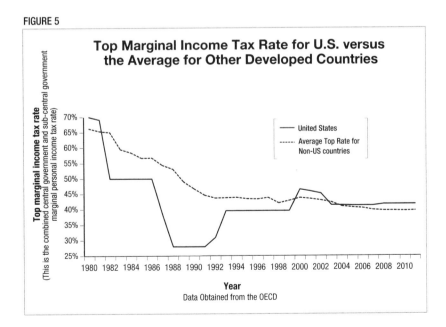

cents of profit as a dividend, you would have to pay personal income tax on that dividend payment. With a 70-percent personal income tax rate, the government would take another thirty-five cents, leaving you with only fifteen cents of that original one dollar of profit. Cutting the personal income tax rate from 70 to 50 percent meant that the profit you got to keep increased from fifteen to twenty-five cents.

Reagan also cut the capital gains tax from 28 to 20 percent, increasing your return on your investment when you sold your stock.[43]

Besides international competition, there is a second reason why higher taxes would have a greater impact today than in the 1950s or even the 1980s. Many more women are now in the labor force, and economic studies consistently show that women are still more willing and able to stop working than men are.[44] Women are more willing than men to stay home raising children. At some point, a higher tax bite makes working outside the home too costly to bother with.

Taxes and Growth

It is a simple notion. Lower corporate tax rates, and people will invest more money. Countries that have lower tax rates get more investments and grow faster. Lower personal income tax rates, which let people keep a greater share of each additional dollar they earn, give them an incentive to work harder and longer.

This intuition is strongly confirmed by the data. Figure 6 uses OECD data to illustrate that the countries with lower average corporate income tax rates from 2000 to 2010 enjoyed greater growth in GDP. Figure 7 on page 206 shows that countries with lower marginal rates for income tax during the same period also had higher growth. In both cases, the relationships are statistically significant.[45]

FIGURE 6

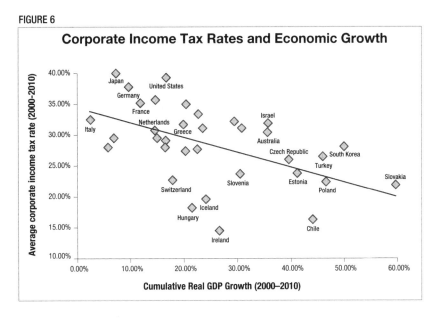

The effect of lower taxes on growth is quite large. In both cases, each 1-percent increase in tax rates reduces GDP growth by about 1 percent, though the effect of higher corporate income tax rates is 25 percent greater. Since money can move more quickly and easily across countries than workers can, we would expect greater sensitivity to higher corporate tax rates. So a country that lowered its corporate income tax rate by 7.1 percentage points (which was the average drop for non-U.S. developed countries from 2000 to 2010) could expect to increase its economic growth by 8.2 percentage points. If that country lowered its top individual marginal rate by the same amount, it could expect to increase its economic growth by an additional 6.6 percentage points.

"An Orgy of Spending"

In his last state of the union address in 2000, Bill Clinton suggested only a few small spending programs, and he voiced no complaint

FIGURE 7

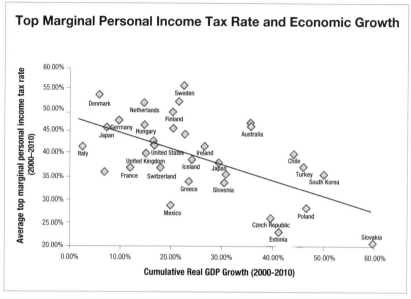

In this figure:

Top Marginal Personal Income Tax Rate and Economic Growth

Y-axis: Average top marginal personal income tax rate (2000-2010)

X-axis: Cumulative Real GDP Growth (2000-2010)

Countries plotted: Sweden, Denmark, Netherlands, Finland, Germany, Japan, Hungary, Australia, Italy, United States, Ireland, United Kingdom, Iceland, Japan, Chile, France, Switzerland, Turkey, South Korea, Greece, Slovenia, Mexico, Poland, Czech Republic, Estonia, Slovakia

that spending was too low. He even boasted, "My fellow Americans, the state of our union is the strongest it has ever been."[46] If federal spending had simply kept pace with inflation and population growth after Clinton left office, it would have risen from $1.86 trillion in 2001 to $2.6 trillion in 2012. The federal deficit for 2012 would have been $150 billion. Instead, the federal government spent $3.54 trillion in 2012 and ran a deficit of $1.1 trillion (Figure 8).[47]

In 2008, Barack Obama attacked Republicans for "an orgy of spending and enormous deficits."[48] In both the second and third presidential debates, he repeatedly promised to cut "net government spending." Instead, real federal spending increased by 21 percent between 2008 and 2011. This was the largest increase in government spending and deficits (adjusted for inflation) in U.S. history, even larger than the increase during the worst part of World War II.[49]

FIGURE 8

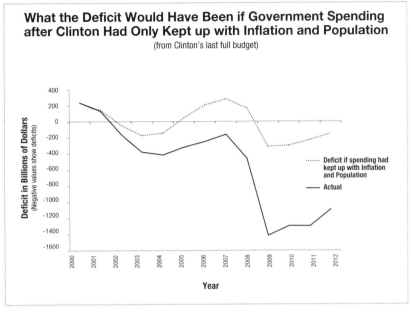

What the Deficit Would Have Been if Government Spending after Clinton Had Only Kept up with Inflation and Population
(from Clinton's last full budget)

The deficit in 2012 would likely have been much worse if Republicans had not won control of the House of Representatives in 2010. After his electoral "shellacking" that year, Obama pledged "to act boldly now" to control the huge deficits.[50] In February and April 2011, he presented budget proposals that supposedly would cut the deficit by $1.1 trillion.[51] Neither one survived scrutiny, however.

The Congressional Budget Office, the White House's designated referee on spending questions, reported that Obama's February plan, which was a formal budget proposal, would have *increased* deficits over the coming decade by $1.2 trillion.[52] Dismissing the president's figures, the CBO reported that he had underestimated the costs of both existing and new programs. The Democratic-controlled Senate voted down the president's budget ninety-seven to zero.

Obama's April plan, presented in a speech at George Washington University, promised a $4 trillion reduction in the deficit over ten years. The CBO was unable to evaluate this "plan" because, as CBO director Douglas Elmendorf told the House Budget Committee, "We don't estimate speeches."[53] The Senate never put the April proposal to a vote.

During Obama's first four years in office, publicly held debt increased by $5.5 trillion.[54] And there is no let-up in sight. If the administration has its way, the debt will grow by another $8 trillion in the decade from 2013 to 2022.[55]

When Obama took office, publicly held debt stood at $20,600 per person. At the end of his first term it had almost doubled to over $37,000 per person. That figure is projected to grow to almost $49,000 by the end of his second term. That's $195,000 for a family of four.

President Obama and his allies in Congress have taken the country on a historic spending binge from which it will be difficult to recover. The word "budget" has ceased to have any meaning in connection with federal spending. And yet they are not chastened. As the consequences of our unprecedented debt come into terrifying focus, Obama refuses to consider cuts to discretionary spending or the reform of entitlement programs.

Our Government Was Already Very Large

About the monstrously bloated federal government over which he presides, we could say to President Obama, "You didn't build that." He *enlarged* it, to be sure, but the government was dangerously overgrown before he took office. As a candidate, Obama even promised to make the government smaller.

From a historical perspective, the growth of the federal government has been simply incredible. Less than a hundred years ago, federal spending exceeded 3 percent of GDP only during wartime,

after which spending would quickly return to pre-war levels. Since the 1920s, however, the federal government has grown dramatically.

The federal government has grown not only in absolute terms but also compared with governments of other countries. This might seem unlikely, since we think of the United States as one of the most free-market countries in the world. Different countries obviously have different answers. Countries run by socialists spend lavishly on cradle-to-grave welfare systems. On the other hand, citizens in non-socialist countries have more choice over how to spend their money. When Americans think of countries with enormous governments, they probably think of Sweden, France, or Finland. Most of Europe, we suppose, is burdened by much larger government than the United States.

Unfortunately, that isn't true anymore. Even after adjusting for differences in the cost of living and population, total government spending—state, local, and federal—accounts for more real resources per capita in the United States than 95 percent of the countries on the planet. In fact, in 2011, 186 out of 195 countries spent less money than the United States. Our government spends almost three times more than the average government. That comes to about $18,940 per person in the United States—almost $76,000 for a family of four.

Even in *France*, per capita non-defense spending in 2011 was 12 percent less than in the United States. The gap is 19 percent if defense spending is included. Non-defense per capita spending for Canada was 22 percent less. Italy, Greece, and Spain—which don't make the top-twenty list of big-spending governments—don't even come close to the U.S. Of the top twenty spenders, the United States experienced the fourth-fastest growth in government spending between 2008 and 2011. With Obamacare, the United States is guaranteed to move up the chart.

Table 3: 2009 per Capita Government Expenditures after Accounting for Price Differences in 2008 and 2011 for Top 20 Countries						
	2011				2008	
Country	Rank	Per Capita non-defense government expenditures	Rank	Per Capita government expenditures	Rank	Per Capita non-defense government expenditures
Luxembourg	1	$29,035	1	$29,454	1	$28,716
Sweden	2	$24,205	3	$24,789	2	$23,909
Norway	3	$24,087	2	$24,892	4	$21,746
Iceland	4	$23,744	5	$23,791	3	$21,973
Denmark	5	$23,398	4	$24,015	5	$21,698
Japan	6	$21,744	6	$22,275	6	$19,017
Finland	7	$20,389	8	$20,910	7	$18,325
Austria	8	$19,185	9	$19,516	8	$17,703
U.S.	9	$18,940	7	$21,314	10	$16,589
U.K.	10	$18,256	10	$19,233	11	$16,459
Netherlands	11	$17,912	11	$18,414	12	$16,381
Belgium	12	$17,566	12	$17,931	13	$16,044
Ireland	13	$17,431	13	$17,651	16	$13,566
Switzerland	14	$16,779	15	$17,187	9	$17,013
France	15	$16,624	14	$17,334	14	$16,000
Germany	16	$16,146	16	$16,600	15	$15,140
Canada	17	$14,839	17	$15,325	17	$13,291
Qatar	18	$13,274	18	$14,388	18	$12,465
Kuwait	19	$12,464	19	$13,636	20	$10,784
Israel	20	$11,579	20	$13,570	19	$11,584

2008 government expenditure data are from the Heritage 2009 Index of World Freedom, available only through the wayback archive.[56] 2011 government expenditure data are from the Heritage 2012 Index of World Freedom.[57] Military spending data 2008 from SIPRI (Stockholm International Peace Research Institute).[58] 2011 Military Spending data (latest year available) are from SIPRI.[59] Per capita GDP data are from the World Bank (chained $2000 dollars were used and then converted to 2012 dollars using the BLS CPI conversion of 1.34).[60]

Two of the eight countries that outrank us in spending do so because of their unique circumstances. In Norway, the government owns the country's oil wealth, and the 500,000 people in tiny Luxembourg specialize in banking.

These comparisons are imperfect. For example, while the Swedish government rewards parents with a check for each additional child, the United States uses the tax credits and the tax code to accomplish the same goal. That would make federal government's expenditures look relatively smaller in the United States, even though the result is the same.

Americans spend more per capita on national defense than most other countries. But the differences in defense expenditures are relatively minor, so limiting our comparisons to non-defense government expenditures actually makes little difference. The federal government's per capita government expenditures still exceed that of 93 percent of other countries. The U.S. government has control over more resources per capita than virtually any other country in the world.

The federal government of the United States is ensnared in a fiscal crisis not because it doesn't take enough from its citizens in taxes but because it spends too much.

CONCLUSION

[Andrew] Bellman [vice president of the Democratic polling company Democracy Corps] said the president has "a lot more work to do" to inform voters of his priorities for the next four years—and added that he is running out of time.... Another Democratic strategist told CBS News that the Obama campaign "made a strategic choice" to avoid talking about the future and instead focus on tearing down his opponent Mitt Romney. The decision, the strategist said, was a response to the mood of the electorate, the status of the economy and likely a host of other factors.

LEIGH ANN CALDWELL, CBS NEWS, OCTOBER 18, 2012, WRITING SHORTLY AFTER THE SECOND PRESIDENTIAL DEBATE BETWEEN OBAMA AND ROMNEY[1]

Obama thinks he has a mandate for change. But this is the man who ran for president in 2008 promising to "cut net spending" and to shrink the federal government, who promised that his "stimulus" spending was only temporary.

He hid regulations from view until after his reelection. The press maintained the fiction that Obama supports the Second Amendment and is no threat to citizens' keeping guns for self-defense. Yet the day after his reelection, Obama called for the UN Arms Trade Treaty negotiations to be started again, and a few weeks later he promised to put the full force of the federal government behind a push for massive new gun control.

Even on taxes, Obama's post-election demands contradicted the positions on which he campaigned. Sure he promised higher taxes on "the rich." But during the campaign he said that he wanted $800 billion from them. As soon as Republican speaker of the House, John Boehner, agreed to raise that amount by eliminating various credits and deductions for high-income taxpayers, Obama announced that he really wanted *twice* that amount.[2]

Does a candidate who won reelection with just under 51 percent of the vote and who has adopted a second-term agenda that he never talked about during the campaign really have a "mandate"?[3] Hardly. Certainly not a mandate for the radical changes that he has in store for Americans. Indeed, the Republican members of Congress have a mandate to stop him.

There is a growing awareness in the United States of the mounting debt problem, and opinion polls show increasing acceptance of budget cuts. But a Barack Obama who will never face the voters again doesn't have to worry about public opinion. He wants to raise taxes to redistribute wealth, not to reduce the deficit. As investments that would have come to the United States are diverted to other countries, federal revenue will fall short of Obama's optimistic estimates. The nation's metastasizing debt will overwhelm the small increases in incomes.

Many Democratic voters naively believe that "the rich"—an undefined group of invisible people who, somehow, must exist—have a lot of extra money that can easily be appropriated through taxation. I'm an economist and a statistician, and I assure you that this is not the case. There is wishful thinking at the other end of the spectrum as well, where some believe we can easily cut "wasteful" government spending. They seem not to realize what a large portion of federal spending goes to transfer payments such as Social Security. People get angry when anyone talks about cutting "their" benefits. It's easier to talk about raising taxes or cutting benefits than to actually do the nitty-gritty work of reaching a compromise on who shall bear the burden.

The United States has been on this unsustainable course for quite a while. What's new is that a true left-wing ideologue is in charge. The one prediction we can make with confidence is that Obama will try to impose a top-down government "solution" for every problem we face. By the end of his second term, we could be left not only with a mountain of debt but also with expanded groups of people who think they "deserve" a government handout. It is going to be very difficult to reverse course.

Unfortunately, the problem goes beyond who gets what handout. Major changes to regulations and taxes create uncertainty and therefore can be implemented only so often. Businesses, especially foreign investors, shy away from gambling with their capital. Why invest in buildings, in research and development, in worker training if they're likely to face new taxes or other disruptions to the business environment? They might be better off delaying those investments or making them in, say, Hong Kong or Singapore.

The United States' fiscal turmoil inspires fear of senseless additional taxes as politicians scramble to finance our mounting debt. The mere proposal of new taxes, even if Congress ultimately votes them down, sends rational investors running for the exits.

Obamacare's 2.5-percent tax on medical devices is a cautionary tale. Most people want to encourage new medical technology, which has made such spectacular contributions to our health care. Ask anyone with an artificial hip or knee. But in the frantic scramble to assemble the financing of Obamacare, some bureaucratic genius came up with the idea of a special tax on medical devices. Now that the tax is about to go into effect, even left-wing Democratics like Senator Al Franken see how foolish it is. Franken provided the crucial sixtieth vote to pass Obamacare, and he didn't demand that this flaw be corrected when he had the chance. Franken's rhetorical shift seems motivated more by concern for his 2014 reelection bid than a true conversion.

International investors see what's going on, and they will vote with their pocket books. In a couple of years, they wonder, which category might their industry find itself in—"worthy of a bailout" or target for taxation? A jungle of complicated taxes and regulations is bad, but constantly changing taxes and regulations make things even worse.

What can we expect of a second Obama term? Obama will continue to try to pick winners and losers. He will continue to pursue the agenda of organized labor at the expense of the unemployed, especially young people. He will continue to try to achieve through the regulatory power of the executive branch what he cannot get through Congress. He will continue to try to grow the government at the expense of the free market and of individual freedoms, especially the free exercise of religion and the right to bear arms.

Our country, in short, is in trouble. Can we pull ourselves back from the brink? Call me a cock-eyed optimist, but I believe that facts can change minds. And the facts are overwhelmingly lined up against Barack Obama.

ACKNOWLEDGMENTS

would like to thank Gertrud Fremling, Roger Lott, Sherwin Lott, and my editor, Tom Spence, for their helpful comments. I also benefited from debates that I had on the economy at Temple University, the University of Arkansas, and the University of Tulsa.

NOTES

Chapter One

1. MSNBC, *Morning Joe*, November 21, 2012.
2. Meena Hart Duerson, "Florida man who warned he wouldn't 'be around' if Barack Obama was reelected kills himself after the election," *New York Daily News*, November 14, 2012, http://www.nydaily news.com/news/national/man-article-1.1201911. Associated Press, "Florida man commits suicide after warning he might harm himself if Obama won," Jacksonville.com, November 14, 2012, http://jackson ville.com/news/crime/2012-11-14/story/florida-man-commits-suicide-after-warning-he-might-harm-himself-if-obama.
3. In 2012, the average insurance premium for a single individual was over $5,615, as seen in, "Employer Health Benefits: 2012 annual survey," Kaiser Family Foundation, 2012, http://ehbs.kff.org/pdf/2012/8345.pdf. As we will see, however, premium inflation is well into double digits.

4. "Estimates for the Insurance Coverage Provisions of the Affordable Care Act Updated for the Recent Supreme Court Decision," Congressional Budget Office, July 2012, http://cbo.gov/sites/default/files/cbo-files/attachments/43472-07-24-2012-CoverageEstimates.pdf.

5. The locations of their forty restaurants are available on their website at, http://www.applemetrorestaurants.com/locations.

6. "Applebee's CEO Announces Hiring Freeze And Layoffs Over Obamacare, Boycott Threatened," Inquisitr.com, November 11, 2012, http://www.inquisitr.com/394524/applebees-ceo-announces-hiring-freeze-and-layoffs-over-obamacare-boycott-threatened/.

7. "CEO of Papa John's says employees' hours will likely be cut due to ObamaCare," Fox News, November 11, 2012, http://www.foxnews.com/us/2012/11/11/ceo-papa-john-says-employees-hours-will-likely-be-cut-due-to-obamacare/.

8. "Applebee's CEO Announces Hiring Freeze And Layoffs Over Obamacare, Boycott Threatened," Inquisitr.com, November 11, 2012, http://www.inquisitr.com/394524/applebees-ceo-announces-hiring-freeze-and-layoffs-over-obamacare-boycott-threatened/.

9. A video of Jon Stewart's segment is available on the *Daily Show* website at, http://www.thedailyshow.com/watch/tue-november-13-2012/post-democalyptic-world---whine-country. For Colbert's discussion, see, News Corpse, "National Papa John's Depreciation Day – Clip This Coupon To Cut 14 Cents & Worker's Health Care," Daily Kos, November 13, 2012, http://www.dailykos.com/story/2012/11/13/1161310/-National-Papa-John-s-Depreciation-Day-Clip-This-Coupon-To-Cut-14-Cents-Worker-s-Health-Care. An example of a columnist's piece may be found here, Leslie Marshall, "Papa John's CEO Should Take a Pay Cut, Not Lay Off Workers," *U.S. News & World Report*, November 16, 2012, http://www.usnews.com/opinion/blogs/leslie-marshall/2012/11/16/papa-johns-ceo-should-take-a-pay-cut-not-lay-off-workers.

10. Boston Scientific, Stryker, and Medtronic announced layoffs respectively of 1,200 to 1,400, 1,170, and another 1,000 on top of 500 this past summer. The tax itself amounts to 2.3 percent. "US Companies plan massive layoffs over new Health Law," MINA breaking News, November 9, 2012, http://macedoniaonline.eu/content/view/22178/61/. IRS, "Medical Device Excise Tax: Frequently Asked Questions," http://www.irs.gov/uac/Medical-Device-Excise-Tax:-Frequently-Asked-Questions.

11. Perry Chiaramonte, "Medical giant Stryker cuts 1,170 jobs, citing ObamaCare," Fox News, November 16, 2012, http://www.foxnews.com/politics/2012/11/16/medical-supply-giant-stryker-corp-makes-pre-emptive-strike-against-pending/?intcmp=trending.

12. Evan Bayh, "ObamaCare's Tax Raid on Medical Devices," *Wall Street Journal*, September 27, 2012, http://online.wsj.com/article/SB10000872396390444620104578012281306687070.html.

13. John Fritze, "Tax on plastic surgery gets ax in final stretch," *USA Today*, December 22, 2009, http://usatoday30.usatoday.com/news/washington/2009-12-21-health-care-plastic-surgery-tax_N.htm.

14. Erin Kim, "Obamacare's 'tanning tax' is here to stay," CNN Money, June 28, 2012, http://money.cnn.com/2012/06/28/pf/taxes/tanning-tax/index.htm.

15. Mary Niederberger, "Health care law brings double dose of trouble for CCAC part-time profs," *Pittsburgh Post-Gazette*, November 19, 2012, http://www.post-gazette.com/stories/local/neighborhoods-city/health-care-law-brings-double-dose-of-trouble-for-ccac-part-time-profs-662697/?print=1.

16. Colleen Flaherty, "So Close Yet so Far," *Inside Higher Ed*, November 20, 2012, http://www.insidehighered.com/news/2012/11/20/college-cuts-adjuncts-hours-avoid-affordable-care-act-costs.

17. "Democrats Post Health Care Bill Online, Starting 72-Hour Clock," Fox News, March 18, 2010, http://www.foxnews.com/politics/2010/03/18/public-awaits-health-care-release-dems-celebrate-cost-estimate/.

18. The Reconciliation Act of 2010 is available online at healthcare.gov, http://www.healthcare.gov/law/resources/authorities/reconciliation-law.pdf.

19. See page 462 in the Compilation of Patient Protection and Affordable Care Act, as Amended through May 1, 2010, http://housedocs.house.gov/energycommerce/ppacacon.pdf.

20. From 2013 to 2022, Medicare outlays are projected to be $7.7 trillion. But over that same period of time Medicare cuts due to Obamacare are $716 billion. That comes to a cut of 8.5% ($716 billion /($7,723 billion + $716 billion)). See Table 1-2 in "An Update to the Budget and Economic Outlook: Fiscal Years 2012 to 2022," available on the Congressional Budget Office website at, http://www.cbo.gov/sites/default/files/cbofiles/attachments/08-22-2012-Update_to_Outlook.

pdf. See also Letter to House Speaker John Boehner from Douglas Elmendorf, Director, Congressional Budget Office, July 24, 2012, http://www.cbo.gov/sites/default/files/cbofiles/attachments/43471-hr6079.pdf.

21. Mary Katharine Ham, "Survey: 46% of Primary Care Physicians Say Health Reform Will Make Them Leave Medicine," *Weekly Standard*, March 17, 2010, http://www.weeklystandard.com/blogs/survey-46-primary-care-physicians-say-health-reform-will-make-them-leave-medicine.

22. Merrit Hawkins, "A Survey of America's Physicians: Practice Patterns and Perspectives," The Physicians Foundation, September 2012, http://www.physiciansfoundation.org/uploads/default/Physicians_Foundation_2012_Biennial_Survey.pdf. Similar numbers have been obtained for surveys done in individual states. In Virginia, a survey found that 23 percent of doctors will refuse to accept new Medicare patients and another 28 percent are placing limits on new Medicare patients. Avik Roy, "In Virginia, Obamacare to Cause 23% of Doctors to Stop Accepting Medicare Patients," *Forbes*, October 30, 2012, http://www.forbes.com/sites/aroy/2012/10/30/in-virginia-obamacare-to-cause-23-of-doctors-to-stop-accepting-medicare-patients/.

23. Based on a conversation with Josh Trent, Senator Coburn's health care advisor.

24. Bret Baier, "President Barack Obama Talks to Bret Baier About Health Care Reform Bill," Fox News, March 17, 2010, http://www.foxnews.com/story/0,2933,589589,00.html.

25. John Lott, "The CBO's sleight of hand on health care," Fox News, March 18, 2010, http://www.foxnews.com/opinion/2010/03/18/john-lott-cbo-pelosi-health-care-costs-medical-care-democrats-vote/.

26. David Gamage, "ObamaCare's Costs to the Working Class," *Wall Street Journal*, October 30, 2012, http://professional.wsj.com/article/SB10001424052970203335504578086702676417058.html.

27. John R. Lott Jr., "Obama's Health Care Bill is Not What He Promised," Fox News, March 29, 2010, http://www.foxnews.com/opinion/2010/03/29/health-care-obama-promised/.

28. Remarks by the President to a Joint Session of Congress, the White House, Office of the Press Secretary, September 9, 2009, http://www.

whitehouse.gov/the_press_office/Remarks-by-the-President-to-a-Joint-Session-of-Congress-on-Health-Care.

29. Letter to House Speaker John Boehner from Douglas Elmendorf, Director, Congressional Budget Office, July 24, 2012, http://www.cbo.gov/sites/default/files/cbofiles/attachments/43471-hr6079.pdf. There are many who think that the CBO estimates dramatically underestimate the costs of Obamacare. For example, Douglas Holtz-Eakin, the former CBO director, writes, "Given the risks of faster than expected health care inflation, slow growth in incomes, and the potential for less employer-sponsored insurance in the future, there is good reason to anticipate that the cost could rise further yet." Douglas Holtz-Eakin, "The Growing Budget Cost of Insurance Subsidies in the Affordable Care Act," American Action Forum, October 2012, http://american actionforum.org/sites/default/files/AAF_Growing%20Cost%20of%20 ACA%20Subsidies_Revised_2012.pdf.

30. Bureau of Labor Statistics data is available on their website at, http://data.bls.gov/pdq/querytool.jsp?survey=cu. See also "Consumer Price Index, September 2012," Bureau of Labor Statistics, October 16, 2012.

31. There is a different set of numbers from the Kaiser Family Foundation that also tries to measure the changing costs of insurance premiums. Their Employer Health Benefits Annual Survey, available at http://ehbs.kff.org/?page=charts&id=1&sn=6&ch=2660, shows that premium increases slowed down during the 2006 to 2010 period before increasing fairly quickly in 2011. The increases in both 2011 and 2012 clearly exceed the increases during those previous five years. While the Kaiser measure also shows an increase in insurance premiums since Obamacare regulations went into effect in 2011, the big difference between the two indexes is that the BLS index tries to account for changing quality in the health insurance plans. The government index might not do a great job of accounting for changing quality, but it is pretty obvious that we have been experiencing large changes in quality, and at least some attempt to account for quality should be made. In any case, whether a flawed measure that accounts for quality is used or another flawed measure is used that ignores quality adjustments completely, the results are qualitatively the same.

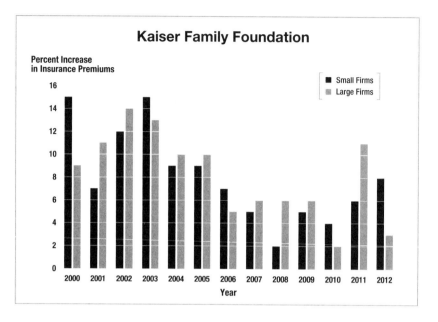

32. "Estimates for the Insurance Coverage Provisions of the Affordable
     Care Act Updated for the Recent Supreme Court Decision,"
     Congressional Budget Office, Table 3, July 2012, http://cbo.gov/sites/
     default/files/cbofiles/attachments/43472-07-24-2012-Coverage
     Estimates.pdf.
33. Jonathan Gruber, "The Senate Finance Committee Proposal Lowers
     Non-Group Premiums," Department of Economics, MIT, October 12,
     2009, http://www.tnr.com/sites/default/files/Gruber%20SFC%20Non
     Group%20Prem%20Analysis.pdf.
34. Ezra Klein, "Does health-care reform do enough on cost control?"
     Washington Post, November 12, 2009, http://voices.washingtonpost.
     com/ezra-klein/2009/11/does_health-care_reform_do_eno.html.
35. We should approach Gruber's figures with caution. In his many media
     appearances and op-eds promoting Obamacare, it was never men-
     tioned that the administration paid him almost $400,000 for his sup-
     port. Gruber defended himself—"I have been completely consistent
     with my academic track record"—and argued that the payment did
     not bias his public statements in favor of Obamacare. If so, he should
     have trusted the public to draw that conclusion themselves. But not
     everyone believed him. Professor Merrill Goozner at New York Uni-
     versity compiled a list of inconsistencies. For example,

What about this March 2007 paper for the National Bureau
of Economic Research, which he co-authored. It looked at
the effect of higher out-of-pocket co-pays for retired public
employees in California. Gruber found that they led to higher
hospitalization rates as old folks with chronic diseases like
diabetes and heart disease cut back on physician visits and
necessary drugs…. What will happen after the excise tax hits
high-cost insurance plans, according to Gruber today? 80
percent of employers will ratchet down plan benefits to keep
their costs under the tax cap. The only way they can do that
is by raising co-pays and deductibles and eliminating benefits. . . . "There's literally no evidence out there that people
are going to suffer," he told the Washington Post earlier this
week. He should re-read his own paper. (David Dayen, "Gruber Did Argue Contrary To Today's Health Care Reform… In
2007," Firedoglake.com, January 8, 2010, http://news.firedo-
glake.com/2010/01/08/gruber-did-argue-contrary-to-todays-
health-care-reform-in-2007/.)

Some reporters expressed dismay over Gruber's failure to inform the
media about the large amount of money he was receiving from the
Obama administration. Ezra Klein at the *Washington Post* wrote: "I
was not aware of [all the money], and if I had been, I would've made
sure it was disclosed when I quoted Gruber." (Ezra Klein, "Jon Gruber," *Washington Post*, January 8, 2010, http://voices.washingtonpost.
com/ezra-klein/2010/01/jon_gruber.html.) Kate Pickert at *Time* magazine noted, "if I had known Gruber had such a contract, I would have
disclosed this fact to readers when I quoted him." (Kate Pickert,
"Jonathan Gruber on the Government Payroll," *Time*, January 8, 2010,
http://swampland.time.com/2010/01/08/jonathan-gruber-on-the-gov
ernment-payroll/.) Still, the reaction was tame. A Google News search
the day after the story broke showed only a small number of news
stories covering the scandal. (The Google News search term was
"'Jonathan Gruber' AND $296,600 OR $400,000 OR $392,600.")
Besides the *Washington Post* and *Time* blog posts, the *Boston Globe*,
ABC News blog post, the *St. Louis Post-Dispatch*, and Reason Online
were the only other media outlets covering the story over the next two
weeks.

36. Avik Roy, "How Obamacare Dramatically Increases The Cost of Insurance for Young Workers," *Forbes*, March 22, 2012, http://www.forbes.com/sites/aroy/2012/03/22/how-obamacare-dramatically-increases-the-cost-of-insurance-for-young-workers/.

37. Gorman Actuarial, Jennifer Smagula, and Jon Gruber, "The Impact of the ACA on Wisconsin's Health Insurance Market," Prepared for the Wisconsin Department of Health Services, July 18, 2011, http://www.dhs.wisconsin.gov/aboutdhs/docs/WI-Final-Report-July-18-2011.pdf. The report was done for the state of Wisconsin.

38. Jeremy Palmer, Jill Herbold, and Paul Houchens, "Assist with the first year of planning for design and implementation of a federally mandated American Health Benefit Exchange," Milliman Client Report, August 31, 2011, http://www.ohioexchange.ohio.gov/Documents/MillimanReport.pdf.

39. President Barack Obama, "Remarks by the President in Health Insurance Reform Town Hall, Portsmouth High School Portsmouth, New Hampshire," the White House, Office of the Press Secretary, August 11, 2009, http://www.whitehouse.gov/the-press-office/remarks-president-town-hall-health-insurance-reform-portsmouth-new-hampshire. Another example of this claim occurred when Obama spoke before the American Medical Association in 2009. Mary Lu Carnevale, "Obama: 'If You Like Your Doctor, You Can Keep Your Doctor,'" *Wall Street Journal*, June 15, 2009, http://blogs.wsj.com/washwire/2009/06/15/obama-if-you-like-your-doctor-you-can-keep-your-doctor/.

40. People can listen to the audio of these remarks themselves, but it certainly appears to me that Pelosi was emphasizing the terms "all" and "every." "House Democrats announce health-care bill," CQ TranscriptsWire, October 29, 2009, http://www.washingtonpost.com/wp-dyn/content/article/2009/10/29/AR2009102902240.html.

41. Alex Nussbaum, "Aetna CEO Sees Obama Health Law Doubling Some Premiums," Bloomberg News, December 13, 2012, http://www.bloomberg.com/news/2012-12-12/aetna-ceo-sees-obama-health-law-doubling-some-premiums.html.

42. Matthew Boyle, "CBO hires Obamacare advocate to provide 'objective' health care budget numbers," *The Daily Caller*, June 6, 2011, http://dailycaller.com/2011/06/06/cbo-hires-obamacare-advocate-to-provide-objective-health-care-budget-numbers/.

43.   Betsi Fores, "Obamacare architects preside over forthcoming CBO cost analysis," *The Daily Caller*, July 23, 2012, http://dailycaller. com/2012/07/23/obamacare-architects-preside-over-forthcoming-cbo-cost-analysis/.

44.   Transcript of Barack Obama's health-care speech, *The Telegraph*, September 9, 2009, http://blogs.telegraph.co.uk/news/tobyharn-den/100009074/transcript-of-barack-obamas-health-care-speech/.

45.   The mandate was something that Obama opposed vigorously many times during the 2008 presidential campaign. During the February 5, 2008, Democratic Presidential debate, Obama argued, "If you haven't made it affordable, how are you going to enforce a mandate? I mean, if a mandate was the solution, we can try that to solve homelessness by mandating everybody to buy a house," http://transcripts.cnn.com/ TRANSCRIPTS/0802/05/ltm.02.html. During the February 21, 2008, Democratic Presidential debate, he said, "And in order for you to force people to get health insurance, you've got to have a very harsh, stiff penalty. And Senator Clinton has said that we will go after their wages," http://www.cfr.org/us-election-2008/democratic-debate-tran script-austin-texas/p15560.

46.   John Merline, "Could Obamacare make the uninsured problem worse?" *Investor's Business Daily*, July 25, 2012, http://news.investors. com/business/072512-619306-obamacare-could-add-to-uninsured. htm.

47.   Sam Baker and Elise Viebeck, "CBO: Supreme Court decision cuts cost of healthcare reform by $84 billion," *The Hill*, July 24, 2012, http:// thehill.com/blogs/healthwatch/health-reform-implementation/ 239887-cbo-supreme-court-cut-cost-of-health-law-by-84b.

48.   "Employer Health Benefits, 2012 Annual Survey," The Kaiser Foundation and Health Research & Educational Trust, 2012, http://ehbs.kff. org/pdf/2012/8345.pdf.

49.   The Patient Protection and Affordable Care Act, p. 83, available online at, http://www.gpo.gov/fdsys/pkg/BILLS-111hr3590enr/pdf/BILLS-111hr3590enr.pdf.

50.   The income above which a percentage tax is levied is the "tax-filing threshold." In 2014, that equals $9,500 for a single filer. In 2016, it rises to $10,250. The percentage income taken by the tax is 1 percent in 2014, 2 percent in 2015, and 2.5 percent in 2016. Paul R. Houchens, "Measuring the Strength of the Individual Mandate," Milliman

Research Report, March 2012, http://publications.milliman.com/
publications/health-published/pdfs/measuring-strength-individual-
mandate.pdf.

51. Paul R. Houchens, "Measuring the Strength of the Individual Man-
     date," Milliman Research Report, March 2012, http://publications.
     milliman.com/publications/health-published/pdfs/measuring-
     strength-individual-mandate.pdf. For the 2012 annual Federal Poverty
     Guidelines, see http://www.familiesusa.org/resources/tools-for-advo
     cates/guides/federal-poverty-guidelines.html.

52. The left wing Urban Institute puts the number of Americans who
     would have an incentive to drop their current health care policies and
     wait until they are sick to buy health insurance at about 18 million,
     though they do not provide the detailed analysis shown by Houchens,
     so it is not possible to check their assumptions. It is not even possible
     to tell what year's tax penalties are being used in the analysis. Yet, even
     if they are right, 18 million people would eliminate virtually all the
     reduction in the number of people uninsured in 2015 and more than
     half the number in 2022. Linda J. Blumberg, Matthew Buettgens, Judy
     Feder, "The Individual Mandate in Perspective," The Urban Institute,
     March 2012, http://www.urban.org/UploadedPDF/412533-the-indi
     vidual-mandate.pdf.

53. David Gregory, *Meet the Press* transcript for April 19, 2009, NBC News,
     www.msnbc.msn.com/id/30291720/page/2/.

54. Reasons for tonsillectomy, www.scribd.com/doc/4705075/Reasons-
     for-Tonsillectomy.

55. President Barack Obama, "Remarks by the President in the Organiz-
     ing for American National Health Care Forum," the White House,
     Office of the Press Secretary, August 20, 2009, www.whitehouse.gov/
     the-press-office/remarks-president-organizating-america-national-
     health-care-forum.

56. One of the times that President Obama made this claim was at the
     Portsmouth High School in Portsmouth, New Hampshire, on August
     11, 2009. Obama claimed: "Take the example of something like dia-
     betes, one of—a disease that's skyrocketing, partly because of obesity,
     partly because it's not treated as effectively as it could be. Right now,
     if we paid a family—if a family care physician works with his or her
     patient to help them lose weight, modify diet, monitors whether
     they're taking their medications in a timely fashion, they might get

reimbursed a pittance. But if that same diabetic ends up getting their foot amputated, that's $30,000, $40,000, $50,000—immediately the surgeon is reimbursed. Well, why not make sure that we're also reimbursing the care that prevents the amputation, right?" The problem that Obama never addresses is: Why would insurance companies or hospitals have an incentive to give doctors the wrong payment scheme? Why would the government have a better incentive than those who have their own money at risk or who are getting the care to get these compensation payments right? President Barack Obama, "Remarks by the President in Health Insurance Reform Town Hall," the White House, Office of the Press Secretary, August 11, 2009, http://www.whitehouse.gov/the-press-office/remarks-president-town-hall-health-insurance-reform-portsmouth-new-hampshire.

57. President Barack Obama, "News Conference by the President, July 22, 2009," the White House, Office of the Press Secretary, July 23, 2009, www.whitehouse.gov/the_press_office/News-Conference-by-the-President-July-22-2009.

58. President Obama, "Remarks by the President on Preventive Care," whitehouse.gov, February 10, 2012, http://www.whitehouse.gov/photos-and-video/video/2012/02/10/president-obama-speaks-contraception-and-religious-institutions#transcript.

59. Transcript of vice presidential debate, Fox News, October 11, 2012, http://www.foxnews.com/politics/2012/10/11/transcript-vice-presidential-debate/.

60. Ruth Marcus, "Obama's contraception fig leaf," *Washington Post*, February 10, 2012, http://www.washingtonpost.com/opinions/obamas-contraception-fig-leaf/2012/02/10/gIQApk6S4Q_story.html.

61. Ibid.

62. *Meet the Press*, February 12, 2012, http://www.msnbc.msn.com/id/46331180/ns/meet_the_press-transcripts/t/meet-press-transcript-february/#.TzhJD5geJFJ.

63. There is another simple reason why a $10 pack of condoms is not covered 100 percent by insurance. Suppose the $10 was completely reimbursed, the cost of insurance would go up by more than $10. The $10 increase is obvious since if the insurance has to pay out $10, they have to charge $10 more for insurance. More paperwork means even higher costs. Someone has to check the forms to make sure that there

is no fraud and give the reimbursement approval. It does not make any sense for insurance to cover low-cost items.

64. *Meet the Press*, February 12, 2012, http://www.msnbc.msn.com/id/46331180/ns/meet_the_press-transcripts/t/meet-press-transcript-february/#.TzhJD5geJFJ.

65. Eva Rodriguez, "Read Before You Vote, Congressman," *Washington Post*, July 28, 2009, http://voices.washingtonpost.com/postpartisan/2009/07/read_before_you_vote.html.

66. Chad Pergram, "House Passes Health Care Bill," Fox News, March 21, 2010, http://politics.blogs.foxnews.com/2010/03/21/house-passes-health-care-bill.

67. John McCormack, "Kathy Dahlkemper: I Wouldn't Have Voted for Obamacare If I'd Known About HHS Rule," *Weekly Standard*, February 7, 2012, http://www.weeklystandard.com/blogs/dem-rep-kathy-dahlkemper-i-wouldnt-have-voted-obamacare-if-id-known-about-hhs-regulation_626302.html.

68. Julian Pecquet and Sam Baker, "Democrats expressing buyers' remorse on Obama's healthcare law," *The Hill*, April 19, 2012, http://thehill.com/blogs/healthwatch/politics-elections/222719-democrats-buyers-remorse-on-obama-health-care-law.

69. Evan Bayh, "ObamaCare's Tax Raid on Medical Devices," *Wall Street Journal*, September 27, 2012, http://online.wsj.com/article/SB10000872396390444620104578012281306687070.html?mod=googlenews_wsj.

70. "No Family Making Less than $250,000 Will See 'Any Form of Tax Increase,'" PolitiFact.com, updated April 8, 2010, www.politifact.com/truth-o-meter/promises/obameter/promise/515/no-family-making-less-250000-will-see-any-form-tax/.

71. Ibid.

72. Peter Roff, "How Obamacare Taxes Hurt Seniors," *U.S. News & World Report*, July 10, 2012, http://www.usnews.com/opinion/blogs/peter-roff/2012/07/10/how-obamacare-taxes-hurt-seniors.

73. Editorial, "Obama's Taxing Logic," *Washington Times*, September 27, 2009.

74. Jordan Fabian, "Obama healthcare plan nixes Ben Nelson's 'Cornhusker Kickback' deal," *The Hill*, February 22, 2010, http://thehill.com/blogs/blog-briefing-room/news/82621-obama-healthcare-plan-nixes-ben-nelsons-cornhusker-kickback-deal.

75. Greg Hitt and Brody Mullins, "Health-Bill Horse Trading: Democrats Broker Deals as Sunday Vote Looms; Republicans Push Back," *Wall Street Journal*, March 19, 2010, http://online.wsj.com/article/SB1000 14240527487035809045751313041165 13076.html.

76. Ibid.

77. Clemente Lisi, "Obama promised 8 times during campaign to televise health care debate," *New York Post*, January 6, 2010, http://www.nypost.com/p/news/national/obama_falls_short_on_campaign_promise_5gFAG1TwuLUSW6Mn7h6hWN. U.S. Senator John Kyl, "President Obama and the C-Span Pledge: Health Care Talks Move Behind Closed Doors," National Ledger, January 11, 2010, http://www.nationalledger.com/news-tech/president-obama-and-the-c-span-151282.shtml#.UNJMfnPjn9s. Editorial, "Obama's record of broken promises: Transparency undermines the Democrats' government expansion," *Washington Times*, January 19, 2010. Angie Drobnic Holan, "Obama said he'd televise health reform negotiations on C-SPAN," Politifact.com, July 10, 2009, http://www.politifact.com/truth-o-meter/promises/obameter/promise/517/health-care-reform-public-sessions-C-SPAN/. Chip Reid, "Obama Reneges on Health Care Transparency," CBS *Evening News*, January 7, 2010, http://www.cbsnews.com/8301-18563_162-6064298.html.

78. John McCormack, "Obama & Democrats Talk for Four Hours; Republicans Talk for Two Hours," *Weekly Standard*, February 25, 2010 (http://www.weeklystandard.com/blogs/obama-democrats-talk-four-hours-republicans-talk-two-hours).

79. Sarah Kliff, "The average employer health plan now costs $15,745, and that's kind of good news," *Washington Post*, September 11, 2012, http://www.washingtonpost.com/blogs/ezra-klein/wp/2012/09/11/the-average-employer-health-plan-now-costs-15980-and-thats-kind-of-good-news/.

80. Paul Krugman, "The Comeback Continent," *New York Times*, January 11, 2008, http://www.nytimes.com/2008/01/11/opinion/11krugman.html?src=recg.

81. "The Health Risks of Obesity Worse Than Smoking, Drinking, or Poverty," The Rand Corporation, 2002, http://www.rand.org/pubs/research_briefs/RB4549/index1.html.

82. See various issues of the FBI's Uniform Crime Report.

83. Baylen Linnekin, "USDA's School Lunch Reforms Earn an 'F' from Students," Reason.com, September 22, 2012, http://reason.com/archives/2012/09/22/usdas-school-lunch-reforms-earning-an-f.

84. Amy Norton, "School ban on sugary drinks shows little effect," Reuters, November 20, 2008, http://www.reuters.com/article/2008/11/20/us-school-ban-idUSTRE4AJ5K420081120.

85. Jennifer Van Hook and Claire E. Altman, "Competitive Food Sales in Schools and Childhood Obesity: A Longitudinal Study," *Sociology of Education*, January 2012, http://www.asanet.org/images/journals/docs/pdf/soe/Jan12SOEFeature.pdf. Benjamin Radford, "Why School Junk Food Isn't Making Kids Fat," DiscoveryNews.com, January 19, 2012, http://news.discovery.com/human/junk-food-not-to-blame-obesity-121901.html.

86. This phenomenon is so pervasive that economists have even given it a name: the Peltzman effect, after the University of Chicago economist who first discovered it in 1975. Sam Peltzman, "The Effects of Automobile Safety Regulation," *Journal of Political Economy*, Vol. 83, No. 4 (August 1975): 677–726. For other research see Leon S. Robertson, "A Critical Analysis of Peltzman's 'The Effects of Automobile Safety Regulation,'" *Journal of Economic Issues*, Vol. 11, No. 3 (September 1977): 587–600; Robert W. Crandall and John D. Graham, "Automobile Safety Regulation and Offsetting Behavior: Some New Empirical Estimates," *The American Economic Review*, Vol. 74, No. 2 (May 1984): 328–331; and Alma Cohen and Liran Einav, "The Effects of Mandatory Seat Belt Laws on Driving Behavior and Traffic Fatalities," *Review of Economics and Statistics*, Vol. 85 (2003).

87. Russell S. Sobel and Todd Nesbit, "Automobile Safety Regulation and the Incentive to Drive Recklessly: Evidence from NASCAR," *Southern Economic Journal*, Vol. 74, No. 1 (2007): 71–84.

88. Clive Thompson, "Bicycle Helmets Put You at Risk," *New York Times*, December 10, 2006, http://www.nytimes.com/2006/12/10/magazine/10bike.html.

89. The basic principle is much broader. Sam Peltzman at the University of Chicago recently noticed the result again in research showing that even great medical breakthroughs have little long-run effect on mortality rates. One of the most significant medical breakthroughs in human history was the development of antibiotics and other anti-infective drugs. Today, people no longer face a high risk of dying from

past scourges like scarlet fever or tuberculosis. But these health benefits were offset when people began taking more risks, which led to more accidents, or when they changed their diet and exercise habits. Sam Peltzman, "Offsetting Behavior and Medical Breakthroughs," University of Chicago Graduate School of Business, undated, http://research.chicagobooth.edu/economy/research/articles/169.pdf.

90. Remarks by the President to a Joint Session of Congress, the White House, Office of the Press Secretary, September 9, 2009, http://www.whitehouse.gov/the_press_office/Remarks-by-the-President-to-a-Joint-Session-of-Congress-on-Health-Care.

91. Scott Harrington, "Fact-checking the president on health insurance," *Wall Street Journal*, September 14, 2009, http://online.wsj.com/article/SB10001424052970203440104574409501904118682.html.

92. See for example, President Barack Obama, "Remarks by the President in Town Hall on Health Care, Gallatin Field Airport Belgrade, Montana," the White House, Office of the Press Secretary, August 14, 2009, http://www.whitehouse.gov/the-press-office/remarks-president-town-hall-health-care-belgrade-montana. These comments were made after the July 27, 2009, testimony that Peggy Raddatz and Robin Beaton gave before Congress.

93. In her testimony to the House, Peggy Raddatz made the following statement:

> Luckily, I am an attorney and was able to aggressively become involved in solving this life-threatening situation for him. I contacted the Illinois Attorney General's office and received immediate and daily assistance from Dr. Babs Waldman, the Medical Director of their Health Insurance Bureau.
>
> During their investigation, they located the doctor who ordered the CT scan. He had no recollection whatsoever of disclosing the information to my brother about an aneurysm and gall stones, or of ever treating him for it. After two appeals by the Illinois Attorney General's office, Fortis Insurance Company overturned their original decision to rescind my brother's coverage, and he was reinstated without any lapse.

> Statement of Peggy Raddatz, testimony before the Subcommittee of Oversight and Investigation of the House Committee on Energy

and Commerce, July 27, 2009, http://www.gpo.gov/fdsys/pkg/CHRG-111hhrg74091/html/CHRG-111hhrg74091.htm. See also Jonathan Weisman, "Obama Used Faulty Anecdote in Speech," *Wall Street Journal*, September 17, 2009, http://online.wsj.com/article/SB125314896131518267.html; Lynn Sweet, "Jab at insurer goes too far?" *Chicago Sun-Times*, September 13, 2009; and Truth-O-Meter, "Insurers delayed an Illinois man's treatment, "and he died because of it,'" Politifact.com, September 17, 2009, http://www.politifact.com/truth-o-meter/statements/2009/sep/17/barack-obama/obama-says-decision-revoke-insurance-led-illinois-/.

94. Ibid. Weisman notes, "Mr. Raddatz was dropped from his insurance plan weeks before a scheduled stem-cell transplant" and that his insurance was reinstated within less than three weeks. See also Truth-O-Meter, "Insurers delayed an Illinois man's treatment, 'and he died because of it,'" Politifact.com, September 17, 2009, http://www.politifact.com/truth-o-meter/statements/2009/sep/17/barack-obama/obama-says-decision-revoke-insurance-led-illinois-/.

95. Scott Harrington, "Fact-checking the president on health insurance," *Wall Street Journal*, September 14, 2009, http://online.wsj.com/article/SB10001424052970203440104574409501904118682.html.

96. Statement of Robin Beaton, Testimony before the Subcommittee of Oversight and Investigation of the House Committee on Energy and Commerce, July 27, 2009, http://www.gpo.gov/fdsys/pkg/CHRG-111hhrg74091/html/CHRG-111hhrg74091.htm.

97. See question 13, but these results differ in that they are conditional on illness.

98. ABC News/*USA TODAY*/Kaiser Family Foundation health care poll conducted by telephone September 7–12, 2006, among a random national sample of 1,201 adults, http://www.usatoday.com/news/health/2006-10-15-health-poll1.htm. See questions 4 and 14.

99. Henry Aaron in telephone conversation with me in June 2009. John R. Lott Jr., "As Obama Pushes National Health Care, Most Americans Already Happy With Coverage," Fox News, June 24, 2009, http://www.foxnews.com/politics/2009/06/24/obama-pushes-national-health-care-americans-happy-coverage/.

100. Al Hunt, "Offering McCain Help in Econ 101," *International Herald Tribune*, July 13, 2008, http://iht.com/articles/2008/07/13/america/letter.php.

101. See question 14, but these results differ in that they are conditional on illness.
102. ABC News/*Washington Post* Poll, "Growing Health Care Concerns Fuel Cautious Support for Change," ABC News/*Washington Post*, October 19, 2003, http://abcnews.go.com/images/pdf/935a3Health Care.pdf.
103. The American Customer Satisfaction Index doesn't ask people about their views on overall health care, but they do ask for their views on hospitals and they rank at the middle of all industries with a 75 percent satisfaction rate.
104. Co-founded by the University of Michigan's Ross School of Business, the American Society of Quality, and the CFI Group.
105. Scores by Industry, The American Customer Satisfaction Index, 2008, http://www.theacsi.org/index.php?option=com_content&task=view&id=148&Itemid=156.
106. Government Satisfaction Scores, The American Customer Satisfaction Index, 2008, http://www.theacsi.org/index.php?option=com_content&task=view&id=27&Itemid=62
107. Paul Krugman, "Death by Ideology," *New York Times*, October 14, 2012, http://www.nytimes.com/2012/10/15/opinion/krugman-death-by-ideology.html?_r=1&src=recg.
108. Jamie L. Freedman, "A Capitol Career," *GW Magazine*, Summer 2005, http://www.gwu.edu/~magazine/archive/2005_law_summer/docs/feat_reid.html.
109. Krugman's piece acknowledges that being uninsured does not mean people do not get health care, but he quickly dismisses the claim that the uninsured really get proper care: "Even the idea that everyone gets urgent care when needed from emergency rooms is false. Yes, hospitals are required by law to treat people in dire need, whether or not they can pay. But that care is not free—on the contrary, if you go to an emergency room you will be billed, and the size of that bill can be shockingly high. Some people cannot or would not pay, but fear of huge bills can deter the uninsured from visiting the emergency room even when they should. And sometimes they die as a result."
110. See, for example, Jack Hadley and John Holahan, "The Cost of Care for the Uninsured: What Do We Spend, Who Pays, and What Would Full Coverage Add to Medical Spending," The Kaiser Commission on Medicaid and the Uninsured, May 10, 2004. Holahan Hadley, et al.,

updated these number in a recent Health Affairs article, "Covering the Uninsured in 2008: Current Costs, Sources of Payments, and Incremental Costs," *Health Affairs*, Vol. 27, No. 5, August 25, 2008.

111. ABC News/*USA TODAY*/Kaiser Family Foundation health care poll, see question 6.

112. The Kaiser survey asked everybody if he was insured as well as if he was satisfied with his health care. For some reason, however, Kaiser publicly reported the satisfaction figures only for the insured. The crucial question of how the uninsured are faring was left unanswered when the results of the survey were reported in the press. A year later, I was able to obtain Kaiser's raw data and to determine the satisfaction rates for the uninsured.

113. This is calculated by using Kaiser estimates for the percent of the population that are uninsured and multiplying it by the share of the uninsured who are very dissatisfied with their health care (see Table 1).

114. "Growing Health Care Concerns Fuel Cautious Support for Change," ABC News/*Washington Post* Poll: Health Care, October 19, 2003, http://abcnews.go.com/images/pdf/935a3HealthCare.pdf.

115. Press Conference by President Obama, President Calderon of Mexico, and Prime Minister Harper of Canada, the White House, Office of the Press Secretary, August 10, 2009, http://www.whitehouse.gov/the-press-office/press-conference-president-obama-president-calderon-mexico-and-prime-minister-harpe.

116. I am relying on two surveys here, one American and one Canadian. The American survey is the Kaiser Family Foundation survey mentioned above, which was conducted by the market research firm TNS Global. The survey polled 1,201 U.S. adults from September 7–12, 2006. The Canadian survey was sponsored by the Institute for Policy Innovation, a Texas-based conservative think tank, and was conducted by Harris/Decima TeleVox. The survey polled 1,022 Canadian adults from May 8–13, 2008.

While some questions that are applicable to Americans are not applicable to Canadians, the Canadian survey was intended to be as similar to the American one as possible. Demographic, income, sex, level of schooling, age, marital status, geographic identifiers (i.e., Canadian province vs. U.S. state), and political views (party identification in Canada and ideology in the United States) are included in both surveys. The Canadian survey asks all respondents whether they have suffered a serious or chronic illness, but the U.S. survey only asks that question of those who have insurance.

The U.S. survey also has information on whether an individual has insurance and which type: private insurance, Medicare, or Medicaid. Canadian surveys do not ask about the respondent's race because a large number of people view the topic as a privacy issue and refuse to answer the question.

Besides these differences and the differences noted in the text, Americans were also asked which type of insurance they had—private insurance, Medicare, or Medicaid—with no corresponding questions for Canadians.

117. The table in this note shows the estimates for these regressions for the United States and Canada. The numbers in the "odds ratio" column express the percentage change in public satisfaction with health care, given a 1 percent change in the various independent variables listed in the left column. For example, the 1.08 odds ratio for U.S. respondents in the 60–69 age group indicates that there would be an eight percent increase in satisfaction if there were a 1 percent increase in the number of respondents age 60–69. Likewise, the 0.96 odds ratio for U.S. respondents age 40–49 indicates that there would be a 4 percent decline in satisfaction if the number of respondents in that age group increased by 1 percent.

It is possible to test whether the coefficients for different levels of education or age are different from each other. The more extreme values are shown at the bottom of the table, even after accounting for all the individual characteristics available in the survey, including whether they have insurance.

Demographics and Health Care Satisfaction **(Also accounting for differences across states or provinces)**					
	United States			Canada	
	Odds Ratio	t-stat		Odds Ratio	t-stat
Age 30–39	0.61	-1.09	Age 30–39	1.17	0.36
Age 40–49	0.96	-0.09	Age 40–49	1.55	1.05
Age 50–59	0.59	-1.15	Age 50–59	1.00	0.01
Age 60–69	1.08	0.14	Age 60–69	1.44	0.81
Age 70 and Older	2.27	1.37	Age 70 and Older	1.43	0.8
Single	1.34	0.76	Single	1.59	0.35

Married			Married	1.77	0.43
Divorced	0.90	-0.25	Divorced	1.41	0.25
Widowed	1.47	0.65	Widowed	0.97	-0.02
Separated	1.60	0.68	Separated	1.18	0.12
Income <$20,000	0.72	-0.66			
$20,000–$35,000	0.59	-1.16	Income <$40,000	0.96	-0.12
$35,000–$50,000	0.82	-0.44	$40,000–$60,000	1.07	0.2
$50,000–$75,000	1.04	0.08	$60,000–$80,000	1.53	1.12
$75,000–$100,000	0.81	-0.41	$80,000–$100,000	1.46	0.84
>$100,000	1.57	0.79	>$100,000	1.57	1.12
Male	0.95	-0.2	Male	1.10	0.47
Liberal	0.24	-1.85	Liberal Party	1.77	1.66
Moderate	0.36	-1.35	Conservative party	1.38	1.03
Conservative	0.29	-1.61	NDP	1.13	0.37
No Label	0.09	-2.51	Bloc Quebec	1.09	0.17
			Green	0.33	-2.12
			None of the Above Parties	2.84	1.32
			Refuse	0.55	-2.03
Black	2.07E-08	-14.36			
White Hispanic	6.41E-08	-12.21			
Hispanic — No additional Racial	7.80E-09	.			
Asian	7.43E-08	-10.49			
Other Race	7.94E-09	-13.39			
White	1.47E-08	-14.4			
Less than High School	2.21E-07	-21.08	Less than High School	0.48	-0.9
Some High School	2.23E-07	-29.33	Some High School	0.50	-1.14
High School Grad	2.27E-07	-34.89	High School Grad	0.40	-1.67
Some College	2.08E-07	-35.67	Some College	0.92	-0.13
College	2.56E-07	-33.8	College	0.39	-1.75
Grad School	4.35E-07	.	Grad School	0.27	-2.23
			Suffer Serious Illness during Last Year	1.18	0.88
Insured	3.172	4.32			
F-test age 30–39 to age >69	6.48	0.019	F-test age 30–39 to age >69	0.28	0.598
F-test <$20,000 to >$100,000	1.81	0.179	F-test <$40,000 to >$100,000	1.91	0.1670
F-test <High Sch to Grad Sch	2.45	0.1174	F-test <High Sch to Grad Sch	0.75	0.3875
F-test Liberal to Conservative	0.39	0.53	F-test Liberal Party to Conservative Party	0.46	0.4987

F-test Black to White	0.90	0.3437			
Number of Observations	1200			1022	
Pseudo R^2	0.1527			0.0722	
Log pseudolikelihood	-295.241			-382.2	

Sources: Kaiser Family Foundation health care poll, conducted September 7–12, 2006; Institute for Policy Innovation poll, conducted May 8–13, 2008

118. Similar regressions were estimated for the other questions on satisfaction, and the results are relatively comparable.
119. In 1986, Congress passed the Emergency Medical Treatment & Labor Act (EMTALA). The act guarantees public access to emergency services regardless of ability to pay or one's legal status and is available on the Centers for Medicare & Medicaid Services website at, http://www.cms.gov/Regulations-and-Guidance/Legislation/EMTALA/index.html?redirect=/emtala/.
120. "Hidden Health Tax: Americans Pay a Premium," Families USA, 2009, http://familiesusa2.org/assets/pdfs/hidden-health-tax.pdf. Peter Suderman, "Wonky Justice," Reason.com, July 2012, http://reason.com/archives/2012/06/15/wonky-justice.
121. Jonathan Gruber and David Rodriguez, "How Much Uncompensated Care Do Doctors Provide?" *Journal of Health Economics*, Vol. 26, No. 6, (December 2007): 1151–69.
122. David Hogberg, "Obama Lawyers Used Faulty Data On Uncompensated Care," *Investor's Business Daily*, March 30, 2012, http://blogs.investors.com/capitalhill/index.php/home/35-politicsinvesting/7083-obama-lawyers-use-faulty-uncompensated-care-data.
123. Jack Hadley, John Holahan, Teresa Coughlin, and Dawn Miller, "Covering the Uninsured in 2008: A Detailed Examination of Current Costs and Sources of Payment, and Incremental Costs of Expanding Coverage," The Kaiser Family Foundation, August 2008, http://www.kff.org/uninsured/upload/7809.pdf.
124. Brief for amici curiae Economists in Support of Respondents Regarding Individual Mandate, filed for the Supreme Court in the case of *United States Department of Health and Human Services et al. v. State of Florida et al.*, http://www.americanbar.org/content/dam/aba/publications/supreme_court_preview/briefs/11-398_respondents_amcu_economists.authcheckdam.pdf.

125. Daniel P. Kessler, "Cost Shifting in California Hospitals: What Is the Effect on Private Payers?" California Foundation for Commerce and Education 1, June 6, 2007, available at, http://news.heartland.org/sites/all/modules/custom/heartland_migration/files/pdfs/21714.pdf

126. Editorial, "Who are the uninsured?" *Washington Times*, June 25, 2009, http://www.washingtontimes.com/news/2009/jun/25/who-are-the-uninsured/.

127. Michael D. Tanner, "Who are the Uninsured?" Cato Institute, August 20, 2009, http://www.cato.org/publications/commentary/who-are-uninsured.

128. Dan Pfeiffer, "More Evidence of an Urgent Problem," the White House Blog, March 7, 2010, http://www.whitehouse.gov/blog/2010/03/07/more-evidence-urgent-problem.

129. Michelle Andrews, "Are Insurance Companies Still Exempt From Antitrust Laws?" *New York Times*, April 23, 2010, http://prescriptions.blogs.nytimes.com/2010/04/23/are-insurance-companies-still-exempt-from-antitrust-laws/.

130. Jesse Lee, "Repealing the Antitrust Exemption for Health Insurance Companies," the White House Blog, February 23, 2010, http://www.whitehouse.gov/blog/2010/02/23/repealing-antitrust-exemption-health-insurance-companies-0.

131. Scott E. Harrington and John R. Lott Jr., "Demonizing the Insurance Industry Is Not the Answer," Fox News, March 19, 2010, http://www.foxnews.com/opinion/2010/03/19/scott-harrington-john-lott-health-care-insurance-obama-monopoly-democrats/.

132. Data here is provided for Wisconsin. Gorman Actuarial, Jennifer Smagula, and Jon Gruber, "The Impact of the ACA on Wisconsin's Health Insurance Market," Prepared for the Wisconsin Department of Health Services, July 18, 2011, http://www.dhs.wisconsin.gov/aboutdhs/docs/WI-Final-Report-July-18-2011.pdf.

133. McKinsey & Company, "How US health care reform will affect employee benefits," *McKinsey Quarterly*, June 2011, https://www.mckinseyquarterly.com/How_US_health_care_reform_will_affect_employee_benefits_2813.

134. CFM Strategic Communications in connection with *Oregon Business* magazine conducted the survey. Tom Eiland, "Business leaders predict health care cost hikes," *Oregon Business*, October 29, 2012 (http://

www.oregonbusiness.com/contributed-blogs/8430-business-leaders-predict-health-care-cost-hikes).

A survey by the Kaiser Family Foundation that interviewed 560 employers who had at least fifty employees each early in 2012 found that 9 percent planned on dropping coverage and another 10 percent were unsure. Chad Terhune, "Nearly 10% of employers to drop health benefits, survey finds," *Los Angeles Times*, July 24, 2012, http://www.latimes.com/business/money/la-fi-mo-employers-health-care-20120724,0,5878835.story.

135. Jim Angle, "Employers Consider Dropping Insurance Plans Once Health Law Provisions Take Effect," Fox News, November 1, 2011, http://www.foxnews.com/politics/2011/11/01/employers-consider-dropping-insurance-plans-once-health-law-provisions-take/. Ricardo Alonso-Zaldivar, "Health overhaul to force changes in employer plans," Associated Press, June 11, 2011, http://www.boston.com/news/nation/washington/articles/2010/06/11/health_overhaul_to_force_changes_in_employer_plans/. One example of Obama's frequent promise that people could keep their health care is available here: President Barack Obama, "Remarks by the President in Town Hall on Health Care, Central High school Grand Junction, Colorado," the White House, Office of the Press Secretary, August 15, 2009, http://www.whitehouse.gov/the_press_office/Remarks-By-The-President-In-Town-Hall-On-Health-Care-Grand-Junction-Colorado/.

136. Ron Suskind, *Confidence Men: Wall Street, Washington, and the Education of a President* (Harper, 2012, Kindle edition), Kindle locations 6515–6522.

137. Michael D. Shear, "Polling Helps Obama Frame Message in Health-Care Debate," *Washington Post*, July 31, 2009, http://www.washingtonpost.com/wp-dyn/content/article/2009/07/30/AR2009073001547.html.

138. Ron Suskind, *Confidence Men: Wall Street, Washington, and the Education of a President* (Harper, 2012), 189–95. Peter Dreier, "Lessons from the Health-care Wars," *The American Prospect*, March 27, 2010, http://prospect.org/article/lessons-health-care-wars-0.

139. Ron Suskind, *Confidence Men: Wall Street, Washington, and the Education of a President* (Harper, 2012), 158.

140. Quote is from Ron Suskind, *Confidence Men: Wall Street, Washington, and the Education of a President* (Harper, 2012), 194. The discussion on whom the deal alienated is from Dreier.

141. Ricardo Alonso-Zaldivar, "Competition lacking among private health insurers," Associated Press, August 22, 2009, http://www.denverpost.com/perspective/ci_13184868.

142. American Medical Association, "Competition in health insurance," American Medical Association, 2007, http://www.ama-assn.org/ama1/pub/upload/mm/368/compstudy_52006.pdf.

143. Agency for Healthcare Research and Quality, Center for Financing, Access and Cost Trends; 2008 Medical Expenditure Panel Survey—Insurance Component, available online at, http://www.meps.ahrq.gov/mepsweb/data_stats/summ_tables/insr/state/series_2/2008/tiib2b1.pdf.

144.

The Entire Insurance Market: Market Concentration Measures When "Self-Insured" Companies Are Included

State	Market share of largest "full" insurance firm in the "full" insurance market	Share of individuals enrolled in private insurance who have "self-insured" plans	Market share of largest "full" insurance firm in the total insurance market	Market share of second largest "full" ins. Firm in the total insurance market	Market share of "full" insurance market for largest two firms
Alabama	83%	57.1%	35.6%	2.1%	37.8%
Rhode Island	79%	38.5%	48.6%	9.8%	58.4%
Hawaii	78%	37.9%	48.4%	12.4%	60.9%
Maine	78%	52.1%	37.4%	4.8%	42.2%
Vermont	77%	54.4%	35.1%	5.9%	41.0%
Montana	75%	49.5%	37.9%	5.1%	42.9%
Arkansas	75%	61.4%	29.0%	2.3%	31.3%
Iowa	71%	67.9%	22.8%	2.9%	25.7%
Wyoming	70%	71.0%	20.3%	4.4%	24.7%
Missouri	68%	61.2%	26.4%	4.3%	30.7%
South Carolina	66%	62.7%	24.6%	3.4%	28.0%
Michigan	65%	51.8%	31.3%	3.9%	35.2%
Louisiana	61%	58.4%	25.4%	5.4%	30.8%

Georgia	61%	65.3%	21.2%	2.8%	23.9%
Alaska	60%	60.7%	23.6%	13.8%	37.3%
Indiana	60%	66.0%	20.4%	5.1%	25.5%
Kentucky	59%	55.9%	26.0%	4.4%	30.4%
Connecticut	55%	49.1%	28.0%	5.6%	33.6%
North Carolina	53%	59.2%	21.6%	8.2%	29.8%
Maryland	52%	54.7%	23.6%	8.6%	32.2%

145. Despite repeated requests, the administration would not respond to my question of how their figures would be affected by including those insured by their own companies. Based on email correspondence with Reed Cherlin at the White House on September 14–15, 2009.

146. "But having a public plan out there that also shows that maybe if you take some of the profit motive out, maybe if you are reducing some of the administrative costs, that you can get an even better deal, that's going to incentivize the private sector to do even better. And that's a good thing," President Obama told the nation during his July 22, 2009, press conference. President Barack Obama, "News Conference by the President," the White House, Office of the Press Secretary, July 22, 2009, http://www.whitehouse.gov/the_press_office/News-Conference-by-the-President-July-22-2009.

147. "Remarks by the President to a Joint Session of Congress on Health Care," the White House, Office of the Press Secretary, September 9, 2009, http://www.whitehouse.gov/video/President-Obama-Address-to-Congress-on-Health-Insurance-Reform#transcript.

148. Paul Krugman, "Why We Reform," *New York Times*, March 19, 2010, http://www.nytimes.com/2010/03/19/opinion/19krugman.html.

149. "National Health Expenditure Accounts: Methodology Paper, 2010 Definitions, Sources, and Methods," Centers for Medicare & Medicaid Services, http://www.cms.gov/Research-Statistics-Data-and-Systems/Statistics-Trends-and-Reports/NationalHealthExpendData/downloads/dsm-10.pdf.

150. Based on a personal conversation from September 2009.

151. OECD Health Data 2012, http://www.oecd.org/health/healthpolicies anddata/oecdhealthdata2012-frequentlyrequesteddata.htm.

152. This regression uses the log of health care expenditures per capita (using purchasing power parity in terms of dollars) on the log of the percentage of health care spending from the government, real per

capita income, real per capita income squared, and year and country fixed effects. Using all the data available from 1960 to 2007 for the OECD countries, each 1 percent increase in a government's share of health care expenditures increases health care expenditures by about 0.4 percent.

	Coef.	Std. Err.	t	P>|t|
log of the percentage of health care spending from the gov	.4116	.0478	8.62	0.000□
real per capita income	.0000428	6.03e-06	7.09	0.000□
real per capita income squared	-5.44e-10	8.48e-11	-6.42	0.000

Number of obs = 969
F(79, 889) = 703.36
Adj R-squared = 0.9829

153. Letter to House Speaker John Boehner from Douglas Elmendorf, Director, Congressional Budget Office, July 24, 2012, http://www.cbo.gov/sites/default/files/cbofiles/attachments/43471-hr6079.pdf.
154. Sarah Kliff, "Romney's right: Obamacare cuts Medicare by $716 billion. Here's how," *Washington Post*, August 14, 2012, http://www.washingtonpost.com/blogs/ezra-klein/wp/2012/08/14/romneys-right-obamacare-cuts-medicare-by-716-billion-heres-how/. See also Jonathan Cohn, "Who's Raiding Medicare? Not Obama," National Public Radio, August 16, 2012, http://www.npr.org/2012/08/16/158919280/new-republic-whos-raiding-medicare-not-obama.
155. Lori Robertson, Robert Farley and Eugene Kiely, "Romney, Obama Uphold Health Care Falsehoods," FactCheck.org, June 28, 2012, http://factcheck.org/2012/06/romney-obama-uphold-health-care-falsehoods/.
156. Jonathan Serrie, "More than 2,200 hospitals face penalties under ObamaCare rules," Fox News, August 23, 2012, http://www.foxnews.com/politics/2012/08/23/more-than-2200-hospitals-face-penalties-for-high-readmissions/.
157. Gene Sperling, Director of the National Economic Council, "The Case for Shared Sacrifice,"Remarks as Prepared for Delivery (Annotated) Association of Magazine Media Washington Media, April 17, 2012.

158. President Barack Obama, "Remarks by the President in the Organizing for America National Health Care Forum," the White House, Office of the Press Secretary, August 20, 2009, www.whitehouse.gov/the-press-office/remarks-president-organizating-america-national-health-care-forum.

159. John Holahan and Linda Blumberg, "Can a Public Insurance Plan Increase Competition and Lower the Costs of Health Reform?" Urban Institute, 2008, http://www.urban.org/UploadedPDF/411762_pub lic_insurance.pdf.

160. Paul Krugman, "Administrative Costs," *New York Times*, July 6, 2009, http://krugman.blogs.nytimes.com/2009/07/06/administrative-costs/.

161. Congressional Budget Office, "Factors Affecting Insurance Premiums," Congressional Budget Office, http://www.cbo.gov/sites/default/files/cbofiles/ftpdocs/99 /doc9924/chapter3.7.1.shtml#82. Others put the range of costs for private insurance companies at between 1–14 percent. Benjamin Zycher, "Comparing Public and Private Health Insurance: Would A Single-Payer System Save Enough to Cover the Uninsured?" Manhattan Institute, October 2007, http://www.manhat tan-institute.org/html/mpr_05.htm.

    One comparison is often made between Medicare Advantage and Medicare. However, there is one important difference between the two plans that helps explain their cost differences: "the incentives that government gives private health plans to expand choice end up undercutting efforts to save money." Dana Goldman, Adam Leive, and Daniel McFadden, "Why Private Medicare Plans Don't Cost Less," *New York Times*, October 16, 2012, http://economix.blogs.nytimes.com/2012/10/16/why-private-medicare-plans-dont-cost-less/.

162. Benjamin Zycher, "Comparing Public and Private Health Insurance: Would A Single-Payer System Save Enough to Cover the Uninsured?" Manhattan Institute, October 2007, http://www.manhattan-institute.org/html/mpr_05.htm, and Ezra Klein, "Administrative Costs in Health Care: A Primer," *Washington Post*, July 7, 2009, http://voices.washingtonpost.com/ezra-klein/2009/07/administrative_costs_in_health.html.

163. Merrill Matthews, "Medicare's Hidden Administrative Costs: A Comparison of Medicare and the Private Sector (Based in Part on a Technical Paper by Mark Litow of Milliman, Inc.)," Council for Affordable

Health Insurance, January 10, 2006, http://www.cahi.org/cahi_con
tents/resources/pdf/CAHI_Medicare_Admin_Final_Publication.pdf.

164. New York State Office for the Aging, "Fraud & Abuse," Health Benefits, http://www.aging.ny.gov/HealthBenefits/FraudIndex.cfm.

165. See footnote 6 and the discussion in the text surrounding it in Merrill
Matthews, "Medicare's Hidden Administrative Costs: A Comparison
of Medicare and the Private Sector (Based in Part on a Technical
Paper by Mark Litow of Milliman, Inc.)," Council for Affordable
Health Insurance, January 10, 2006, http://www.cahi.org/cahi_con
tents/resources/pdf/CAHI_Medicare_Admin_Final_Publication.pdf.

166. See footnote 6 and the discussion in the text surrounding it in Merrill
Matthews, ibid.

167. John Goodman and Thomas Saving, "Is Medicare More Efficient
Than Private Insurance?" Health Affairs blog, August 9, 2011, http://
healthaffairs.org/blog/2011/08/09/is-medicare-more-efficient-than-
private-insurance/.

168. Benjamin Zycher, "Comparing Public and Private Health Insurance:
Would A Single-Payer System Save Enough to Cover the Uninsured?"
Manhattan Institute, October 2007, http://www.manhattan-institute.
org/html/mpr_05.htm. Milliman, the actuarial firm discussed earlier,
puts private sector administrative costs at 8.9 percent, slightly higher
than the 6–8 percent range for Medicare. But the report talks about
the benefits from those expenditures and the difference is more than
offset by the much higher rates of fraud in the public sector. Merrill
Matthews, "Medicare's Hidden Administrative Costs: A Comparison
of Medicare and the Private Sector (Based in Part on a Technical
Paper by Mark Litow of Milliman, Inc.)," Council for Affordable
Health Insurance, January 10, 2006, http://www.cahi.org/cahi_con-
tents/resources/pdf/CAHI_Medicare_Admin_Final_Publication.pdf.

Chapter Two

1. "Transcript of Second Presidential Debate," Fox News, October 16,
2012, http://www.foxnews.com/politics/2012/10/16/transcript-second-
presidential-debate/.

2. "Remarks by the President on the Economy in Osawatomie, Kansas,"
the White House, Office of the Press Secretary, December 6, 2011,

http://www.whitehouse.gov/the-press-office/2011/12/06/remarks-pres-ident-economy-osawatomie-kansas.

3. Data on the 2008 and 2012 voter exit poll surveys are available here, "Fox New Exit Poll: Results for the 2008 General Election," Fox News, http://www.foxnews.com/politics/elections/2008-exit-poll, and here, "2012 Fox News Exit Polls," Fox News, http://www.foxnews.com/politics/elections/2012-exit-poll.

4. "Complete final debate transcript: John McCain and Barack Obama," *Los Angeles Times*, October 15, 2008, http://latimesblogs.latimes.com/washington/2008/10/debate-transcri.html.

5. "The Second Presidential Debate," *New York Times*, October 7, 2008, http://elections.nytimes.com/2008/president/debates/transcripts/second-presidential-debate.html.

6. The federal deficit reached $54.6 billion dollars in 1943. After adjusting for inflation that would have been $669 billion in 2009. Yet, the actual 2009 federal deficit was $1.41 trillion, more than twice as large. As to the increase in government spending, during World War II federal government spending increased by $43.4 billion in 1943, the equivalent of $532.5 billion in 2009. Still this increase was slightly less than the $535 billion in spending during Obama's first year. Office of Management and Budget, "Fiscal Year 2012 Historical Tables, Budget of the US Government," Office of Management and Budget, budget. gov, http://www.whitehouse.gov/sites/default/files/omb/budget/fy2012/assets/hist.pdf.

7. "Obama's aides have begun working on a plan to spend up to $500 billion in new funds if the economy continues to worsen. That's well over the roughly $300 billion House Speaker Nancy Pelosi (D-Calif.) had initially considered for a new package—a figure that had been viewed as the outside limit until now." Jane Sasseen, "How Obama Will Stoke the Economy," *Business Week*, November 12, 2008, http://www.businessweek.com/magazine/content/08_47/b4109026234142.htm.

8. Martin Crutsinger, "Obama aides cite need for big stimulus program," *Boston Globe*, November 17, 2008, http://www.boston.com/business/articles/2008/11/17/obama_aides_cite_need_for_big_stimulus_program/.

9. "Estimated Impact of the American Recovery and Reinvestment Act on Employment and Economic Output from April 2011 Through June

2011," Congressional Budget Office, August 24, 2011, http://www.cbo. gov/ftpdocs/123xx/doc12385/08-24-ARRA.pdf.

10. At least once in each of the three presidential debates during September and October 2008, Obama claimed that we were in the "worst financial crisis since the Great Depression." "September 26, 2008 Debate Transcript: The First McCain-Obama Presidential Debate," Commission on Presidential Debates, September 26, 2008, www. debates.org/index.php?page=2008-debate-transcript; "October 7, 2008 Debate Transcript: The Second McCain-Obama Presidential Debate," Commission on Presidential Debates, October 7, 2008, http://www. debates.org/index.php?page=october-7-2008-debate-transcrip; and "October 15, 2008 Debate Transcript: The Third McCain-Obama Presidential Debate," Commission on Presidential Debates, October 15, 2008, www.debates.org/index.php?page=october-15-2008-debate-transcript.

11. Associated Press, "Obama: Stimulus will create 4.1 million jobs," MSNBC, January 10, 2009, http://www.msnbc.msn.com/id/28590554/ ns/business-stocks_and_economy/t/obama-stimulus-will-create-mil lion-jobs/#.UNMfGeTAevg. The "Stimulus" had been so large when some of his aides pushed for another round of spending in October 2009, Obama is quoted as saying: "I said it before, I'll say it again. It's not going to happen."

12. Sam Gustin, "Obama Signs $26 Billion Public Sector Jobs Bill Into Law," *Daily Finance*, August 10, 2010, http://www.dailyfinance. com/2010/08/10/public-sector-jobs-bill-passes-house/?icid=sphere_ copyright.

13. Catherine Clifford, "House OKs small biz jobs bill," CNNMoney.com, September 23, 2010, http://money.cnn.com/2010/09/23/smallbusiness/ small_business_legislation_house/index.htm.

14. "Disaster Relief and Summer Jobs Act," Fox News, March 24, 2010, http://www.foxnews.com/topics/politics/disaster-relief-and-summer-jobs-act.htm. See also "H.R.4899–Disaster Relief and Summer Jobs Act of 2010," OpenCongress.org, http://www.opencongress.org/ bill/111-h4899/show.

15. Associated Press, "Obama: Stimulus will create 4.1 million jobs," MSNBC, January 10, 2009, http://www.msnbc.msn.com/id/28590554/ ns/business-stocks_and_economy/t/obama-stimulus-will-create-mil lion-jobs/#.UNMfGeTAevg. There was the $42 billion "Small Business

Jobs Act of 2010," which was supposed to create or save another 500,000 jobs. Finally, the "Disaster Relief and Summer Jobs Act of 2010" that contained a hodgepodge of items, such as $24 billion to help keep teachers, police, and firefighters employed during the recession and $600 million to create 300,000 jobs for youth ages 16 to 24. "Disaster Relief and Summer Jobs Act," Fox News, March 24, 2010, http://www.foxnews.com/topics/politics/disaster-relief-and-summer-jobs-act.htm. See also "H.R.4899–Disaster Relief and Summer Jobs Act of 2010," OpenCongress.org, http://www.opencongress.org/bill/111-h4899/show. Catherine Clifford, "House OKs small biz jobs bill," CNNMoney.com, September 23, 2010, http://money.cnn.com/2010/09/23/smallbusiness/small_business_legislation_house/index.htm.

16. The working age population during this period increased by 8.8 million, but not everyone who is in that age group works. The 5.7 million additional jobs assumes that the labor force participation rate stayed the same.

17. George Stephanopoulos, "'This Week' Transcript: EXCLUSIVE: Vice President Joe Biden," *This Week with George Stephanopoulos*, ABC News, July 5, 2009, http://abcnews.go.com/ThisWeek/Politics/Story?id=8002421&page=3.

18. Deborah Solomon, "Calls Grow to Increase Stimulus Spending," *Wall Street Journal*, July 6, 2009, http://online.wsj.com/article/SB124680904844296383.html#mod=loomia?loomia_si=t0:a16:g2:r1:c0.0529546:b26214120.

19. Jared Bernstein, "PRESS BRIEFING BY PRESS SECRETARY ROBERT GIBBS AND THE VICE PRESIDENT'S CHIEF ECONOMIST, JARED BERNSTEIN," the White House, Office of the Press Secretary, whitehouse.gov, June 8, 2009, http://www.whitehouse.gov/the_press_office/Briefing-by-Press-Secretary-Robert-Gibbs-with-Jared-Bernstein-the-Vice-Presidents-Chief-Economist-6-8-09/.

20. Chuck Todd, Mark Murray, Domenico Montanaro, and Ali Weinberg, "First thoughts: Obama on Putin," MSNBC, July 7, 2009, http://firstread.msnbc.msn.com/_news/2009/07/07/4431468-first-thoughts-obama-on-putin.

21. "Notes Projections and the Budget Outlook," the White House, whitehouse.gov, February 28, 2009, http://www.whitehouse.gov/administration/eop/cea/Economic-Projections-and-the-Budget-Outlook/. "A New

Era of Responsibility: Renewing America's Promise," Office of Management and Budget, whitehouse.gov, February 26, 2009, see Table S-8, http://www.whitehouse.gov/sites/default/files/omb/assets/fy2010_new_era/A_New_Era_of_Responsibility2.pdf.

22. WSJ Staff, "Fourth-Quarter GDP: Worse and Worse," *Wall Street Journal*, December 11, 2008, http://blogs.wsj.com/economics/2008/12/11/fourth-quarter-gdp-worse-and-worse/.

23. Paul Krugman was actually even more bullish than Summers in terms of how quickly the economy would start benefitting from the stimulus. On the day that the stimulus bill was signed by Obama, Krugman told CNBC: "Actually we are already seeing some positive effects." Paul Krugman appearing on CNBC on Tuesday, February 17, 2009, "Paul Krugman: Stimulus Too Small, Second Package Likely (VIDEO)," *Huffington Post*, March 20, 2009, http://www.huffingtonpost.com/2009/02/17/paul-krugman-stimulus-too_n_167721.html.

24. "A New Era of Responsibility: Renewing America's Promise," Office of Management and Budget, whitehouse.gov, February 26, 2009, see Table S-8, http://www.whitehouse.gov/sites/default/files/omb/assets/fy2010_new_era/A_New_Era_of_Responsibility2.pdf.

25. These numbers were correct as of November 3, 2011. The data are available from the Bureau of Economic Analysis, U.S. Department of Commerce, http://www.bea.gov/newsreleases/national/gdp/gdpnews-release.htm.

26. "September 26, 2008 Debate Transcript: The First McCain-Obama Presidential Debate," Commission on Presidential Debates, September 26, 2008, http://www.debates.org/index.php?page=2008-debate-transcript, "October 7, 2008 Debate Transcript: The Second McCain-Obama Presidential Debate," Commission on Presidential Debates, October 7, 2008, http://www.debates.org/index.php?page=october-7-2008-debate-transcrip, and "October 15, 2008 Debate Transcript: The Third McCain-Obama Presidential Debate," Commission on Presidential Debates, October 15, 2008, http://www.debates.org/index.php?page=october-15-2008-debate-transcript.

27. "EDITORIAL: Revisionist history on unemployment," *Washington Times*, June 23, 2010, http://www.washingtontimes.com/news/2010/jun/23/revisionist-history-on-unemployment/.

28. President Barack Obama, "President Obama delivers Your Weekly Address," White House Blog, January 24, 2009, http://www.white

house.gov/blog/2009/01/24/president-obama-delivers-your-weekly-address.

29. President Barack Obama, "Transcript: Obama takes questions on economy," CNN Politics, February 9, 2009, http://www.cnn.com/2009/POLITICS/02/09/obama.conference.transcript/.

30. President Barack Obama, "Transcript: Remarks by President Obama, Home Mortgage Crisis, Mesa, Arizona—February 18, 2009," White House, Press Office, February 18, 2009, available on the C2: Clips & Comment website, http://www.clipsandcomment.com/2009/02/18/transcript-remarks-by-president-obama-home-mortgage-crisis-mesa-arizona-february-18-2009/.

31. President Barack Obama, "Remarks of President Barack Obama—As Prepared for Delivery, Address to Joint Session of Congress," White House Press Office, February 24, 2009, whitehouse.gov, http://www.whitehouse.gov/the_press_office/Remarks-of-President-Barack-Obama-Address-to-Joint-Session-of-Congress/.

32. "Pelosi says job creation key to Stimulus proposals," Fox News, January 25, 2009.

33. Sheryl Gay Stolberg, "In a World Not Wholly Cooperative, Obama's Top Economist Makes Do," *New York Times*, February 16, 2009, http://www.nytimes.com/2009/02/17/us/politics/17summers.html?pagewanted=all. Garrett Jones and Daniel M. Rothschild, "No such thing as shovel ready: the supply side of the recovery act," Mercatus Center, George Mason University, September 2011, http://mercatus.org/sites/default /files/publication/No_such_thing_as_shovel_ready_WP1118.pdf. For a related earlier discussion see: Lawrence H. Summers, "The State of the US Economy," Presentation at Brookings Institution forum, December 19, 2007, http://www.brookings.edu/events/2007/1219_us_economy.aspx.

34. Laura Meckler, "Obama Signs Stimulus into Law," *Wall Street Journal*, February 18, 2009, http://online.wsj.com/article/SB123487951033799545.html. Further, Ron Suskin's book reveals that in a private White House meeting in June, Summers predicted "a quick bounce-back" in jobs. Ron Suskind, *Confidence Men: Wall Street, Washington, and the Education of a President* (Harper Perennial, 2011), Kindle Locations 6894–6895.

35. "Biden: Stimulus to 'drop-kick' U.S. out of recession," WRAL, February 25, 2009, http://www.wral.com/news/political/story/4609630/.

36. President Barack Obama, "Transcript: President Obama's Press Conference," *Washington Post*, March 24, 2009, http://www.washington post.com/wp-dyn/content/article/2009/03/24/AR2009032403036.html. Summers declared even earlier: "some of the things that the president is doing are starting to have effects." "'This Week' Transcript: Larry Summers & Mitch McConnell," *This Week with George Stephanopoulos*, ABC News, March 15, 2009, http://abcnews.go.com/ThisWeek/story?id=7085991&page=3.

37. "Why is Obama Touting Stimulus After 1.6M Jobs Lost?" Fox Nation, Fox News, May 28, 2009, http://nation.foxnews.com/politics/2009/05/28/why-obama-touting-stimulus-after-16m-jobs-lost. For a discussion of the Obama administration talking about the "green shoots" of recovery see Martin Wolf, "Why the 'green shoots' of recovery could yet wither," *Financial Times*, April 21, 2009, http://www.ft.com/intl/cms/s/0/1ed88b70-2ea9-11de-b7d3-00144feabdc0.html#axzz1aNqnJJfL.

38. Elizabeth Williamson, "Biden on Stimulus: 'Never Thought It Would Work This Well,'" *Wall Street Journal*, September 24, 2009, http://blogs.wsj.com/washwire/2009/09/24/biden-on-stimulus-never-thought-it-would-work-this-well/.

39. Mimi Hall, "Biden touts 'Summer of Recovery,'" *USA Today*, June 17, 2010, http://content.usatoday.com/communities/theoval/post/2010/06/biden-touts-summer-of-recovery/1.

40. Austan Goolsbee, "The Employment Situation in April," Council of Economic Advisers, whitehouse.gov, May 6, 2011, http://www.white house.gov/blog/2011/05/06/employment-situation-april.

41. Don Lee, "Economy shows solid job growth for a third straight month," *Los Angeles Times*, May 7, 2011, http://articles.latimes.com/2011/may/07/business/la-fi-april-jobs-report-20110506, and Motoko Rich, "Payrolls Show Strong Growth but Jobless Rate Rises," *New York Times*, May 6, 2011, http://www.nytimes.com/2011/05/07/business/economy/07jobs.html?_r=1.

42. President Barack Obama, "Statement by the President, Rose Garden," the White House, Office of the Press Secretary, whitehouse.gov, August 2, 2011, http://www.whitehouse.gov/the-press-office/2011/08/02/statement-president.

43. Using the Bureau of Labor Statistics international unemployment rates adjusted to U.S. concepts, the Japanese unemployment rate fell from 4.3 percent in March 2011 to 4.0 percent in August 2011.

44. Using the Bureau of Labor Statistics international unemployment rates adjusted to U.S. concepts, the German, Italian, and Swedish unemployment rates fell from 6.9, 8.2, and 7.7 percent in January 2011 to 6.5, 8.0, and 7.3 percent in August 2011.

45. John Lott, "Obama's Stimulus Package Will Increase Unemployment," Fox News, February 3, 2009, http://www.foxnews.com story/0,2933, 487425,00.html.

46. President Obama, "Remarks by the President, James S. Brady Press Briefing Room," the White House, Office of the Press Secretary, whitehouse.gov, June 8, 2012, http://www.whitehouse.gov/the-press-office/2012/06/08/remarks-president.

47. "Bill Clinton: Obama Has 'Not Fixed' Economy, 'Middle Class Incomes Are Not Yet Rising,'" Fox Nation, Fox News, October 18, 2012, http://nation.foxnews.com/bill-clinton/2012/10/18/clinton-were-not-where-we-ought-be-middle-class-incomes-are-not-yet-rising.

48. Rasmussen Reports, "Rasmussen Consumer Index," October 17, 2012.

49. Alan S. Blinder, "A Slow but Steady Climb to Prosperity," *Wall Street Journal*, October 31, 2012, http://online.wsj.com/article/SB10001424 052970203922804578080920652419526.html?mod=WSJ_Opinion_LEFTTopOpinion.

50. The other way of measuring job growth is to use the Establishment Survey, but doing that shows similar weak growth in the current recovery relative to either the average recovery or recoveries after severe recessions. See figure on page 256.

51. Because the size of the job market has changed so much over the last forty years, job growth is expressed as a percentage of the number of people employed.

52. From its peak, the percent of the unemployed who had been unemployed for more than twenty-six weeks had fallen by 25 percent.

53. Jordan Weissmann, "53% of Recent College Grads Are Jobless or Underemployed—How?" *The Atlantic*, April 23, 2012, http://www.theatlantic.com/business/archive/2012/04/53-of-recent-college-grads-are-jobless-or-underemployed-how/256237/.

54. Charley Stone, Carl Van Horn, and Cliff Zukin, "Chasing the American Dream: Recent College Graduates and the Great Recession," Work Trends, Rutgers University, May 2012, http://www.heldrich.rutgers.edu/sites/default/files/content/Chasing_American_Dream_Report.pdf.

55.   Philip Oreopoulos, Till von Wachter, and Andrew Heisz, "The Short-
      and Long-Term Career Effects of Graduating in a Recession: Hyster-
      esis and Heterogeneity in the Market for College Graduates," NBER
      Working Paper No. 12159, National Bureau of Economic Research,

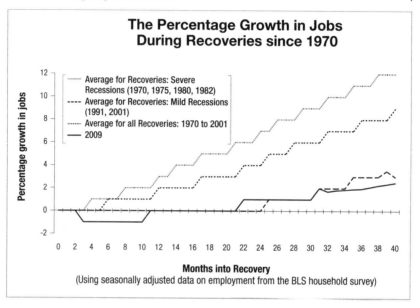

The Percentage Growth in Jobs
During Recoveries since 1970

      April 2006, http://www.nber.org/papers/w12159.pdf?new_window=1.
56.   Chris Isidore, "The Great Recession's lost generation," CNN Money,
      May 17, 2011 http://money.cnn.com/2011/05/17/news/economy/reces-
      sion_lost_generation/index.htm, and Robert J. Samuelson, "Is the
      economy creating a lost generation?" *Washington Post*, December 10,
      2012, http://www.washingtonpost.com/opinions/robert-samuelson-
      is-the-economy-creating-a-lost-generation/2012/12/09/41683956-409
      3-11e2-bca3-aadc9b7e29c5_story.html.
57.   Tim Kane, "The Importance of Startups in Job Creation and Job
      Destruction," Kauffman Foundation Research Series: Firm Founda-
      tion and Economic Growth, Kauffman: The Foundation of Entrepre-
      neurship, July 2010, Table 2, http://www.kauffman.org/uploadedfiles/
      firm_formation_importance_of_startups.pdf.
58.   William T. Dickens, "Structural Unemployment: Stubborn Myths and
      Elusive Realities," Milken Institute Review, First Quarter 2012, http://
      www.milkeninstitute.org/publications/review/2012_1/42-51MR53.pdf.

59. "Household Income Trend Series: August 2012: Household Income Down by 1.1 Percent Between July 2012 and August 2012," Sentier Research, September 25, 2012, http://www.sentierresearch.com/pressreleases/Sentier_Household_Income_Trends_Press_Release_August2012_09_25_12.pdf.

60. Ibid.

61. "Tracking the Recovery after the Great Recession," National Employment Law Project (NELP), August 2012, http://www.nelp.org/index.php/content/content_about_us/tracking_the_recovery_after_the_great_recession.

62. The stimulus and the various other jobs programs might have continued until the end of 2011, but real hourly wages have fallen consistently from the middle of 2010 on. People have offset these lower wages by working longer hours. See figure below.

63. Milton Friedman, "The 'Plucking Model' of Business Fluctuations Revisited," *Economic Inquiry*, 1993.

64. To estimate this relationship, I estimated the natural log of GDP on a time trend from the first quarter of 1965 to the last quarter of 2007. The coefficient on the time-trend was .0076698 and a t-statistic of 228.65. During the 1947 through 2007 period, GDP was growing at an annual rate of 3.26 percent.

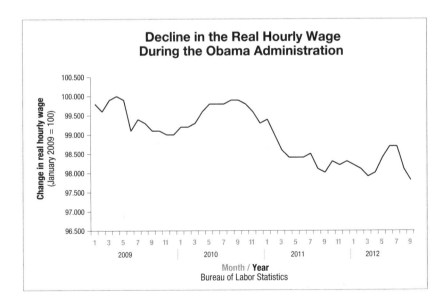

Decline in the Real Hourly Wage During the Obama Administration

Bureau of Labor Statistics

65. Paul Krugman has used similar figures himself. Paul Krugman, "New Deal economics," *New York Times*, November 8, 2008, http://krugman. blogs.nytimes.com/2008/11/08/new-deal-economics/.

66. Some argue that the recovery during the Great Depression would have been even stronger if it weren't for Franklin Roosevelt's stimulative policies. Harold Cole and Lee Ohanian, "New Deal Policies and the Persistence of the Great Depression: A General Equilibrium Analysis", *Journal of Political Economy*, Vol. 112, No. 4, August 2004, 779–816. See also Harold Cole and Lee Ohanian, "Stimulus and the Depression: The Untold Story," *Wall Street Journal*, September 26, 2011, http:// online.wsj.com/article/SB10001424053111904787404576532141884 735626.html.

67. Historical data on U.S. GDP is available from deceased Angus Maddison's homepage, http://www.ggdc.net/maddison/Maddison.htm at this page www.ggdc.net/maddison/Historical_Statistics/horizontal-file_02-2010.xls. He is a former economics professor at the University of Groningen in the Netherlands.

68. Joseph E. Stiglitz, "Political Causes, Political Solutions," *New York Times*, October 24, 2012, http://www.nytimes.com/roomforde bate/2012/10/18/shrink-inequality-to-grow-the-economy/political-causes-political-solutions.

69. Lynn Neary, "Why One Economist Pushed Cash For Clunkers," National Public Radio, August 11, 2009, http://www.npr.org/templates/ story/story.php?storyId=111781653. In an interview with Neary, liberal economics professor Alan Blinder states: "one of its objectives was to assist poor people who tend to own the clunkers."

70. The final way that the government can transfer money is by printing it up. Printing up money also acts as a tax on money that is already held by people. When you print up money, it lowers the value of other money that people hold. Reducing the value of money that people hold by 10 percent is no different than imposing a 10 percent tax on the money that people hold.

71. Fareed Zakaria, "Watch GPS: Krugman calls for space aliens to fix U.S. economy?" CNN World, August 12, 2011, http://globalpublic-square.blogs.cnn.com/2011/08/12/gps-this-sunday-krugman-calls-for-space-aliens-to-fix-u-s-economy/. John Lott, "Cash for Clunkers Falls Flat," Fox News, August 3, 2009, available here, http://johnrlott.tripod. com/op-eds/FoxNewsCasForClunkers080309.html.

72. John Lott, "Cash for Clunkers Falls Flat," Fox News, August 3, 2009, available here, http://johnrlott.tripod.com/op-eds/FoxNewsCasForClunkers080309.html.

73. John R. Lott Jr., "John R. Lott, Jr.: Ethanol Mandates Cause Rising Food Prices," Fox News, April 28, 2008, http://www.foxnews.com/story/0,2933,352968,00.html; James Shell, "The Ethanol Disaster And The Ramifications For Producers," Seeking Alpha, August 1, 2012, http://seekingalpha.com/article/769871-the-ethanol-disaster-and-the-ramifications-for-producers, and Chris Hurt, Wally Tyner, and Otto Doering, "Economics of Ethanol," Department of Agricultural Economics, Purdue Extension, Purdue University, June 2006, http://www.extension.purdue.edu/extmedia/ID/ID-339.pdf.

74. Among those who have made this argument is Edward Conard. See Edward Conard, *Unintended Consequences: Why Everything You've Been Told About the Economy Is Wrong* (Portfolio Hardcover, 2012).

75. Even the liberal Center for American Progress could only muster claiming that the data "facing the United States is not entirely clear." Heather Boushey and Adam Hersh, "The American Middle Class, Income Inequality, and the Strength of Our Economy," Center for American Progress, May 17, 2012, http://www.americanprogress.org/issues/economy/report/2012/05/17/11628/the-american-middle-class-income-inequality-and-the-strength-of-our-economy/.

76. Paul Krugman interviewed by Martin Bashir on MSNBC on May 18, 2012, watch it here, http://www.msnbc.msn.com/id/21134540/vp/47480484#47480484.

77. "The euro crisis: Bad Medicine," *The Economist*, July 11, 2012, http://www.economist.com/blogs/freeexchange/2012/07/euro-crisis-1?fsrc=scn/tw/te/bl/badmedicine.

78. "US Deficit 'Higher than Euro Zone's': Germany Rejects Obama's Criticism in Euro Crisis," Spiegel Online International, June 25, 2012, http://www.spiegel.de/international/europe/german-finance-minister-rejects-obama-criticism-of-crisis-management-a-840749.html.

79. There is another consideration. When the economy comes tumbling down, there are automatic triggers that increase government spending and decrease revenue. So deficits are not entirely under the immediate control of the government and cannot all be viewed as "stimulus policies." Likewise, surpluses (or decreasing deficits) during boom times may reflect a decline in automatic spending on such items as

unemployment benefits, food stamps, etc. Such surpluses may also reflect an increase in tax revenue from higher incomes.

80. For comparison, here are the figures if the same time periods are used for both the change in government spending and income and employment growth.

81. I can redo the figures showing the year-by-year changes, though that doesn't really make it feasible to identify the changes for individual countries. Doing this produces very similar results to those that are shown in the text. Here is one example showing that the results for changes lagged behind government spending as a share of GDP and the change in per capita GDP.

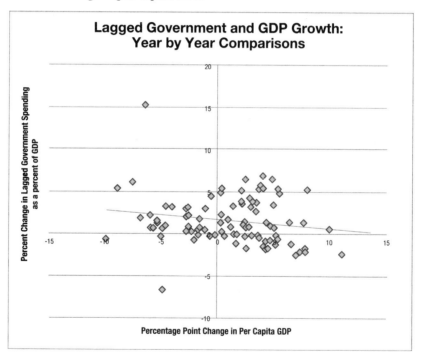

82. Milton Friedman, "An argument that the balanced-budget amendment would be a rare merging of public and private interests," *The Atlantic*, 1983.

83. Paul Krugman, "Austerity and Growth, Again (Wonkish)," *New York Times*, April 24, 2012, http://krugman.blogs.nytimes.com/2012/04/24/austerity-and-growth-again-wonkish/. Krugman's assumption of

2 percent growth was for European countries. So the figure below
shows what the relationship would be for just European countries.

84. There are two sets of European countries reported by Eurostat: the
seventeen country Euro area and the twenty-seven EU countries.
Strangely, Krugman uses neither and instead uses data for only
twenty-three countries. No explanation is provided for why he did
this and no list of which countries he dropped out is given. Eurostat,
"Euro area and EU27 government deficit at 4.1% and 4.5% of GDP
respectively," Eurostat News Release, April 23, 2012, http://epp.euro-
stat.ec.europa.eu/cache/ITY_PUBLIC/2-23042012-AP/EN/2-
23042012-AP-EN.PDF, and Eurostat, "Provision of deficit and debt
data for 2009—first notification Euro area and EU27 government
deficit at 6.3% and 6.8% of GDP respectively Government debt at
78.7% and 73.6%," Eurostat News Release, April 22, 2010, http://
europa.eu/rapid/press-release_STAT-10-55_en.htm.

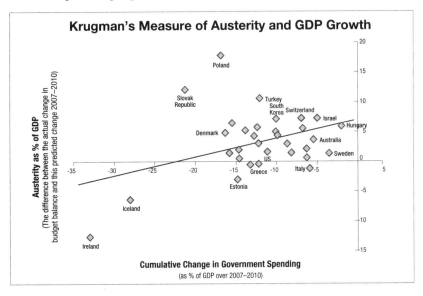

85. Using the changes between 2007 and 2010, regressing percentage
point change in per capita GDP on Krugman's measure of "Austerity"
produced the following result (absolute t-statistics are in parentheses).
Change in GDP per capita = .2854 (2.04) Austerity + 6.74 (3.53)
N= 32 Adj-R2 = 0.0929 F-statistic = 4.17

86. Using the changes between 2007 and 2010, regressing percentage point change in the percent of the working age population that is employed on Krugman's measure of "Austerity" produced the following result (absolute t-statistics are in parentheses).

    Change in percent of the working age population employed = .2203 (3.27) Austerity + .82399 (0.89)

    N= 32 Adj-R2 = 0.2385 F-statistic = 10.71

87. These regressions account for what is called country and year fixed effects. Regressing real per capita GDP on the previous year's government expenditures as a percent of GDP as well as these fixed effects shows:

    Change in GDP per capita = -184 (3.69) previous year's government expenditures as a percent of GDP + 46712 (28.08)

    N= 128 Adj-R2 = 0.9944 prob >F-statistic = 0.00

88. Regressing the percentage of the working age population that is employed on the previous year's government expenditures as a percent of GDP as well as these fixed effects shows:

    Change in percent of the working age population employed = -.445 (8.00) previous year's government expenditures as a percent of GDP + 87.8 (47.33)

    N= 128 Adj-R2 = 0.9799 prob >F-statistic = 0.00

89. Author's telephone conversation with Stephen Bronars on June 22, 2012.

90. W. Craig Riddell, "Why Is Canada's Unemployment Rate Persistently Higher than that in the US?" Centre for the Study of Living Standards, 2003, 3 (http://www.csls.ca/events/cea2003/riddell-cea2003.pdf). See also "Job Search," National Longitudinal Survey, Bureau of Labor Statistics, U.S. Department of Labor, http://www.nlsinfo.org/nlsy97/nlsdocs/nlsy97/topicalguide/jobsearch.html.

91. W. Craig Riddell, "Why Is Canada's Unemployment Rate Persistently Higher than that in the US?" Centre for the Study of Living Standards, 2003, http://www.csls.ca/events/cea2003/riddell-cea2003.pdf.

92. An Angus-Reid Survey conducted during December 17 to 18, 2008, found that 56 percent of Canadians thought that their economy was "bad," and 49 percent of Canadians thought that the economy was going to get worse. A Gallup Survey from December 18 to 20, 2008, found that 57 percent of Americans described their economy as "poor." Another Gallup Survey found that in 2009 35 percent thought

that the economy was getting worse. "Canadians Head to 2009 with Gloomy Forecast for the National Economy," Angus Reid Strategies, December 30, 2008, http://www.angus-reid.com/wp-content/uploads/archived-pdf/2008.12.30_EcoIndex.pdf). "Gallup Daily: U.S. Economic Conditions," Gallup Economy, http://www.gallup.com/poll/110821/Gallup-Daily-US-Economic-Conditions.aspx). Jeffrey M. Jones, "In U.S., 6 in 10 Do Not Expect Economy to Improve Soon," Gallup Economy, September 21, 2011, http://www.gallup.com/poll/149576/not-expect-economy-improve-soon.aspx.

93. For a discussion of Canada's debt and deficits over the last few decades see David R. Henderson, "Canada's Budget Triumph," Working Paper, No. 10–52, Mercatus Center, George Mason University, August 2010, http://mercatus.org/sites/default/files/publication/Canada's%20Budget%20Triumph.WP_.pdf.

94. "Gallup Daily: U.S. Economic Conditions," Gallup Economy, http://www.gallup.com/poll/110821/Gallup-Daily-US-Economic-Conditions.aspx.

95. Angus Reid Public Opinion conducted surveys both before and after the third quarter of 2011, doing the surveys in April and October 2011. In April, 61 percent of Canadians said that economic conditions in Canada were "Good/Very Good." That percent rose to 63 percent in October. "Three-in-Five Canadians Satisfied with Country's Economic Conditions," AngusReidPublicOpinion, October 19, 2011, http://www.angus-reid.com/polls/44091/three-in-five-canadians-satisfied-with-countrys-economic-conditions/.

96. Information was available from Recovery.gov's "Quarterly Summary" page, http://www.recovery.gov/Transparency/RecoveryData/Pages/QuarterlySum.aspx. Also by that time 87 percent of the stimulus dollars had been received.

97. William L. Watts, "Clash over stimulus spending clouds G20 outlook," MarketWatch, March 13, 2009, http://www.marketwatch.com/story/clash-over-stimulus-spending-clouds-g20.

98. "The US treasury secretary talks about permanent action and we at our [EU summit] were quite alarmed by that. He talks about an extensive US stimulus campaign. All of these steps are the road to hell," Mirek Topolanek, the Czech prime minister, warned. Ian Traynor, "Obama's rescue plan is 'road to hell', claims EU president," *The*

Guardian, March 25, 2009, http://www.guardian.co.uk/business/2009/mar/25/obama-rescue-eu-criticism.

99. Craig Whitlock, "European Union President Criticizes Obama's Economic Policies," *Washington Post*, March 26, 2009, http://www.washingtonpost.com/wp-dyn/content/article/2009/03/25/AR2009032502074.html.

100. For the 2008 to 2010 period, stimuluses as a percentage of GDP by country were: Australia, 4.6; Japan, 2.0; France, .6; Germany, 3; Italy, 0; the Netherlands, 1.5; Sweden, 2.8; the UK, 1.4; and the US, 5.6. See Table 3.1 on page 110, "OECD Economic Outlook," Interim Report, March 2009, http://www.iier.org/i/uploadedfiles/publication/real/1300670938_010309EconomicOutlookOECD4B.pdf.

101. European Commission, "Employment Statistics," Eurostat, http://epp.eurostat.ec.europa.eu/statistics_explained/index.php/Employment_statistics.

102. The data on the Current Population Survey from the Bureau of Labor Statistics is available here, "Data Retrieval: Labor Force Statistics (CPS)," Bureau of Labor Statistics, http://www.bls.gov/webapps/legacy/cpsatab1.htm.

103. President Barack Obama, "Remarks by President Obama at Press Conference After G20 Summit, Convention Center, Los Cabos, Mexico," the White House, June 19, 2012, whitehouse.gov, click "Read the Transcript," http://www.whitehouse.gov/photos-and-video/video/2012/06/19/president-obama-holds-press-conference-g20-summit#transcript.

104. Tiffany Hsu, "Think 8.2% unemployment is bad? It's a record 11.1% in Europe," *Los Angeles Times*, July 2, 2012, http://articles.latimes.com/2012/jul/02/business/la-fi-mo-euro-unemployment-20120702.

105. Paul Krugman surely thinks the answer to this question is "yes." In November 2012, while acknowledging "initially some of the drop in unemployment was basically people leaving the labor force," he thinks that the graph demonstrates: "America is doing the least worst among major economies." Paul Krugman, "Transatlantic Divergence," *New York Times*, November 17, 2012, http://krugman.blogs.nytimes.com/2012/11/17/transatlantic-divergence/.

106. "'Ranks of Discouraged Workers and Others Marginally Attached to the Labor Force Rise During Recession,' Issues in Labor Statistics"

Bureau of Labor Statistics, April 2009, http://www.bls.gov/opub/ils/ils74abs.htm.

107. Just between January 2011 and October 2012, another million people have taken part-time work for other reasons.

108. Paul Krugman, "That '30s Feeling," *New York Times*, June 17, 2010, http://www.nytimes.com/2010/06/18/opinion/18krugman.html.

109. Krugman wrote: "If there's a slam-dunk argument for austerity in there, it's remarkably well hidden." Paul Krugman, "What About Germany?" *New York Times*, August 24, 2010, http://krugman.blogs.nytimes.com/2010/08/24/what-about-germany/.

110. Yet, even if it were only true that Germany's economy was doing relatively well without a "real" stimulus, that would still represent a real problem for Keynesians.

111. John F. Burns and Landon Thomas Jr., "Britain Unveils Emergency Budget," *New York Times*, June 22, 2010, http://www.nytimes.com/2010/06/23/world/europe/23britain.html?pagewanted=all&_r=0.

112. Paul Krugman, "British Fashion Victims," *New York Times*, October 21, 2010, http://www.nytimes.com/2010/10/22/opinion/22krugman.html. They also increased taxes to cut down the deficit, but, as our earlier discussion on Milton Friedman noted, it is the level of government spending that determines the level of taxes. Financing government spending by borrowing doesn't eliminate taxes, it only means higher taxes in the future. Britain's tax rate was already very high and would discourage work, but at least it wasn't going to be even higher.

113. Paul Krugman, "Cameron's Remarkable Achievement," *New York Times*, April 25, 2012, http://krugman.blogs.nytimes.com/2012/04/25/camerons-remarkable-achievement/.

114. Timothy Geithner, "Remarks by Secretary Geithner before the Economic Club of New York," U.S. Department of the Treasury, Press Center, March 15, 2012, http://www.treasury.gov/press-center/press-releases/Pages/tg1452.aspx.

115. See for example Chapter 2, "The Year in Review and the Years Ahead," of the 2012 Economic Report of the President by the Council of Economic Advisers, whitehouse.gov, http://www.whitehouse.gov/sites/default/files/microsites/ERP_2012_ch_2.pdf.

116. President Barack Obama, "Remarks by the President at a Facebook Town Hall," the White House, Office of the Press Secretary, whitehouse.gov, April 20, 2011, http://www.whitehouse.gov/the-press-office/2011/04/20/remarks-president-facebook-town-hall.

117. None of Reinhart's and Rogoff's evidence covers anything remotely close to five hundred years of employment data. With the exception of the U.S.'s Great Depression, their international employment data goes back to about 1981. Here are just a few of the many times that former President Clinton made this claim. "Clinton: 10 years to get out of recession, housing crisis," CBS *Evening News*, June 5, 2012, http://www.cbsnews.com/8301-18563_162-57447748/clinton-10-years-to-get-out-of-recession-housing-crisis/. President Bill Clinton, "Remarks by President Obama and Former President Clinton at a Campaign Event," the White House, Office of the Press Secretary, whitehouse.gov, April 29, 2012, http://www.whitehouse.gov/the-press-office/2012/04/29/remarks-president-obama-and-former-president-clinton-campaign-event. "Bill Clinton wants to get America 'Back to Work,'" *Today Show*, NBC News, November 8, 2011, http://today.msnbc.msn.com/id/45195220/ns/today-books/t/bill-clinton-wants-get-america-back-work/.

118. Often Reinhart and Rogoff have described academic critics as blinded by support for Republican politicians. In an op-ed in Bloomberg shortly before the election, Reinhart and Rogoff wrote: "Some of these authors, including Kevin Hassett, Glenn Hubbard and John Taylor—who are advisers to the Republican presidential nominee, Mitt Romney—as well as Michael Bordo, who supports the candidate, have stressed that the U.S. is also 'different' in that its recoveries from recessions associated with financial crises have been rapid and strong." Carmen M. Reinhart and Kenneth S. Rogoff, "Sorry, U.S. Recoveries Really Aren't Different," Bloomberg, October 15, 2012, http://www.bloomberg.com/news/2012-10-15/sorry-u-s-recoveries-really-aren-t-different.html.

119. John Lott, Jerry Dwyer, and James Lothian, "The financial crisis can't explain the current slow recovery," Fox News, November 5, 2012, http://www.foxnews.com/opinion/2012/11/05/financial-crisis-cant-explain-current-slow-recovery/.

120. Milton Friedman, "The Monetary Studies of the National Bureau," Chapter twelve in *The Optimum Quantity of Money and Other Essays* (Aldine Publishing Company, 1969) (Originally from The National Bureau Enters its 45th year, annual report, 1964).

121. Michael D. Bordo and Joseph G. Haubrich, "Deep Recessions, Fast Recoveries, and Financial Crises: Evidence from the American

Record," Federal Reserve Bank of Cleveland, June 2012, http://www.clevelandfed.org/research/workpaper/2012/wp1214.pdf. The quote is from Michael Bordo, "Michael Bordo: Financial Recessions Don't Lead to Weak Recoveries," *Wall Street Journal*, September 27, 2012, http://online.wsj.com/article/SB10000872396390444506004577613122591922992.html.

122. Gerald P. Dwyer and James R. Lothian, "The Financial Crisis and Recovery: Why so Slow?" Federal Reserve Bank of Atlanta, September/October 2011, http://www.frbatlanta.org/cenfis/pubscf/nftv_1110.cfm. John B. Taylor, "Simple Proof That Strong Growth Has Typically Followed Financial Crises," Economics One, October 11, 2012, http://johnbtaylorsblog.blogspot.com/2012/10/simple-proof-that-strong-growth-has.html.

123. Carmen M. Reinhart and Kenneth Rogoff, *This Time Is Different: Eight Centuries of Financial Folly* (Princeton University Press, 2009, Kindle Edition), 11. Similarly, for Domestic public debt crises, they write: "it is very difficult to date these episodes, and in many cases (such as those of banking crises) it is impossible to ascertain the data of the final resolution." John Cochrane, an economist at the University of Chicago Business School, notes: "Me, I'm still waiting for an economically meaningful *definition* of 'systemic' better than 'we'll know it when we see it.'" John Cochrane, "Are recoveries always slow after financial crises and why," The Grumpy Economist, October 17, 2012 (http://johnhcochrane.blogspot.com/2012/10/are-recoveries-always-slow-after.html). See also John Cochrane, "Slow recoveries after financial crises?" The Grumpy Economist, May 4, 2012, http://johnhcochrane.blogspot.com/2012/05/slow-recoveries-after-financial-crises.html.

124. A timeline of the financial crisis is available from the St. Louis Federal Reserve, "The Financial Crisis: A Timeline of Events and Policy Actions," Federal Reserve Bank of St. Louis, http://timeline.stlouisfed.org/index.cfm?p=timeline.

125. See pp. 98–100 in Grover Norquist and John R. Lott Jr., *Debacle* (John Wiley & Sons, 2012). It should also be noted that countries identified as suffering a financial crisis by Reinhart and Rogoff also did not experience slower Gross Domestic Product (GDP) growth during their recoveries. From the third quarter of 2009, when the U.S. recovery

started, the difference in GDP growth between the two sets of nations averaged just one-tenth of 1 percent.

126. Eurostat, Statistics Canada, Statistics New Zealand, the Australian Bureau of Statistics, and Statistics South Africa provide quarterly labor force participation rate data for most countries through the middle of 2012. Strangely enough, Reinhart and Rogoff recognize the differences in how unemployment is measured across countries, but even in the few comparisons they make, they never try to do anything about it. Figures and tables in Reinhart's and Rogoff's book contain notes stating, "The figures reflect differences in the definition of unemployment and in the methods of compiling the statistics" (e.g., Carmen M. Reinhart and Kenneth Rogoff, *This Time Is Different: Eight Centuries of Financial Folly* (Princeton University Press, 2009), Kindle Edition), 269. They also acknowledge one problem with cross-country comparisons: "Notably, widespread 'underemployment' in many emerging markets and the vast informal sector are not fully captured in the official unemployment statistics" (p. 292). But the problems with the different definitions of unemployment are much broader than that. One very big problem is simply that in the U.S. people are only classified as unemployed as long as they are actively looking for work. That means that they have to be sending out resumes and doing job interviews. In other countries, simply saying that someone is looking for a job is enough to be classified as unemployed.

127. Austria, Belgium, Germany, Hungary, Iceland, Ireland, Japan, the Netherlands, Spain, and the United Kingdom.

128. Australia, Canada, Czech Republic, Denmark, Estonia, France, Finland, Norway, Portugal, Poland, Latvia, Lithuania, Italy, New Zealand, Sweden, Slovenia, South Africa, and Switzerland.

129. A simple t-test that compares the ten foreign countries Reinhart and Rogoff label as facing a financial crisis in 2007–2008 with the eighteen countries that I have data for that didn't implies a t-statistic = 1.1855 with a probability to 12.7 percent.

130. By the second quarter of 2012, the average labor force participation rate for the countries without financial crises had fallen to 97.2 percent. For Austria, Belgium, Germany, Hungary, Iceland, Ireland, Japan, Netherlands, Spain, and the United Kingdom, their labor force participation rates ranged from a low of 97.5 percent for the UK to 104.8 percent for Germany.

131. A simple t-test that compares the countries Reinhart and Rogoff label as not facing a financial crisis in 2007–2008 with the eight foreign countries that say they did face such a crisis (excluding Ireland and Spain) is statistically significant at being much better than the 0.01 percent level for a two-tailed t-test (t = 7.1403).

132. President Barack Obama, "In Obama's Words: Feb. 17, 2009—Denver, Colo.," *Washington Post*, February 17, 2009, http://projects.washing tonpost.com/obama-speeches/speech/78/.

133. Prepared for California Energy Commission, "Federal Economic Recovery Program American Recovery and Reinvestment Act of 2009 Program Support Services," Perry-Smith, NewPoint Group, McGladrey, December 29, 2010, p. 2, http://www.energy.ca.gov/recov ery/documents/DBA_Toolkit_Combined.pdf.

134. United States Department of Labor, "Notification of Employee Rights Under Federal Labor Laws; Final Rule [5/20/2010]," *Federal Register*, Vol. 75, No. 97, May 20, 2010, http://webapps.dol.gov/federalregister/ HtmlDisplay.aspx?DocId=23890&AgencyId=12&DocumentType=2.

Chapter Three

1. "Fireworks: Piers Morgan Battles Gun Advocate Again," RealClear-Politics, December 20, 2012, http://www.realclearpolitics.com/ video/2012/12/20/fireworks_piers_morgan_battles_gun_advocate_ again.html.

2. "Soledad O'Brien To Gun Advocate John Lott: Your Position 'Bobbles' Me (VIDEO), December 17, 2012, *Huffington Post*, http://www.huff ingtonpost.com/2012/12/17/soledad-obrien-john-lott-newtown_n_ 2315710.html.

3. "Barack Obama on Gun Control," On the Issues, http://www.ontheis-sues.org/2012/Barack_Obama_Gun_Control.htm. A Youtube of this interview is available here, "Obama Supports DC Handgun Ban:" http://youtu.be/-wu9jE1MnAE.

4. Jodi Kantor, "Teaching Law, Testing Ideas, Obama Stood Slightly Apart," *New York Times*, July 30, 2008, http://www.nytimes. com/2008/07/30/us/politics/30law.html?pagewanted=all. Ms. Kantor interviewed me for the story in the summer of 2008. I shared these and a couple of other stories with her. But my examples were not

included in her final article. Ms. Kantor said in e-mail correspondence: "the Obama people denied that the conversation ever took place." In a follow-up conversation with her, I asked what exactly they were denying. That I ever talked to Obama? That we ever talked about guns? That we knew each other at Chicago? But the only statement she ever received back from the Obama camp was that they "denied that the conversation ever took place." A key point of my account was how different Obama was from academics in his unwillingness to discuss things with those who held opposing views. As I pointed out, Obama would just turn his back and walk away from conversations. Kantor noted that others had told her similar things and that was another reason my anecdotes were not crucial: "There was, frankly, a fair amount of other evidence, independent of the incident you told me about, that Sen. Obama did not engage much with conservatives/libertarians."

5. The video of the news broadcast is available here, "Barack Obama: Presumptive Democratic presidential candidate discusses North Korea, the Second Amendment and tax cuts," Fox News, May 3, 2011, http://video.foxnews.com/v/3907719/.

6. Saira Anees, "Obama Explains Why Some Small Town Pennsylvanians Are 'Bitter,'" ABC News, April 11, 2008, http://abcnews.go.com/blogs/politics/2008/04/obama-explains-2/.

7. Jason Horowitz, "Over a barrel? Meet White House gun policy adviser Steve Croley," *Washington Post*, April 11, 2011, http://www.washingtonpost.com/lifestyle/style/over-a-barrel-meet-white-house-gun-policy-adviser-steve-croley/2011/04/04/AFt9EKND_story.html.

8. Charles C. Johnson, "Full audio of 1998 'redistribution' speech: Obama saw welfare recipients as 'majority coalition,'" Daily Caller, September 24, 2012, http://dailycaller.com/2012/09/24/full-audio-of-1998-redistribution-speech-obama-saw-welfare-recipients-as-majority-coalition/#ooid=w4N2d5NTpRvoDqq-uk56825aahsPQkDa.

9. Kenneth P. Vogel, "Obama had greater role on liberal survey," Politico, March 31, 2008, http://dyn.politico.com/printstory.cfm?uuid=03FA375F-3048-5C12-00CC7D33B6E8E59E.

10. "Barack Obama on Gun Control," OnTheIssues, http://www.ontheissues.org/2008/barack_obama_gun_control.htm.

11. Tracy Baim, "Obama changed views on gay marriage; 1996 statement: 'I favor legalizing same-sex marriage,'" *Windy City Times*, January 14, 2009, 6–8.

12. Jim Geraghty, "Obama's Efforts to Fund the Self-Described 'Most Aggressive Group in the Gun Control Movement'," National Review Online, June 26, 2008, http://www.nationalreview.com/campaign-spot/9396/obamas-efforts-fund-self-described-most-aggressive-group-gun-control-movement.

13. President Barack Obama, "Remarks by the President at the National Urban League Convention," the White House, Office of the Press Secretary, whitehouse.gov, July 25, 2012, click "Read the Transcript," http://www.whitehouse.gov/photos-and-video/video/2012/07/25/president-obama-speaks-national-urban-league-convention#transcript.

14. Transcript of second presidential debate, Fox News, October 16, 2012, http://www.foxnews.com/politics/2012/10/16/transcript-second-presidential-debate/.

15. President Barack Obama, "Remarks by the President on the Nomination of Dr. Jim Kim for World Bank President," March 23, 2012, click "Read the Transcript," http://www.whitehouse.gov/photos-and-video/video/2012/03/23/president-obama-nominates-jim-yong-kim-world-bank-president#transcript.

16. Chad Sinclair, "Biden: Trayvon case could spur Fla. gun law debate," CBS News, March 31, 2012, http://www.cbsnews.com/8301-3460_162-57407389/biden-trayvon-case-could-spur-fla-gun-law-debate/?tag=mncol;lst;3.

17. See Chapter 10 in John R. Lott Jr., *More Guns, Less Crime* (University of Chicago Press, 2010), third edition.

18. Ibid. for a survey of the research on defensive gun use. See also John R. Lott Jr., "What a balancing test will show for Right-to-Carry Laws," *University of Maryland Law Review*, 2012: 1205–18.

19. Erik Wasson, "Obama says he's not bound by Guantanamo, gun-control provisions," *The Hill*, December 23, 2011, http://thehill.com/blogs/on-the-money/budget/201245-obama-says-he-wont-be-bound-by-guantanamo-gun-control-portions-of-omnibus.

20. John R. Lott Jr., *The Bias Against Guns* (Regnery, 2003), Chapter 3.

21. "EDITORIAL: Obama's backdoor gun ban," *Washington Times*, September 3, 2010, http://www.washingtontimes.com/news/2010/sep/3/obamas-backdoor-gun-ban/.

22. Mike Levine, "Guns Groups to Sue Over New Obama Regulations, DOJ Vows To 'Vigorously Oppose,'" Fox News, August 3, 2011, http://www.foxnews.com/politics/2011/08/03/guns-groups-to-sue-over-new-obama-regulations-doj-vows-to-vigorously-oppose/.

23. "Barack Obama proposes major cuts to federal 'Armed Pilots Program,'" PolitiFact.com, June 12, 2012, http://www.politifact.com/truth-o-meter/statements/2012/jun/14/national-rifle-association/barack-obama-proposes-major-cuts-federal-armed-pil/.

24. Paul Bedard, "Obama Pushing Shooters Off Public Lands," *U.S. News and World Report*, November 16, 2011, http://www.usnews.com/news/blogs/washington-whispers/2011/11/16/obama-pushing-shooters-off-public-lands. Paul Bedard, "Shooters Heard: Interior Will Not Ban Target Practice," *U.S. News and World Report*, November 17, 2011, http://www.usnews.com/news/blogs/washington-whispers/2011/11/17/shooters-heard-interior-will-not-ban-target-practice.

25. Sam Salzwedel, "Drivers go through checkpoint at Redington Pass," KVOA NBC Channel 4, Tucson, Arizona, November 10, 2012 (http://www.kvoa.com/news/drivers-go-through-checkpoint-at-redington-pass/#!prettyPhoto/0/).

26. Ibid.

27. Brian Wingfield, "Rifle-Toting Terrorists Called Major Threat to U.S. Power Grid," *San Francisco Chronicle*, November 23, 2012, http://www.sfgate.com/business/bloomberg/article/Rifle-Toting-Terrorists-Called-Major-Threat-to-4062094.php.

28. At least as of December 21, 2012, the Bureau of Alcohol, Tobacco, Firearms and Explosives website still listed B. Todd Jones as Acting Director: http://www.atf.gov/about/executive-staff/.

29. Nita Ghei, "GHEI: ATF's latest gun grab," *Washington Times*, September 6, 2012, http://www.washingtontimes.com/news/2012/sep/6/atfs-latest-gun-grab/.

30. John R. Emshwiller and Gary Fields, "Federal Asset Seizures Rise, Netting Innocent With Guilty," *Wall Street Journal*, August 22, 2011, http://online.wsj.com/article/SB10001424053111903480904576512253265073870.html.

31. John Lott Jr., "A Vote for Kagan Is a Vote to Take Away Your Guns," Fox News, June 30, 2010, http://www.foxnews.com/opinion/2010/06/30/john-lott-elena-kagan-sonia-sotomayor-gun-ownership-self-defense-second/.

32. "Dissent" written by Justice Stephen Breyer, with whom Justice Gins-
     burg and Justice Sotomayor join, in the case "OTIS McDONALD, et
     al ., PETITIONERS v. CITY OF CHICAGO, ILLINOIS, et al.," U.S.
     Supreme Court, June 28, 2010, available on the Cornell University
     Law School website, http://www.law.cornell.edu/supremecourt/
     text/08-1521/#writing-ZD1.

33. Dan Rivoli, "Obama's Pick to Influential Court Becomes Latest to Face
     GOP Obstruction," *International Business Times*, December 6, 2011,
     http://www.ibtimes.com/obamas-pick-influential-court-becomes-
     latest-face-gop-obstruction-379626. "Grassley Statement on the Nom-
     ination of Caitlin Joan Halligan to be U.S. Circuit Judge for the D.C.
     Circuit," Senator Chuck Grassley of Iowa's website, December 6, 2011,
     http://www.grassley.senate.gov/news/Article.cfm?customel_data-
     PageID_1502=38160.

34. Hillary Rodham Clinton and Goodwin Liu, "Separation Anxiety:
     Congress, the Courts, and the Constitution," 91 *Georgetown Law
     Journal* 439 (Jan. 2003).

35. Associated Press, "Gun Issue Represents Tough Politics for Obama,"
     Fox News, November 24, 2011, http://www.foxnews.com/poli
     tics/2011/11/24/gun-issue-represents-tough-politics-for-obama/.

36. Jake Tapper, "White House Suggests President Obama Will Not Push
     for More Gun Control," ABC News, July 22, 2012, http://abcnews.
     go.com/blogs/politics/2012/07/white-house-suggests-president-obama-
     will-not-push-for-more-gun-control/.

37. Charles M. Blow, "The Gun Frenzy," *New York Times*, November 29,
     2012, http://www.nytimes.com/2012/11/29/opinion/blow-the-gun-
     frenzy.html?src=recg. See also Rachel Weiner, "Where Obama and
     Romney stand on gun control," *Washington Post*, July 20, 2012, http://
     www.washingtonpost.com/blogs/the-fix/post/where-obama-and-rom-
     ney-stand-on-gun-control/2012/07/20/gJQAwMpNyW_blog.html.

38. This protection of Obama has been occurring for years. For an early
     example of this see: "Fact Check: Does Obama want to ban guns and
     rifles?" CNN, September 23, 2008, http://politicalticker.blogs.cnn.
     com/2008/09/23/fact-check-does-obama-want-to-ban-guns-and-rifles/.

39. Clare Kim, "Costas: We need to talk about America's gun culture,"
     MSNBC, December 4, 2012, http://tv.msnbc.com/2012/12/04/ccostas-
     i-can-think-of-dozens-where-by-virtue-of-having-a-gun-a-profes
     sional-athlete-wound-up-in-a-tragic-situation/.

40.   "Transcript: Obama's Speech at Sandy Hook Interfaith Prayer Vigil,"
        Wall Street Journal, December 16, 2012, http://blogs.wsj.com/wash-
        wire/2012/12/16/transcript-obamas-speech-at-sandy-hook-interfaith-
        prayer-vigil/.

41.   Here is the relevant part of the Colorado law on the ability of private
        businesses to restrict concealed carry. 18-12-214 Authority granted
        by permit - carrying restrictions.(5) Nothing in this part 2 shall be
        construed to limit, restrict, or prohibit in any manner the existing
        rights of a private property owner, private tenant, private employer,
        or private business entity.

42.   The killer's apartment was at: 1690 Paris Street, Aurora, CO 80010-
        2900. Elizabeth Flock, " Who Is James Holmes? Suspected Shooter
        Is 24, Was University Of Colorado Student," U.S. News & World
        Report, July 20, 2012, http://www.usnews.com/news/arti
        cles/2012/07/20/who-is-james-holmes-suspected-shooter-is-24-may-
        have-house-full-of-explosives-.
        The theaters were as follows:
        1) Cinema Latino de Aurora/Aurora Plaza 8 Cinemas, 777 Peoria
        Street, Aurora, CO 80011 888-588-2463/(303) 991-7022 (Lou Sullivan-
        Olmos)/ Not posted (Theater visited by Michael McNulty), Showing
        The Dark Knight Rises, 1.22 miles (3 minutes).
        2) Century Cinemark Theater—where the attack occurred, 14300 East
        Alameda Avenue, Aurora, CO 80012, No weapons allowed sign,
        Showed Dark Knight Rises, 3.97 miles (8 minutes).
        3) Harkins Northfield 18 (Billed as the home of Colorado's largest
        auditorium), 8300 E. Northfield Boulevard, Denver, CO 80238, (303)
        595-4275, 720-374-3118, Not posted at the time of the attack, the
        manager (Erin Griffie) indicated that the policy had been changed
        since the Cinemark attack. Showing The Dark Knight Rises, 5.13
        miles (10 minutes).
        4) Aurora Movie Tavern, 18605 East Hampden Avenue, Aurora, CO
        80013-3533, (303) 680-9913, Not posted Showing Dark Knight Rises,
        10.04 miles (18 minutes).
        5) THE MOVIE TAVERN AT SEVEN HILLS, 18305 E. Hampden
        Avenue, Aurora, CO 80013, (303) 680-9913, Not posted, Showing The
        Dark Knight Rises, 10.02 miles (19 minutes).
        6) Landmark Theatre Greenwood Village, 5415 Landmark Place,
        Greenwood Village, CO 80111, (303) 352-1908, (303) 779-0584, Not
        posted, Showing The Dark Knight Rises, 12.88 miles (19 minutes).

7) UA Colorado Center Stadium 9 and IMAX, 2000 S. Colorado Blvd., Denver, CO 80222, (303) 757-8665, Not posted, Showing The Dark Knight Rises, 9.66 miles (20 minutes).

43. Maxim Lott, "Temple massacre has some Sikhs mulling gun ownership," Fox News, August 21, 2012, http://www.foxnews.com/us/2012/08/21/temple-massacre-has-some-sikhs-mulling-gun-owner ship/. Sharif Durhams, "Azana Salon banned concealed-carry weapons," Journal Sentinel, October 22, 2012, http://www.jsonline.com/news/crime/azana-salon-banned-concealedcarry-weapons-k07age6-175281811.html.

44. Pam Belluck and Jodi Wilgoren, "SHATTERED LIVES — A special report.; Caring Parents, No Answers, In Columbine Killers' Pasts," *New York Times*, June 29, 1999, http://www.nytimes.com/1999/06/29/us/shattered-lives-special-report-caring-parents-no-answers-colum bine-killers-pasts.html?pagewanted=all&src=pm.

45. Josh White, "Law School Shooter Pleads Guilty," *Washington Post*, February 28, 2004. Rusty Surette, "Marine Allegedly Upset With Military Status Opens Fire in Northwest OKC," News9.com, December 18, 2009, http://www.news9.com/Global/story.asp?S=11696830&Call=Email&Format=Text%5D. John Lott, "Media Coverage of Mall Shooting Fails to Reveal Mall's Gun-Free-Zone Status," Fox News, December 6, 2007, http://www.foxnews.com/story/0,2933,315563,00.html. See my books More Guns, Less Crime and The Bias Against Guns for many additional examples.

46. Associated Press, "Pastor: Man opened fire after crashing near church," CNSNews.com, April 23, 2012, http://cnsnews.com/news/article/pastor-man-opened-fire-after-crashing-near-church. Associated Press, "Year after attack, Colo. church guard reflects," PoliceOne.com, December 8, 2008, https://secure.policeone.com/preview/patrol-issues/articles/1763667-Year-after-attack-Colo-church-guard-reflects.

47. Shenna Stout, "RV PARK KILLINGS: 'Witness shooter' recounts shootout with gunman who killed two in Early," KTXS.com, August 1, 2012, http://www.ktxs.com/news/RV-PARK-KILLINGS-Witness-shooter-recounts-shootout-with-gunman-who-killed-two-in-Early/-/14769632/15933066/-/30wo2o/-/index.html. Jack Blood, "Armed Citizen in TX Stops Shooting Spree and Saves Cop by Making 150+ Yard Shot With a Pistol," DeadlineLive.info, August 7, 2012, http://deadlinelive.info/2012/08/07/armed-citizen-in-tx-stops-shooting-spree-and-saves-cop-by-making-150-yard-shot-with-a-pistol/.

48. "22nd Annual National Survey Questions," National Association of Chiefs of Police, 2010, http://www.nacoponline.org/22nd.pdf.

49. "Shooting Straight," *Police* magazine, March 1, 2007, http://www.policemag.com/channel/weapons/articles/2007/03/editorial.aspx. San Diego Police Officers Association, "Assault Weapons Survey Results," The Informant, January/February 1997, http://nrawinningteam.com/awsurvey.html. Stephen L. Christopoulos, "Survey of Police Officers in Lehigh and Northampton Counties Pennsylvania," SightM1911.com, October 1997, http://www.sightm1911.com/lib/rkba/police_survey.htm.

50. John R. Lott Jr., "Gun Control and Mass Murders," *National Review*, June 11, 2010, http://www.nationalreview.com/articles/229929/gun-control-and-mass-murders/john-r-lott-jr#.

51. "Transcript of second presidential debate, Fox News, October 16, 2012, http://www.foxnews.com/politics/2012/10/16/transcript-second-presidential-debate/.

52. Jeffrey A. Roth and Christopher S. Koper, "Impacts of the 1994 Assault Weapons Ban: 1994–96," National Institute of Justice, March 1999.

53. See the conclusion in Christopher Koper, Daniel Woods, and Jeffrey Roth, "An Updated Assessment of the Federal Assault Weapons Ban: Impacts on Gun Markets and Gun Violence, 1994–2003," Report to the National Institute of Justice, United States Department of Justice, June 2004.

54. The data is available from various issues of the FBI's Uniform Crime Reports.

55. The second edition of *More Guns, Less Crime* dealt with the initial implementation of the Assault Weapons Ban. The third edition also studied the ban being sunset. See also my book *The Bias Against Guns*. John R. Lott Jr., *More Guns, Less Crime* (University of Chicago Press, 2000, 2010). John R. Lott Jr., *The Bias Against Guns* (Regnery, 2003).

56. Louis Charbonneau, "After Obama win, U.S. backs new U.N. arms treaty talks," Reuters, November 7, 2012, http://www.reuters.com/article/2012/11/07/us-arms-treaty-un-idUSBRE8A627J20121107.

57. Rick Gladstone, "U.N. Misses Its Deadline for Arms Pact," *New York Times*, July 27, 2012, http://www.nytimes.com/2012/07/28/world/proponents-of-arms-trade-treaty-urge-final-approval.html?_r=1.

58. Ibid.

59. Foreign & Commonwealth Office, "Support for a global Arms Trade Treaty," United Kingdom, gov.uk, November 8, 2012, http://www.fco.gov.uk/en/news/latest-news/?id=833244682&view=News.

60. Maxim Lott, "Proposed U.N. Treaty to Regulate Global Firearms Trade Raising Concerns for U.S. Gun Makers," Fox News, August 5, 2011, http://www.foxnews.com/world/2011/08/05/proposed-un-treaty-to-regulate-global-firearms-trade-raising-concerns-for-us/.

61. "The Global Regime for Armed Conflict," Council on Foreign Relations, July 25, 2012, http://www.cfr.org/global-governance/global-regime-armed-conflict/p24180 and Global Burden of Armed Violence, Geneva Declaration, 2008, http://www.genevadeclaration.org/fileadmin/docs/Global-Burden-of-Armed-Violence-full-report.pdf.

62. "Sweden asks Venezuela to explain FARC weapons find," AFP, July 27, 2009, http://www.google.com/hostednews/afp/article/ALeqM5jg-mUhszbB9C53sLHMP2Pea4c9CfQ.

63. John R. Lott and Gary Mauser, "Ask Canada -- gun registration won't make D.C. safer," *Washington Examiner*, March 27, 2012, http://washingtonexaminer.com/ask-canada-gun-registration-wont-make-d.c.-safer/article/412041.

64. Chip Todd, "Replacing Missing Firing Pins," Gun Reports, May 8, 2012, http://www.gunreports.com/special_reports/accessories/american-gunsmith-magazine-firing-pin-missing-replacement-fix1655-1.html.

65. A survey of this literature on background checks and gun show regulations is available here John R. Lott Jr., *More Guns, Less Crime: Understanding Crime and Gun Control Laws* (University of Chicago Press, 2010), third edition, e.g., pp. 327–30.

66. Sharyl Attkisson, "Documents: ATF used 'Fast and Furious' to make the case for gun regulations," CBS News, December 7, 2011, http://www.cbsnews.com/8301-31727_162-57338546-10391695/documents-atf-used-fast-and-furious-to-make-the-case-for-gun-regulations/.

67. Ibid. One Fortune article by Katherine Eban went so far as declaring that the ATF "never intentionally allowed guns to fall into the hands of Mexican drug cartels." Her article never mentioned a critical point: that there are emails with and testimony from gun dealers who were ordered to make sales to Mexican drug cartels. Katherine Eban, "The truth about the Fast and Furious scandal," Fortune, CNNMoney, June 27, 2012, http://features.blogs.fortune.cnn.com/2012/06/27/fast-and-furious-truth/.

68. Ibid.

69. Ibid.

70. Cristina Rayas, "ATF agents, Terry family blast 'gun-walking' investigation," Tucson Sentinel, June 16, 2011, http://www.tucsonsentinel.com/local/report/061611_atf_congress/atf-agents-terry-family-blast-gun-walking-investigation/.

71. John Malcolm, "Showstopper: Department of Justice Report on Operation Fast and Furious," Heritage Foundation, September 20, 2012, http://www.heritage.org/research/reports/2012/09/department-of-justice-report-on-operation-fast-and-furious#_edn3.

72. Shannon Bream, "Updates on Justice Department's Newest Gun Regulations," *Special Report with Bret Baier*, Fox News, July 12, 2011, watch on YouTube, http://youtu.be/cLn04WZN6hk.

73. Sharyl Attkisson, "Documents: ATF used 'Fast and Furious' to make the case for gun regulations," CBS News, December 7, 2011, http://www.cbsnews.com/8301-31727_162-57338546-10391695/documents-atf-used-fast-and-furious-to-make-the-case-for-gun-regulations/.

74. Judson Berger, "ATF whistle-blower fired, claims complaints about 'Fast and Furious' played role," Fox News, October 11, 2012 (http://www.foxnews.com/politics/2012/10/11/atf-whistle-blower-fired-claims-furious-complaints-played-role/). "Lawmakers: 'Ominous' video a warning to ATF whistle-blowers after 'Furious,'" Fox News, July 19, 2012, http://www.foxnews.com/politics/2012/07/19/lawmakers-ominous-video-warning-to-atf-whistleblowers-after-furious/.

75. William La Jeunesse, "ATF official tied to 'Furious' sting on leave, earning second paycheck, lawmakers allege," Fox News, August 23, 2012, http://www.foxnews.com/politics/2012/08/22/atf-official-tied-to-fast-and-furious-on-leave-earning-second-paycheck/.

76. "Mexico analyzing U.S. probe on Fast and Furious," Fox News Latino, September 22, 2012, http://latino.foxnews.com/latino/news/2012/09/22/mexico-analyzing-us-probe-on-fast-and-furious/.

77. Devlin Barrett, "Suit Seeks Documents in Gun-Trafficking Case," *Wall Street Journal*, August 13, 2012, http://online.wsj.com/article/SB10000872396390444318104577587291192295730.html?mod=WSJ_article_LatestHeadlines.

78. "CNN LARRY KING LIVE: Interview With Barack Obama," CNN, March 19, 2007, http://transcripts.cnn.com/TRANSCRIPTS/0703/19/lkl.01.html. Conor Friedersdorf, "The 'Most Transparent Administra-

tion Ever' Doctors Its Quotes," The Atlantic, July 16, 2012, http://www. theatlantic.com/politics/archive/2012/07/the-most-transparent-admin istration-ever-doctors-its-quotes/259857/.

79. Morton Rosenberg, "Presidential Claims of Executive Privilege: History, Law, Practice and Recent Developments," CRS Report for Congress, Congressional Research Service, August 21, 2008, http://www. fas.org/sgp/crs/secrecy/RL30319.pdf. Peter Grier, "On Fast and Furious, Obama invokes 'executive privilege.' What's that?" *Christian Science Monitor*, June 20, 2012, http://www.csmonitor.com/USA/DC-Decoder/Decoder-Wire/2012/0620/On-Fast-and-Furious-Obama-invokes-executive-privilege.-What-s-that.

80. David Codrea deserves special praise because he broke the story on the website examiner.com. See also Maxim Lott, "Senator Calls ATF on Allegations Agency Is Allowing Guns Into Mexico," Fox News, February 2, 2011, http://www.foxnews.com/politics/2011/02/02/senator-calls-atf-allegations-agency-allowing-guns-mexico/ and James V. Grimaldi and Sari Horwitz, "ATF gunrunning probe strategy scrutinized after death of Border Patrol agent," *Washington Post*, February 1, 2011, http://www.washingtonpost.com/national/atf-gunrunning-probe-strategy-scrutinized-after-death-of-border-patrol-agent/2011/02/01/ABFUe0Q_story.html.

81. Sharyl Attkisson, "Memos contradict Holder on 'Fast and Furious,'" CBS News, October 3, 2011, http://www.cbsnews.com/video/watch/?id=7383343n.

82. Mike Levine, "Emails Show Justice Officials Drawing Blanks on 'Fast and Furious' Despite Memos," Fox News, October 13, 2011, http://www.foxnews.com/politics/2011/10/13/emails-justice-officials-blank-memos/.

83. Even President Obama gave an interview in March where he indicated that at that time Holder knew about the operation. With the president on record saying that he knew about the operation before April, Holder conceded in November 2011 that he probably knew about the operation at least a month earlier than he had previously testified. "Obama Spoke About 'Fast & Furious' Before Holder Claimed He Knew," RealClearPolitics Video, October 13, 2011, http://www.real clearpolitics.com/video/2011/10/13/obama_spoke_about_fast__furi ous_before_holder_claimed_he_knew.html.

84. Rep. Jason Chaffetz's (R-UT) questioning of Holder on Operation Fast and Furious during the June 7, 2012, House Judiciary hearing is available on YouTube, "Chaffetz: Will AG Holder Explain His 'Reasonable' Conclusion From New…" http://www.youtube.com/watch?v=NaUXOHYbE9M.

85. Matt Cover, "Holder Claims Emails Using Words 'Fast and Furious' Don't Refer to Operation Fast and Furious," CNSNews.com, June 7, 2012, http://cnsnews.com/news/article/holder-claims-emails-using-words-fast-and-furious-don-t-refer-operation-fast-and.

86. Rep. Jason Chaffetz's (R-UT) questioning of Holder on Operation Fast and Furious during the June 7, 2012 House Judiciary hearing is available on YouTube, "Chaffetz: Will AG Holder Explain His 'Reasonable' Conclusion From New…" (http://www.youtube.com/watch?v=NaUXOHYbE9M).

87. Sharyl Attkisson, "Fast and Furious: GOP says wiretaps revealed 'Gunwalking' early on," CBS News, June 29, 2012, http://www.cbsnews.com/8301-31727_162-57464139-10391695/fast-and-furious-gop-says-wiretaps-revealed-gunwalking-early-on/.

88. Jonathan Strong, "Darrell Issa Puts Details of Secret Wiretap Applications in Congressional Record," Roll Call, June 29, 2012, http://www.rollcall.com/news/darrell_issa_puts_details_of_secret_wiretap_applications_in_congressional-215828-1.html.

89. "Pelosi: GOP is attacking Eric Holder because of his efforts on voter fraud," C-SPAN TV, available on YouTube, June 21, 2012, http://youtu.be/ENFA8PC-wQ8.

90. Charlie Savage, "A Partisan Lightning Rod Is Undeterred," *New York Times*, December 17, 2011, http://www.nytimes.com/2011/12/18/us/politics/under-partisan-fire-eric-holder-soldiers-on.html?_r=1&pagewanted=all.

91. Mike Levine, "Holder 'Regrets' Death Of Border Patrol Agent, Stands By Response In Aftermath," Fox News, November 8, 2011, http://www.foxnews.com/politics/2011/11/08/after-fast-and-furious-holder-to-blame-congress-for-not-supporting-atf/.

92. Cristina Rayas, "ATF agents, Terry family blast 'gun-walking' investigation," *Tuscon Sentinel*, June 16, 2011, http://www.tucsonsentinel.com/local/report/061611_atf_congress/atf-agents-terry-family-blast-gun-walking-investigation/. Indeed, at least one supervisory special

agent, Peter Forcelli, in desperation went to his local Radio Shack in an unsuccessful attempt to jury rig a GPS tracking bug for the guns.

93. Peter Yost, "Fast And Furious-Like 'Gun-Walking' Probe Mentioned In 2007 Bush Administration Memo," *Huffington Post*, November 4, 2011, http://www.huffingtonpost.com/2011/11/04/fast-and-furious-bush-administration_n_1076148.html. See also Sari Horwitz, "Earlier ATF gun operation 'Wide Receiver' used same tactics as 'Fast and Furious,'" *Washington Post*, October 6, 2011, http://www.washington post.com/politics/earlier-atf-gun-operation-wide-receiver-used-same-tactics-as-fast-and-furious/2011/10/06/gIQAuRHIRL_story.html, and Evan Perez, "Justice Faces 'Sting' Grilling," *Wall Street Journal*, November 7, 2011, http://online.wsj.com/article/SB10001424052970 204621904577017941485938760.html.

94. Senator John Cornyn (R-TX) presses Obama Attorney General Eric Holder, "Cornyn Grills Holder on Wide Receiver vs Fast and Furious," testimony before Senate Judiciary Committee, November 8, 2011, available on YouTube, http://www.youtube.com/watch?v=s1G5x0XmNiA.

95. Jake Tapper, "President Obama Falsely Claims Fast and Furious Program 'Begun Under the Previous Administration,'" September 21, 2012, http://abcnews.go.com/blogs/politics/2012/09/president-obama-falsely-claims-fast-and-furious-program-begun-under-the-previous-administration/.

96. Office of the Inspector General, "A Review of ATF's Operation Fast and Furious and Related Matters," U.S. Department of Justice, September 2012, http://www.justice.gov/oig/reports/2012/s1209.pdf. The report is less meaty than its page count suggests, as a great deal of material is repeated two, three, or even four times. The authors seem to have thought that a lengthy report would convince the public that they had done a thorough job.

97. Consider, for example, the puzzling April 2010 briefings that Jason Weinstein gave his boss, Lanny Breuer, the assistant attorney general for the criminal division. Weinstein clearly knew about both "gun walking" operations Fast and Furious and Wide Receiver. He knew that Wide Receiver entailed at least some attempts to trace the guns. He knew that Mexican authorities were informed about Wide Receiver. And he knew by March 4 and 11, 2010, that Fast and Furious didn't do either of those things (p. 257).

On April 19, 2010, the report finds, Weinstein briefed Breuer about Wide Receiver (pp. 73–75). The Department of Justice report further reveals that after the April briefing, Breuer agreed with Weinstein that Wide Receiver was "obviously flawed" and ordered Weinstein to communicate this conclusion to the ATF.

So here is the problem: If Breuer agreed with Weinstein that Wide Receiver was flawed, why didn't Weinstein tell Breuer that the Obama administration was engaged in an operation that was even more flawed? The inspector general simply takes Weinstein's and Breuer's word that they talked only about Wide Receiver.

The inspector general's report lets Weinstein take the fall, limiting the damage to political appointees in the Obama administration. If Breuer knew about Fast and Furious, that creates problems for Attorney General Eric Holder because Breuer reports directly to him. Holder and Breuer are extremely close, having been partners for years at the Washington law firm Covington & Burling.

98. See, for example, pp. 298, 431, and 441.
99. William La Jeunesse and Maxim Lott, "The Myth of 90 Percent: Only a Small Fraction of Guns in Mexico Come From U.S.," Fox News, April 2, 2009, (http://www.foxnews.com/politics/2009/04/02/myth-percent-small-fraction-guns-mexico-come/).
100. Sen. Charles Grassley (R-Iowa) is quoted by CBS News as saying: "There's plenty of evidence showing that this administration planned to use the tragedies of Fast and Furious as rationale to further their goals of a long gun reporting requirement. But, we've learned from our investigation that reporting multiple long gun sales would do nothing to stop the flow of firearms to known straw purchasers because many Federal Firearms Dealers are already voluntarily reporting suspicious transactions. It's pretty clear that the problem isn't lack of burdensome reporting requirements." A similar quote was also given by Congressman Darrell Issa (R-CA). Sharyl Attkisson, "Documents: ATF used 'Fast and Furious' to make the case for gun regulations," CBS News, December 7, 2011, http://www.cbsnews.com/8301-31727_162-57338546-10391695/documents-atf-used-fast-and-furious-to-make-the-case-for-gun-regulations/.
101. William La Jeunesse, "EXCLUSIVE: Long-awaited 'Furious' report places blame on ATF, Justice," Fox News, September 11, 2012, http://www.foxnews.com/politics/2012/09/11/exclusive-long-awaited-furious-report-spreads-blame-across-agencies/.

Chapter Four

1.   "Press Release—FAA Proposes to Raise Airline Pilot Qualification Standards," Federal Aviation Administration, February 27, 2012, https://www.faa.gov/news/press_releases/news_story.cfm?newsId=13373. And "Pilot Certification and Qualification Requirements for Air Carrier Operations," Federal Register, February 29, 2012, http://www.faa.gov/regulations_policies/rulemaking/recently_published/media/2120-AJ67NPRM.pdf.

      What often happens now is that people will get the first 250 hours of training and then become a flight instructor. But it usually takes someone a total of 400 to 500 hours of flight experience before they are hired by a commuter airline. The new rule will effectively increase training by 3 to 4 times. Many people currently pay for the current difference between 250 and 400 to 500 hours by becoming flight instructors. But there is simply no way that all the new entrants can be instructors for the new required amount of time.

2.   Ibid.

3.   The FAA has proposed lowering the requirement for military pilots to 750 hours, but it has yet to be approved and it is unlikely to make a big difference in the number of new pilots. Susan Carey, Jack Nicas, and Andy Pasztor, "Airlines Face Acute Shortage of Pilots," *Wall Street Journal*, November 12, 2012, http://online.wsj.com/article/SB10001424052970203937004578079391643223634.html.

4.   Associated Press, "List of Deadly Commercial U.S. Airline Crashes," Fox News, February 13, 2009, http://www.foxnews.com/story/0,2933,492206,00.html. For more recent events, see Airsafe.com, "The Most Recent Fatal or Significant US Plane Crashes," http://airsafe.com/events/us_ten.htm.

5.   Matthew L. Wald, "Safety Net for Airlines Has Holes, a Crash Shows," *New York Times*, May 11, 2009, http://www.nytimes.com/2009/05/12/nyregion/12pilot.html.

6.   Ibid.

7.   One pilot who has been involved with hiring at a major airline wrote me: "But firing a pilot in a union environment takes a long time, concerted effort and there is no guarantee you'll get rid of the pilot in the long run. Building a case that the pilot is not good at flying airplanes takes a long period of many checkride failures. Everything

must be carefully documented. When the action is taken to fire the pilot, the union will quickly file a grievance. There will be numerous meetings with union officials and the union will transmit one-sided information to the pilot group about the termination, thus inflaming the pilot group at the airline and building an atmosphere of distrust that is corrosive and expensive for the airline. The next step is a System Board of Adjustment usually comprised of two people selected by the union and two selected by airline management. In termination cases, the System Board normally deadlocks and the issue is presented to an arbitrator. The arbitrator's livelihood depends upon being selected by airline managements as well as union leadership, so they tend to be very careful to build 'middle of the road' reputations, thus their decisions are usually coin tosses regardless of how strong a case airline management has built. Once the arbitrator makes his decision, it is binding to both parties. If the pilot is reinstated, the airline pays him back pay for the 10–18 months it took to go through the process."

8. Airline Pilots Association International, "ALPA's FTDT Comparison: New FAR vs. Existing Rules," FASTREAD, December 23, 2011, http://www.alpa.org/portals/alpa/fastread/2011/FastReadNewsflash_20111223.htm. And "No more falling asleep on the job," Flight Training Blog, http://blog.aopa.org/flighttraining/?p=805. The new rules now limit all passenger and cargo pilots to one hundred hours during any 28-day period, one thousand hours in any 12-month period—an average of five hours a day for a five-day work week, 19.2 hours per week over a year. The minimum rest between flights is now ten hours, two more than the previous mandate. There are now hard limits on maximum flight times, whereas before pilots could work past eight hours if there were "unforeseen circumstances."

9. Susan Carey, Jack Nicas, and Andy Pasztor, "Airlines Face Acute Shortage of Pilots," *Wall Street Journal*, November 12, 2012, http://online.wsj.com/article/SB10001424052970203937004578079391643223634.html.

10. "RAA Touts Safety, Growth and Resiliency of Regional Airlines But Warns of Flight Cuts from Pilot Shortfall," Regional Airline Association, July 17, 2012, http://www.raa.org/Media/RAAHeadlines/tabid/114/articleType/ArticleView/articleId/122/Default.aspx.

11. Michael Cooper, "Inspector General Questions Value of Some Airport Stimulus Projects," *New York Times*, August 11, 2009, http://www.nytimes.com/2009/08/12/us/12airports.html.

12. Jim Acosta and Janet Rodriguez, "Remote Murtha airport lands big bucks from Washington," CNN, April 23, 2009, http://articles.cnn.com/2009-04-23/politics/murtha.airport_1_stimulus-funds-faa-spokeswoman-laura-brown-airport?_s=PM:POLITICS.

13. Michael Grabell, "Tiny Airports Take Off With Stimulus," ProPublica, July 13, 2009, http://www.propublica.org/article/tiny-airports-take-off-with-stimulus-713.

14. Ibid.

15. Steve Wynn, "I'll Be Damned If I Want To Have Him Lecture Me," RealClearPolitics Video, October 9, 2012, http://www.realclearpolitics.com/video/2012/10/09/steve_wynn_on_obama_ill_be_damned_if_ill_have_him_lecture_me.html.

16. Congressional Quarterly Transcripts, "Obama Remarks on Economy," *Washington Post*, March 27, 2008, http://www.washingtonpost.com/wp-dyn/content/article/2008/03/27/AR2008032701631.html.

17. Ibid.

18. Ibid.

19. Walter Isaacson, *Steve Jobs* (Simon and Schuster, 2011).

20. CNBC Transcript, "Investing in America: A CNBC Town Hall Event with President Obama," Monday, September 20, 2010, http://www.cnbc.com/id/39211696/CNBC_EXCLUSIVE_CNBC_TRANSCRIPT_CNBC_BROADCASTS_INVESTING_IN_AMERICA_A_CNBC_TOWN_HALL_EVENT_WITH_PRESIDENT_OBAMA_TODAY_MONDAY_SEPTEMBER_20TH_AT_12PM_ET.

21. Sudeep Reddy, "Big Interview: Goolsbee Defends Obama Record on Business," *Wall Street Journal*, October 1, 2010, http://blogs.wsj.com/economics/2010/10/01/big-interview-goolsbee-defends-obama-record-on-business/. And Larry Kudlow, "An Interview with Austan Goolsbee," *National Review*, August 18, 2011, http://www.nationalreview.com/kudlows-money-politics/274931/interview-austan-goolsbee.

22. Carrie Budoff Brown, "President Obama at war with himself over Wall Street," Politico, October 21, 2011, http://www.politico.com/news/stories/1011/66514.html.

23. Brian Montopoli, "Obama Versus the 'Fat Cats,'" CBS News, December 13, 2009, http://www.cbsnews.com/8301-503544_162-5975318-503544.html?tag=contentMain;contentBody. And editorial, "About those 'Speculators,'" *Wall Street Journal*, May 21, 2009.

24. Sara Kugler, "NYC mayor defends Wall Street before Obama's visit," Associated Press, April 21, 2010, http://www.breitbart.com/article.php?id=D9F7LQ7O1&show_article=1.

25. President Barack Obama, "Remarks by the President in Town Hall Meeting on Health Care," the White House, Office of the Press Secretary, June 11, 2009, http://www.whitehouse.gov/the_press_office/Remarks-by-the-President-in-Town-Hall-Meeting-on-Health-Care-in-Green-Bay-Wisconsin/.

26. President Barack Obama, "Obama's Speech on Overhauling Financial Regulation," *New York Times*, April 22, 2010, http://www.nytimes.com/2010/04/23/business/economy/23prexy-text.html?pagewanted=all.

27. Douglas Schoen, "Polling the Occupy Wall Street Crowd," *Wall Street Journal*, October 18, 2011, http://online.wsj.com/article/SB10001424052970204479504576637082965745362.html?mod=WSJ_hp_mostpop_read.

28. Doyle McManus, "Pre-occupied: Obama finds sympathy loves company," *Sydney Morning Herald*, October 22, 2011, http://www.smh.com.au/business/world-business/preoccupied-obama-finds-sympathy-loves-company-20111021-1mcee.html. And Carrie Budoff Brown, "President Obama at war with himself over Wall Street," Politico, October 21, 2011, http://www.politico.com/news/stories/1011/66514.html.

29. Zeke Miller, "White House Draws Closer To Occupy Wall Street, Says Obama Is Fighting For The Interests Of The 99%," *Business Insider*, October 16, 2011, http://articles.businessinsider.com/2011-10-16/politics/30285591_1_house-spokesman-josh-earnest-president-barack-obama-class-warrior.

30. Sophie Quinton and Lara Seligman, "Who Are the Small-Business Owners Obama Hosted? White House lines up stalwart supporters to counter anti-business image," *National Journal*, November 28, 2012, http://www.nationaljournal.com/politics/who-are-the-small-business-owners-obama-hosted--20121127. A more typical headline was given by *Businessweek*: John Tozzi, "Obama Tries to Assuage Small Busi-

nesses' Fiscal Fears," Bloomberg *Businessweek*, November 27, 2012, http://www.businessweek.com/articles/2012-11-27/obama-tries-to-assuage-small-businesses-fiscal-fears.

31. United States District Court Southern District of New York, *U.S. Securities and Exchange Commission v. Edward S. Steffelin*, http://www.sec.gov/litigation/complaints/2011/comp-pr2011-131-steffelin.pdf.

32. Editorial, "Where Are the Criminals?" *Wall Street Journal*, November 25, 2012, http://online.wsj.com/article/SB10001424127887323353204578129182913327340.html?mod=WSJ_Opinion_AboveLEFTTop.

33. Ibid.

34. Average U.S. retail gas price data is available here: http://ycharts.com/indicators/gas_price.

35. President Barack Obama, "Remarks by the President on Increasing Oversight on Manipulation in Oil Markets," the White House, Office of the Press Secretary, April 17, 2012, http://www.whitehouse.gov/photos-and-video/video/2012/04/17/president-obama-speaks-increasing-oversight-manipulation-oil-marke#transcript.

36. Ben Sharples, "Oil Trades Near One-Week Low on Rising U.S. Stockpiles," Bloomberg *Businessweek*, April 19, 2012, http://www.businesweek.com/news/2012-04-18 oil-trades-near-one-week-low-in-new-york-on-rising-u-dot-s-dot-supplies. And Wendy Koch, "U.S. oil production is up, so why are gas prices so high?" *USA Today*, April 19, 2012, http://usatoday30.usatoday.com/money/industries/energy/story/2012-04-21/global-factors-gasoline-prices/54421804/1.

37. "Commodity prices mixed amid weak Chinese, US data," *Daily Times* (Pakistan), April 15, 2012, http://www.dailytimes.com.pk/default.asp?page=2012%5C04%5C15%5Cstory_15-4-2012_pg5_32.

38. Ibid. See also Richard Wolf, "Obama on rising gas prices: 'No silver bullet,'" *USA Today*, April 23, 2011, http://content.usatoday.com/communities/theoval/post/2011/04/obama-on-rising-gas-prices-no-silver-bullet/1.

39. President Barack Obama, "Remarks by the President at a Town Hall in Annandale, Virginia," the White House, Office of the Press Secretary, April 19, 2011, http://www.whitehouse.gov/the-press-office/2011/04/19/remarks-president-town-hall-annandale-virginia. "And I know that if you've got a limited budget and you just watch that hard-earned money going away to oil companies that will once again probably make record profits this quarter, it's pretty frustrating."

40. President Barack Obama, "Remarks by the President at a Campaign Event in Roanoke, Virginia," the White House, Office of the Press Secretary, July 13, 2012, http://www.whitehouse.gov/the-press-office/2012/07/13/remarks-president-campaign-event-roanoke-virginia.

41. Natalie Gewargis, "'Spread the Wealth'?" ABC News, October 14, 2008, http://abcnews.go.com/blogs/politics/2008/10/spread-the-weal/.

42. Gerald Prante, "Obama and Gibson Capital Gains Tax Exchange," Tax Foundation, April 17, 2008, http://taxfoundation.org/blog/obama-and-gibson-capital-gains-tax-exchange.

43. John R. Lott Jr., "Why is Education Publicly Provided? A Critical Survey," *Cato Journal*, Fall 1987, http://www.cato.org/pubs/journal/cj7n2/cj7n2-14.pdf.

44. "Elevated Seeks Loan From RFC To Pay Taxes and Run Own Lines; Manhattan Company Is Asking $12,000,000-Looks to Higher Fare-Plan Would Give U.S. Lien and Complicate Unification," *New York Times*, April 20, 1938, http://select.nytimes.com/gst/abstract.html?res=F6071FF83C55157A93C2AB178FD85F4C8385F9.

45. Ronald A. Reis, "The New York City Subway System," Infobase Publishing, October 7, 2009, http://issuu.com/ilovegraffiti/docs/the_new_york_city_subway_system__2009__-__malestro. And Mark S. Feinman, "History of the Independent Subway," Subway, http://www.nycsubway.org/wiki/History_of_the_Independent_Subway. The subways did receive a government subsidy in getting set up.

46. Dan Klein, "Private Highways in America, 1792-1916," *The Freeman*, http://www.fee.org/the_freeman/detail/private-highways-in-america-1792-1916/. And Dan Klein, "The Voluntary Provision of Public Goods? The Turnpike Companies of Early America," *Economic Inquiry*, October 1990, http://econfaculty.gmu.edu/klein/PdfPapers/VoluntaryProvisionPublicGoods.pdf. And Marlon G. Boarnet and Joseph F. Dimento, "The Private Sector's Role in Highway Finance: Lessons from SR91," *Access*, Fall 2004, http://www.uctc.net/access/25/Access%2025%20-%2005%20-%20Lessons%20From%20SR%2091.pdf. And Eduardo Engel, Ronald Fischer, and Alexander Galetovic, "A New Approach to Private Roads," *Regulation*, Fall 2002, http://www.cato.org/pubs/regulation/regv25n3/v25n3-6.pdf.

47. Robert M. Shea, "American Fire Marks—A Good Story," the Fire Mark Circle of the Americas, http://www.firemarkcircle.org/documents/

goodstory.htm. And "A little fire service history," Fire Service Information, 2011, http://www.fireserviceinfo.com/history.html.

48. A history of New York City's fire department is available here: http://www.nyc.gov/html/fdny/html/history/fire_service.shtml. New York City's population in 1865 is available here: http://query.nytimes.com/mem/archive-free/pdf?res=F10915FC3E59137A93CBA9178AD85F428684F9.

49. Histories of Philadelphia's fire department are available here from Robert M. Shea, "American Fire Marks—A Good Story," the Fire Mark Circle of the Americas. Philadelphia's population in 1870 is available here: http://physics.bu.edu/~redner/projects/population/cities/philadelphia.html.

50. John P. McIver, "History of Policing," Police Science 5108, University of Colorado, 2007, sobek.colorado.edu/~mciverj/History%20of%20Policing.pps.

51. Terry L. Anderson and P. J. Hill, *The Not So Wild, Wild West: Property Rights on the Frontier* (Stanford University, 2004). See also Terry L. Anderson and P. J. Hill, *An American Experiment in Anarcho-Capitalism: The Not So Wild, Wild West* (*Journal of Libertarian Studies*, 1978), http://mises.org/journals/jls/3_1/3_1_2.pdf.

52. Press Conference by the President, "Transcript of Obama News Conference," *Wall Street Journal*, June 29, 2011, http://blogs.wsj.com/washwire/2011/06/29/transcript-of-obama-news-conference/.

53. Paul Krugman, "Phony Fear Factor," *New York Times*, September 29, 2011, http://www.nytimes.com/2011/09/30/opinion/krugman-phony-fear-factor.html?_r=1. See also Lawrence Mishel, "Regulatory Uncertainty: A phony explanation for our jobs problem," Economic Policy Institute, Briefing Paper No. 330, September 27, 2011, http://w3.epi-data.org/temp2011/EPIBriefingPaper330b.pdf. "I do have genuine contact with both the White House and with congressional leadership," Paul Krugman in his interview with Alison van Tiggelen. Alison van Tiggelen, "Paul Krugman: Transcript—Will Climate Legislation kill the Economy," Fresh Dialogues, December 2, 2009, http://www.freshdialogues.com/2009/12/09/paul-krugman-transcript-will-climate-legislation-kill-the-economy/.

54. "Members Show Overwhelming Opposition to Federal Regulations," National Federation of Independent Business, September 2011, http://www.nfib.com/nfib-in-my-state/nfib-in-my-state-content?cmsid=58245.

55. Geiger is the executive director of the National Federation of Inde-
     pendent Business. Roger R. Geiger, "Small business struggles under
     thumb of regulators," Cincinnati.com, September 27, 2011, http://
     news.cincinnati.com/article/20110928/EDIT02/109280336/Guest-
     Column-Regulators-hinder-small-businesses?odyssey=mod%7Cnew
     swell%7Ctext%7CFRONTPAGE%7Cs.

56. The previous quarter's survey results were fairly similar, so even
     though these survey data came out right after the column, he could
     have used the Chamber of Commerce's previous survey. U.S. Chamber
     of Commerce, "Q3 Small Business Outlook Survey," Harris Interac-
     tive, October 12, 2011, http://www.uschambersmallbusinessnation.
     com/uploads/US%20Chamber%20Small%20Business%20Survey%20
     Q3%20Report.pdf. Still another survey done by Gallup in October
     2011 found that the biggest concern of small businesses was "comply-
     ing with government regulation." Joshua Altman, "Democrat criticizes
     Obama for '4,200 pages' of pending regulations," *The Hill*, November
     22, 2011, http://thehill.com/video/in-the-news/195091-dem-criticizes-
     obama-admin-for-4200-pages-of-pending-regulations.

57. See http://www.reginfo.gov/public/do/eoHistReviewSearch.

58. Byron York, "New report cites 'regulatory tsunami' under Obama,"
     Washington Examiner, September 13, 2011.

59. I should also mention that I have known Cass Sunstein very well over
     the years.

60. Sunstein headed up the Office of Information and Regulatory Affairs.
     Darren Samuelsohn and Jonathan Allen, "President Obama's admin-
     istration slow-walks new rules," Politico, July 12, 2012, http://www.
     politico.com/news/stories/0712/78419.html.

61. Editorial, "Here comes the regulatory flood," *Wall Street Journal*,
     November 23, 2012, http://online.wsj.com/article/SB1000142412788
     7324439804578115001809986588.html.

62. Patrick McLaughlin and Jerry Ellig, "Does Haste Make Waste in
     Regulatory Analysis?" Social Science Research Network, July 13,
     2010, http://papers.ssrn.com/sol3/papers.cfm?abstract_id=1646743.

63. The biggest last year of term increases occur right before a president
     leaves office—either when a president is in the eighth and final year
     of his administration or, in George H. W. Bush's case, about to be
     defeated. In that case, the number of significant regulations during
     these years was 32 percent higher than during the previous three

years. If you look at the years when they ran for reelection and were not defeated, the number of significant regulations falls by 19 percent. Since all the data are not yet available for 2012, I assumed that the regulations during November and December would be released at the same rate that they were from January through October. Doing that implies that during 2012, Obama was producing regulations by over 36 percent of the rate that they were being produced annually during 2009 to 2011.

So there are two sets of comparisons. If you compare the drop in Obama's rate of issuing regulations to those for the last years of terms from Reagan through George W. Bush, the t-statistic is 3.65 and it is significant for a two-tailed t-test at the 1 percent level. If you compare Obama's drop with when Reagan, Clinton, and George W. Bush were running for reelection, the t-statistic is 3.11 and it is significant for a two-tailed t-test at the 10 percent level.

64. The website for the National Federation of Independent Businesses concerns about regulations is http://stopthetidalwave.org

65. "Cherry-picking on Regulation," FactCheck.org, September 22, 2011, http://www.factcheck.org/2011/09/cherry-picking-on-regulation/.

66. Susan Dudley, "Perpetuating Puffery: An Analysis of the Composition of OMB's Reported Benefits of Regulation," *Business Economics*, July 2012, Vol. 47 No. 3, pp 165–76.

67. C. J. Ciaramella, "Obama Regulations Adding $2K to Cost of Cars," Fox News, November 17, 2011, http://nation.foxnews.com/govern ment-regulations/2011/11/17/obama-regulations-adding-2k-cost-cars.

68. The information on how they define regulations on property rights is available here: http://www.heritage.org/Index/Property-Rights.

69. The information on how they define regulations on investments and financial markets is available here: http://www.heritage.org/Index/ Investment-Freedom and http://www.heritage.org/Index/Financial-Freedom.

70. How many days does it take to go through the red tape to start a business? How many procedures have to be done to start a business or obtain a license? How costly are those regulations to meet? Explanation of their measure of "Business Freedom," http://www.heritage.org/ Index/Business-Freedom.

71. The World Economic Forums' rankings are available at http://reports. weforum.org/global-competitiveness-report-2012-2013/. See also

Anita Greil, "U.S. Competitiveness Slips," *Wall Street Journal*, September 5, 2012, http://online.wsj.com/article/SB10000872396390443686 0045776334100660666848.html?mod=WSJ_article_LatestHeadlines.

72. See the Economic Freedom of the World: 2010 Annual Report for 2008, http://www.cato.org/pubs/efw/efw2010/EFW2010-chapter1.pdf, and Economic Freedom of the World: 2012 Annual Report for 2010, http://www.cato.org/pubs/efw/efw2012/efw-2012-chapter-1.pdf. See also "US Slips in Report's Ranking of Free Economies," Fox News, September 18, 2012, http://www.foxnews.com/politics/2012/09/18/us-free-economy-slide/.

73. Ibid.

74. Michael E. Porter and Jan W. Rivkin, "Prosperity at Risk: Findings of Harvard Business School's Survey on U.S. Competitiveness," Harvard Business School, January 2012, http://www.hbs.edu/competitiveness/pdf/hbscompsurvey.pdf.

75. Sudeep Reddy, "Big Interview: Goolsbee Defends Obama Record on Business," *Wall Street Journal*, October 1, 2010, http://blogs.wsj.com/economics/2010/10/01/big-interview-goolsbee-defends-obama-record-on-business/.

76. Robb Mandelbaum, "What's in the Senate Small-Business Jobs Bill for You," *New York Times*, July 1, 2010, http://boss.blogs.nytimes.com/2010/07/01/whats-in-the-senate-small-business-jobs-bill-for-you/. John R. Lott Jr., "Another Proposal From Obama to Throw Your Money Down the Drain," Fox News, September 8, 2010, http://www.foxnews.com/opinion/2010/09/08/john-lott-economy-unemployment-rate-cleveland-tax-law-obama-stimulus/.

77. Paul Bedard, "6 Pages of Obamacare Equals 429 Pages of Regulations," *US News*, April 7, 2011, http://www.usnews.com/news/washington-whispers/articles/2011/04/07/6-pages-of-obamacare-equals-429-pages-of-regulations.

78. Ed Henry, "Obama Cuts Red Tape, But Businesses Want More," Fox News, August 23, 2011, http://politics.blogs.foxnews.com/2011/08/23/obama-cuts-red-tape-businesses-want-more.

79. Henry J. Pulizzi, "Obama Signs Credit-Card Overhaul Legislation Into Law," *Wall Street Journal*, May 22, 2009, http://online.wsj.com/article/SB124302235634548041.html. And Clayton Closson, "President Obama Signs New Mortgage Law To Prevent Further Foreclosures," Associated Press, May 22, 2009, http://www.quickenloans.com/blog/

ap-president-obama-signs-new-mortgage-law-to-prevent-further-foreclosures-5607.

80. "Cheerios are a Drug? FDA's Surprising Letter to General Mills," Agence France Presse, May 13, 2009, available on AlterNet.org, http://www.alternet.org/health/139990. "General Mills' CEO Discusses Q1 2012 Results—Earnings Call Transcript," Seeking Alpha, September 21, 2011, http://seekingalpha.com/article/295088-general-mills-ceo-discusses-q1-2012-results-earnings-call-transcript.

81. Based on a telephone conversation with Susan Cruzan in the FDA's press office, on June 18, 2009. See also a piece that I wrote for the *Washington Times*. Editorial, "Uh-oh, Cheerios," June 21, 2009.

82. John Stossel, "Government Crushes Innovative Online Prediction Market," Fox Business, November 26, 2012, http://www.foxbusiness.com/on-air/stossel/blog/2012/11/26/government-crushes-innovative-online-prediction-market.

83. Press Release, "CFTC Charges Ireland-based 'Prediction Market' Proprietors Intrade and TEN with Violating the CFTC's Off-Exchange Options Trading Ban and Filing False Forms with the CFTC," U.S. Commodity Futures Trading Commission, November 26, 2012, http://www.cftc.gov/PressRoom/PressReleases/pr6423-12.

84. James M. O'Neil, "New federal law may make replacing your furnace much costlier," NorthJersey.com, November 23, 2012, http://www.northjersey.com/news/bergen/New_federal_law_may_make_replacing_your_furnace_much_costlier.html?page=all.

85. Editorial, "Obamacare's pizza price," *Washington Times*, November 23, 2012, http://www.washingtontimes.com/news/2012/nov/23/obamacares-pizza-price/.

86. Hoag Levins, "FDA Rolls Out Menu-Labeling Rules: But Does It Really Work?" LDI Health Economist, April 4, 2011, http://ldihealtheconomist.com/he000001.shtml.

87. Any time a family farm is set up as a business partnership or a corporation, children would be banned from doing chores. Even if the farms are not incorporated, children would not be allowed to work on other people's farms, even the farms of their grandparents. Rick Barrett, "Farms could face new rules for kid workers," *Milwaukee Journal Sentinel*, November 22, 2011, http://www.jsonline.com/business/farms-could-face-new-rules-for-kid-workers-i3337e7-134368758.html.

88. Editorial, "Inside the EPA," *Wall Street Journal*, September 26, 2011, http://online.wsj.com/article/SB100014240531119041946045765828 14196136594.html?mod=opinion_newsreel.

89. Mary Williams Walsh, "A.I.G. Reaches Deal to Repay Treasury and Fed for Bailout," *New York Times*, September 30, 2010, http://www.nytimes.com/2010/10/01/business/01aig.html?_r=1&hp. And Mike Allen, "White House hopes for business help," Politico, September 29, 2010, http://www.politico.com/news/stories/0910/42805.html.

90. Bill Canis and Baird Webel, "The Role of TARP Assistance in the Restructuring of General Motors," Congressional Research Service, September 7, 2012 , http://www.fas.org/sgp/crs/misc/R41978.pdf.

91. "Hedge Fund Leader Blasts Obama for 'Bullying' and 'Abuse of Power,'" Yahoo Finance, May 6, 2009, http://finance.yahoo.com/tech-ticker/article/241837/Hedge-Fund-Leader-Blasts-Obama-for-%22Bullying%22-and-%22Abuse-of-Power%22?tickers=%5Edji,%5Egspc,GM,ARM,DAN,GT,XLF?sec=topStoriesccode=.

92. The entire quotation from Lauria is this: "was directly threatened by the White House and in essence compelled to withdraw its opposition to the deal under the threat that the full force of the White House press corps would destroy its reputation if it continued to fight. That's how hard it is to stand on this side of the fence." "Frank talks with Tom Lauria, who represents a group of lenders that object to the Chrysler sale," WJR Radio, May 1, 2009, http://www.wjr.com/Article.asp?id=1301727&spid=6525. And ABC News' Jake Tapper reported that Steven Rattner, Obama's car czar, made the threat. See Theresa Cook, "White House Denies Charge By Attorney that Administration Threatened to Destroy Investment Firm's Reputation," ABC News *Political Punch*, May 2, 2009, http://abcnews.go.com/blogs/politics/2009/05/bankruptcy-atto/.

93. For GM that amounted to $6.5 billion in preferred stock paying a 9 percent dividend, $2.5 billion in debt, 17.5 percent of the new company and future warrants allowing purchase of another 2.5 percent. The United Auto Workers was originally going to get 39 percent of GM stock, but it decided that GM's future was simply too risky. Jerry Shenk, "Detroit High Life," *American Thinker*, February 8, 2011, http://www.americanthinker.com/blog/2011/02/detroit_high_life.html. John D. Stoll, Jeff McCracken, and Neil King Jr., "GM-Union Deal Raises

U.S. Stake," *Wall Street Journal*, May 27, 2009, http://online.wsj.com/article/SB124335377570854805.html#mod=testMod.

94. James Kelleher and David Bailey, "U.S. automakers see tests from old, new threats," Reuters, January 11, 2011, http://www.reuters.com/article/2011/01/11/retire-us-autoshow-idUSTRE7090AN20110111?pageNumber=2. Originally, the union was supposed to get 55 percent of Chrysler. John D. Stoll and Sharon Terlep, "GM Offers U.S. a Majority Stake," *Wall Street Journal*, April 28, 2009, http://online.wsj.com/article/SB124083476254259049.html.

95. John Stoll, Jeff McCracken, Kate Linebaugh, "U.S. Squeezes Auto Creditors," *Wall Street Journal*, April 10, 2009, http://online.wsj.com/article/SB123932036083306929.html.

96. The *Wall Street Journal*'s Holman Jenkins summarized the fight this way: "[GM bondholders] have been intransigent precisely because they calculate the UAW is too important to Democratic electoral politics for Mr. Obama to risk losing control of the reorganization process to a bankruptcy judge. The GM bailout has become a political operation run out of the White House." Holman Jenkins, "GM Bankruptcy? Tell Me Another," *Wall Street Journal*, April 1, 2009, http://online.wsj.com/article/SB123853988781575499.html.

97. Editorial, "Kicking the Tires on the General Motors Deal," *Washington Post*, June 3, 2009, http://www.washingtonpost.com/wp-dyn/content/article/2009/06/02/AR2009060203217.html.

98. Austan Goolsbee interview, "Obama Unveils Tough Terms for GM, Chrysler Recovery Efforts," PBS *Newshour*, March 30, 2009, http://www.pbs.org/newshour/bb/business/jan-june09/ledeautos_03-30.html.

99. Goolsbee also pretty much repeated what he had said in his PBS *Newshour* interview: "What we've seen over past months is the bondholders in some cases holding out thinking that the government will step in and bail out the car companies and we'll get paid off.... I think what the president outlined in his remarks pretty clearly was that that's not going to happen and everybody has got to put some skin in the game." Reuters, "GM talks likely to June 1, not past: Obama adviser," May 22, 2009, http://www.reuters.com/article/2009/05/22/us-gm-bankruptcy-goolsbee-idUSTRE54L0T120090522.

100. Theresa Cook, "White House Denies Charge By Attorney that Administration Threatened to Destroy Investment Firm's Reputation," ABC

News *Political Punch*, May 2, 2009, http://abcnews.go.com/blogs/politics/2009/05/bankruptcy-atto/.

101. Holman Jenkins, "GM Is Becoming a Royal Debacle," *Wall Street Journal*, April 22, 2009, http://online.wsj.com/article/SB124035637935940943.html.

102. Theresa Cook, "White House Denies Charge By Attorney that Administration Threatened to Destroy Investment Firm's Reputation."

103. Dealbook, "Chrysler's Holdout Lenders Feel the Heat," *New York Times*, May 1, 2009, http://dealbook.nytimes.com/2009/05/01/are-chrysler-hedge-funds-being-unfairly-blamed/. And Steven Pearlstein, "Claiming Unfairness, Hedge Funds Miss the Point," *Washington Post*, May 1, 2009, http://www.washingtonpost.com/wp-dyn/content/article/2009/04/30/AR2009043003898.html?wprss=rss_business.

104. The economics here is pretty straightforward. In exchange for the protections normally provided bondholders, they earn less money. Shareholders take the risks and on average they earn more. Sometimes if the company goes bankrupt, shareholders lose everything. For bondholders, they don't face the downside risk of shareholders, but they also don't rake in the earnings when things go well. Taking away this protection from bondholders may let the Obama administration give money to those they like, but it raises the costs for companies to borrow in the future.

105. Craig Karmin and Peter Lattman, "White House Says It Stands Behind Rattner," *Wall Street Journal*, April 18, 2009, http://online.wsj.com/article/SB124001459464430971.html.

106. Ashby Jones, "Quadrangle Settles Pay-For-Play Charges; Partners Rip Rattner," *Wall Street Journal*, April 16, 2010, http://blogs.wsj.com/law/2010/04/16/quadrangle-settles-pay-for-play-charges-partners-rip-rattner/.

107. Dan Primack, "Ex-car czar Steve Rattner settles pay-to-play scandal," Fortune.com, December 30, 2010, http://finance.fortune.cnn.com/2010/12/30/ex-car-czar-steve-rattner-settles-pay-to-play-scandal/.

108. The Obama administration has removed the links that it had for these claims during the campaign. The claim about GM being the "number-one automaker" is available here: President Barack Obama, "Remarks by the President at a Campaign Event," the White House, Office of the Press Secretary, April 27, 2012, http://www.whitehouse.gov/the-press-office/2012/04/27/remarks-president-campaign-event-0. The

original ad claiming, "saving over 1 million jobs" is available here, http://youtu.be/rgjTYFE2aYc, and one can see similar statements such as this weekly radio address by Obama: President Barack Obama, "Weekly Address: President Obama Hails Successes of the Restructuring of the Auto Industry, Calls on GOP Leaders to Stop Blocking Aid for Small Businesses," the White House, Office of the Press Secretary, July 31, 2010, http://www.whitehouse. gov/the-press-office/weekly-address-president-obama-hails-successesrestructuring-auto-industry-calls-go. Another ad had text on it saying: "U.S. automakers are hiring hundreds of thousands of new workers." Here is a Youtube version of the ad, though it doesn't have the text, http://youtu.be/ny1PCCU-BRWI. The quote "Three years later, all loans have been repaid to the federal government and U.S. automakers are hiring hundreds of thousands of new workers" was obtained from, http://www.barack obama.com/forward#auto-recovery. Another citation that obtained the same quote is available here: http://bestsocialprogram.wordpress. com/2012/05/21/lies-on-obamas-campaign-site/. See also John Lott, "Obama and GM Cook the Books," *National Review*, May 16, 2012, http://www.nationalreview.com/articles/300075/obama-and-gm-cook-books-john-lott-jr.

109. The Editors, "Sorry, GM, It's 'Government Motors' Awhile Longer," Bloomberg View, September 23, 2012, http://www.bloomberg.com/news/2012-09-23/sorry-gm-it-s-government-motors-awhile-longer-view.html.

110. Randall Smith and Sharon Terlep, "GM Could Be Free of Taxes for Years," *Wall Street Journal*, November 3, 2010, http://online.wsj.com/article/SB10001424052748704462704575590642149103202.html.

111. The product liabilities from pre-bankruptcy sales were assigned to the "Old GM" version of the company after bankruptcy.

112. The information on stimulus dollars given to GM is available from Recovery.gov, http://www.recovery.gov/Transparency/RecoveryData/Pages/RecipientSearch.aspx?recipname=GEneral%20Motors.

113. Peter Valdes-Dapena, "Don't buy a Chevy Volt, lease it," CNN Money, October 2, 2012, http://money.cnn.com/2012/10/02/autos/chevy-volt-lease/index.html.

114. Ryan Chittum, "Calculating the Clunkers' Real Cost to Taxpayers," *Columbia Journalism Review*, September 2, 2009, http://www.cjr.org/the_audit/calculating_the_clunkers_real.php.

115. Interview by Neil Cavuto of Neil Barofsky on Fox News, *Your World with Neil Cavuto*, at 4:23 p.m., April 21, 2010, http://www.pddnet.com/news/2010/04/interview-troubled-asset-relief-program-special-inspector.

116. "Number of GM Employees in the US," Numberof.net, April 16, 2010, http://www.numberof.net/number-of-gm-employees-in-the-us/.

117. Blade Staff and News Services, "Sales fueling surge in auto industry hiring," ToledoBlade.com, February 28, 2012, http://www.toledoblade.com/Automotive/2012/02/28/Sales-fueling-surge-in-auto-industry-hiring.html.

118. Rattner writes: "Their original estimate for a Chrysler liquidation had been a net job loss in a wide range. . . . Now Goolsbee said that the job loss from Plan A would be around 25,000 and the loss from Plan B would be about 60,000, a difference of around 35,000 jobs—and a far cry from the 300,000 that had practically knocked Larry off his chair when the subject of a Chrysler liquidation first came up." Steven Rattner, *Overhaul: An Insider's Account of the Obama Administration's Emergency Rescue of the Auto Industry* (Houghton Mifflin Harcourt, 2010), 164.

119. Mike Ramsey, "GM's 2011 Auto Sales Spark Feud Over Count," *Wall Street Journal*, January 20, 2012, http://online.wsj.com/article/SB10001424052970204616504577171031057829416.html.

120. "Global 500: Our ranking of the world's largest corporations," *Fortune*, 2011 http://money.cnn.com/magazines/fortune/global500/2011/full_list/index.html.

121. Editorial, "Kicking the Tires on the General Motors Deal," *Washington Post*.

122. It hasn't just been the Obama administration that has pushed for these write-offs. In 2010, with the Democrats completely controlling Congress, there was a similar push there. "House Financial Services Committee Chairman Barney Frank is going after the four largest providers of U.S. mortgages to write down second mortgages to prevent 'a deepening crisis' in the U.S. housing market." In Corbett B. Daly, "Pressure Builds for Us Mortgage Loan Write-downs," Reuters, March 8, 2010, http://www.reuters.com/article/2010/03/08/usa-housing-secondlien-idUSN0818028120100308. A more recent discussion on the Obama administration policy is available here: "Delinquent

Homeowners to Get Mortgage Aid from Government," Reuters, June 4, 2011, http://www.cnbc.com/id/43281199.

"'They seem to just try to coerce the industry into the loan-modi-fication program,' said David Watts, a strategist at analysis firm CreditSights Inc. 'They're saying, 'We want you to do this program, and we're going to make sure you do it by helping you, possibly with money and possibly with a big fat stick.'" "CitiGroup Expands Loan Modification Program After FDIC Pressure," Federal Loan Modifica-tion, February 4, 2009, http://fedmod.tv/citigroup-expands-loan-mod ification-program-after-fdic-pressure/.

123. Nelson Schwartz and Shaila Dewan, "States Negotiate $26 Billion Agreement for Homeowners," *New York Times*, February 8, 2012, http://www.nytimes.com/2012/02/09/business/states-negotiate-25-bil lion-deal-for-homeowners.html.

124. Editorial, "Kneecapping Financial Bosses," *Washington Times*, Decem-ber 23, 2009, http://www.washingtontimes.com/news/2009/dec/23/ kneecapping-financial-bosses/.

125. Lynn Sweet, "Obama tells bankers: make loans, modify mortgages," the White House, Office of the Press Secretary, December 14, 2009, http://blogs.suntimes.com/sweet/2009/12/obama_kicks_bankers_ make_loans.html.

126. Louise Story, "US Inquiry Eyes S&P Ratings of Mortgages," *New York Times*, August 17, 2011, http://www.cnbc.com/id/44184348.

127. Ben Smith, "White House Denies Eyeing Koch Tax Returns," Politico, September 21, 2010, http://www.politico.com/blogs/bensmith/0910/ White_House_denies_eyeing_Koch_tax_returns.html.

128. Glenn Thrush, "Treasury analyzes Goolsbee remark," Politico, Octo-ber 6, 2010, http://www.politico.com/politico44/perm/1010/tax_ claims_reviewed_42857716-18fe-483d-9869-7cead282dd31.html.

129. Letter from Russell George, Inspector General, IRS, to Senator Charles E. Grassley, dated September 28, 2010, http://www.week lystandard.com/sites/all/files/docs/Sen.%20Grassley%20-%20 Acknowledgement%20Letter.pdf.

130. "Walking Dead: Congress Edition," Mother Jones, December 7, 2010.

131. Paul Bedard, "Ford TV Ad Slams Obama Auto Bailouts," *US News & World Report*, September 16, 2011, http://www.usnews.com/news/ blogs/washington-whispers/2011/09/16/ford-tv-ad-slams-obama-auto-bailouts.

132. Frank Beckman, "White House wrong to lean on Ford," *Detroit News*, September 30, 2011, http://detnews.com/article/20110930/OPIN-ION03/109300331/1008/opinion01/White-House-wrong-to-lean-on-Ford. And Daniel Howes, "Ford pulls its ad on bailouts," *Detroit News*, September 27, 2011, http://www.detnews.com/article/20110927/OPIN-ION03/109270322/Howes--Ford-pulls-its-ad-on-bailouts). The *Washington Post*'s Greg Sargent reported that Ford and the Obama administration denied that there had been any pressure from the White House on Ford to pull the ad. Yet, sometimes a few well placed, pointed questions are enough to make people get a message. Greg Sargent, "Another White House scandal ... that is being denied by the parties on both sides," *Washington Post*, September 27, 2011, http://www.washingtonpost.com/blogs/plum-line/post/another-white-house-scandal--that-is-being-denied-by-the-parties-on-both-sides/2011/03/03/gIQAM5tY2K_blog.html.

133. Editorial, "Government thuggishness," *Washington Times*, August 24, 2009, http://www.washingtontimes.com/news/2009/aug/24/government-thuggishness/.

134. Mike Allen, "House demands compensation data," Politico, August 19, 2009, http://www.politico.com/politico44/perm/0809/compensationn_watch_d4882f2f-46d6-413f-9679-f518a7e923b3.html.

135. President Obama said: "Right now, at the time when everybody's getting hammered, [insurance companies are] making record profits and premiums are going up." Congressional Quarterly, "Transcript of Obama Prime-Time News Conference," *Washington Post*, July 22, 2009, http://voices.washingtonpost.com/44/2009/07/22/transcript_of_obama_prime-time.html.

136. "Insurance Co. Profits: Good, But Not Breaking Records," FactCheck.org, August 5, 2009.

137. Democratic House Speaker Nancy Pelosi claimed: "[Insurance companies] are the villains. They have been part of the problem in a major way. They are doing everything in their power to stop a public option from happening." "Pelosi lashes out against insurance companies," Reuters, July 30, 2009, http://in.reuters.com/article/2009/07/30/usa-healthcare-insurance-idINWNA021320090730.

138. David Kirkpatrick and Duff Wilson, "One Grand Deal Too Many Costs Lobbyist His Job," *New York Times*, February 12, 2010, http://www.nytimes.com/2010/02/13/health/policy/13pharm.html.

139. Editorial, "Kathleen Spitzer: The Administration targets a drug CEO in a troubling precedent," *Wall Street Journal*, May 2, 2011, http://online.wsj.com/article/SB10001424052748703655404576293232066996982.html.

140. Sam Baker, "HHS grants 106 new healthcare waivers," *The Hill*, August 19, 2011, http://thehill.com/blogs/healthwatch/health-reform-implementation/177581-hhs-grants-106-new-healthcare-waivers.

141. Information on the percent of the private sector population belonging to unions is available here: Bureau of Labor Statistics, "Union Members Survey," United States Department of Labor, January 21, 2011, http://www.bls.gov/news.release/union2.nr0.htm. The share of waivers granted to unions is available here: Tom Fitton, "Why Did Unionized Companies Get so Many Obamacare Waivers?" Biggovernment.com, September 12, 2011, http://biggovernment.com/tfitton/2011/09/12/why-did-unionized-companies-get-so-many-obamacare-waivers/.

142. David Willman, "Cost, need questioned in $433-million smallpox drug deal," *Los Angeles Times*, November 13, 2011, http://www.latimes.com/news/nationworld/nation/la-na-smallpox-20111113,0,6456082,full.story. "Questions Arise Over $433M Smallpox Drug Contract to Company Tied to Donor," Fox News, November 12, 2011, http://topstories.foxnews.mobi/quickPage.html?page=17224&external=1214818.proteus.fma&pageNum=-1.

143. Montana Farm Bureau Federation, "Montana farmers and ranchers urged to communicate with consumers," November 13, 2012, http://www.kxlo-klcm.com/site/index.php?option=com_content&view=article&id=454:montana-farmers-and-ranchers-urged-to-communicate-with-consumers&catid=8:ag-news-pod&Itemid=115. A discussion of the cost estimate is available from University of Chicago economist John Cochrane. John Cochrane, "Predictions," The Grumpy Economist, November 7, 2012, http://johnhcochrane.blogspot.com/2012/11/predictions.html?m=1.

144. Robert Brown, "Pollutants in Wyoming groundwater linked to 'fracking,'" Examiner.com, September 29, 2012, http://www.examiner.com/article/pollutants-wyoming-groundwater-linked-to-fracking. Brigham A. McCown, "Lack of Environmental Evidence Fails to Stop Proposed Fracking Regulations," *Forbes*, August 8, 2012, http://www.forbes.com/sites/brighammccown/2012/08/10/fracking-regulations-stalled-despite-lack-of-evidence/.

145. "Clean Energy," U.S. Environmental Protection Agency, site last visited on December 3, 2012, http://www.epa.gov/cleanenergy/energy-and-you/affect/water-discharge.html.

146. Eric Pfeiffer, "Endangered crocodile finds new life at nuclear power plant," Yahoo News, December 6, 2011, http://news.yahoo.com/blogs/sideshow/endangered-crocodile-finds-life-nuclear-power-plant-174148153.html.

147. "New Senate Report Reveals Economic Pain of Obama-EPA Regulations Put on Hold Until After the Election," U.S. Senate Committee on Environment & Public Works, October 18, 2012, http://epw.senate.gov/public/index.cfm?FuseAction=Minority.PressReleases& ContentRecord_id=743423ef-07b0-4db2-bced-4b0d9e63f84b.

148. A discussion of the cost estimate of the financial market regulations is available from University of Chicago economist John Cochrane, "Predictions," The Grumpy Economist.

Chapter Five

1. Jim Zarroli, "Companies Rush Dividends To Beat Possible Tax Hike," National Public Radio, November 29, 2012, http://www.npr.org/2012/11/29/166139907/companies-rush-dividends-to-beat-possible-tax-hike.

2. The 44.7-percent claim is from Ernst & Young as quoted by Jonathan Weisman, "Democrats Propose Plan to Sidestep Anti-Tax Pledge," *New York Times*, July 17, 2012, http://www.nytimes.com/2012/07/18/us/politics/senate-democrats-propose-letting-all-tax-cuts-expire.html?pagewanted=all.

3. Jeff Macke, "Why Apple Investors Are Owed $30 a Share by Christmas," Yahoo Finance, November 29, 2012, http://finance.yahoo.com/blogs/breakout/why-apple-investors-owed-30-share-christmas-170140899.html. Patti Domm, "Companies Gifting Shareholders Ahead of Tax-Law Change," CNBC, November 27, 2012, http://www.cnbc.com/id/49982523. Rich Miller and Alex Kowalski, "Rich Gain as Companies Seek to Beat Obama Tax Increases," Bloomberg, December 10, 2012, http://www.bloomberg.com/news/2012-12-10/rich-gain-as-companies-seek-to-beat-obama-tax-increases.html.

4. Matt Krantz, "Oracle pays dividend early to beat Uncle Sam," *USA Today*, December 3, 2012, http://www.usatoday.com/story/money/business/2012/12/03/oracle-dividend-tax-hike/1743877/.

5. "Washington Post to Pay Dividend Early," Associated Press, December 7, 2012, http://hosted.ap.org/dynamic/stories/U/US_WASHINGTON_POST_DIVIDEND?SITE=AP&SECTION=HOME&TEMPLATE=DEFAULT&CTIME=2012-12-07-16-53-14. "Washington Post endorsement: Four more years for President Obama," *Washington Post*, October 25, 2012, http://articles.washingtonpost.com/2012-10-25/opinions/35500076_1_fiscal-commission-entitlement-reform-and-revenue-president-barack-obama.

6. Mike Thiessen, "What's With All the Special Dividends?" The Motley Fool, December 6, 2012, http://beta.fool.com/mthiessen/2012/12/06/whats-all-special-dividends/18170/?ticker=AAPL&source=eogyholnk0000001. For information on Peter Lewis's donations see "Present Progressive," Snopes.com, September 8, 2012, viewed on December 6, 2012, http://www.snopes.com/politics/business/peterlewis.asp.

7. "Costco's Dividend Tax Epiphany," *Wall Street Journal*, November 30, 2012, http://online.wsj.com/article/SB10001424127887324705104578149012514177372.html.

8. Quentin Fottrell, "George Lucas's Jedi estate planning: 'Star Wars' creator's deal with Disney is a savvy move," MarketWatch, November 13, 2012, http://www.marketwatch.com/story/george-lucass-jedi-estate-planning-2012-11-01?link=MW_home_latest_news.

9. Krystal Peak, "Apple execs race to sell stock before reaching the fiscal cliff," *Business Journal*, December 5, 2012, http://www.bizjournals.com/sanjose/news/2012/12/05/apple-execs-race-to-cash-dividents.html.

10. Karen Smith Conway and Jonathan Rork, "State 'Death' Taxes and Elderly Migration—The Chicken or the Egg?" *National Tax Journal* (March 2006): 97–128.

11. Laura Saunders, "Rich Cling to Life to Beat Tax Man," *Wall Street Journal*, December 30, 2009, http://online.wsj.com/article/SB126213588339309657.html.

12. Wojciech Kopczuk and Joel Slemrod, "Dying to Save Taxes: Evidence from Estate Tax Returns on the Death Elasticity," *Review of Economics and Statistics* (May 2003), 85(2): 256–65.

13. Ben Berkowitz and Lauren Tara LaCapra, "Berkshire buyback seen clashing with estate tax push," Reuters, December 12, 2012, http://www.reuters.com/article/2012/12/12/berkshire-buyback-idUSL1E8N CITK20121212?feedType=RSS&feedName=rbssFinancialServicesA ndRealEstateNews&rpc=22.

14. Stacy Dickert-Conlin and Amitabh Chandra, "Taxes and the Timing of Births," *Journal of Political Economy* (February 1999), 107(1), 161–77.

15. "France's richest man applies to be Belgian, says not a tax move," Reuters, September 8, 2012, http://www.reuters.com/arti cle/2012/09/08/us-france-tax-lvmh-idUSBRE88709520120908.

16. Hugh Carnegy, "Hollande faces questions on tax pledge," *Financial Times*, September 6, 2012, http://www.ft.com/intl/ cms/s/0/0e7ed63a-f84f-11e1-b0e1-00144feabdc0.html.

17. "France's proposed tax hikes spark 'exodus' of wealthy," *The Telegraph*, July 16, 2012, http://www.telegraph.co.uk/news/worldnews/europe/ france/9404209/Frances-proposed-tax-hikes-spark-exodus-of-wealthy. html.

18. The *New York Times* quotes one tax specialist in France as saying: "Even young, dynamic people pulling in 200,000 euros are wondering whether to remain in a country where making money is not consid- ered a good thing." Liz Alderman, "Indigestion for 'les Riches' in a Plan for Higher Taxes," *New York Times*, August 7, 2012, http://www. nytimes.com/2012/08/08/business/global/frances-les-riches-vow-to- leave-if-75-tax-rate-is-passed.html.

19. Andrew Ross Sorkin, "Welcoming Higher Taxes, but Not That High," *New York Times*, October 8, 2012, http://dealbook.nytimes. com/2012/10/08/welcoming-higher-taxes-but-not-that-high/.

20. Hugh Carnegy, "Hollande faces questions on tax pledge," *Financial Times*, September 6, 2012, http://www.ft.com/intl/ cms/s/0/0e7ed63a-f84f-11e1-b0e1-00144feabdc0.html.

21. Robert Winnett, "Two-thirds of millionaires left Britain to avoid 50p tax rate," *The Telegraph*, November 27, 2012, http://www.telegraph. co.uk/news/politics/9707029/Two-thirds-of-millionaires-left-Britain- to-avoid-50p-tax-rate.html. The tax year in the UK goes from April 6th to April 5th.

22. President Barack Obama, "WEEKLY ADDRESS: Passing the Buffett Rule so that Everyone Pays Their Fair Share," the White House, Office

of the Press Secretary, whitehouse.gov, March 31, 2012, http://www.whitehouse.gov/the-press-office/2012/03/31/weekly-address-passing-buffett-rule-so-everyone-pays-their-fair-share.

23. Former President Clinton, "Remarks by President Obama and Former President Clinton," the White House, Office of the Press Secretary, whitehouse.gov, December 10, 2010, http://www.whitehouse.gov/the-press-office/2010/12/10/remarks-president-obama-and-former-president-clinton.

24. See the Congressional Budget Office Distribution of Household Income and Federal Taxes, "The Distribution of Household Income and Federal Taxes, 2008 and 2009," Congressional Budget Office, July 10, 2012, http://cbo.gov/publication/43373.

25. TurboTax TaxCaster can be found here, http://turbotax.intuit.com/tax-tools/calculators/taxcaster/?s=1.

26. The maximum taxable earnings is indexed so that it changes over time. "2012 Social Security tax rate and maximum taxable earnings," Social Security Administration, updated December 4, 2012, http://ssa-custhelp.ssa.gov/app/answers/detail/a_id/240/~/2012-social-security-tax-rate-and-maximum-taxable-earnings.

27. Six academics from Cornell, Boston University, and the Federal Reserve Bank of Cleveland assumed that there was a 5-percent discount rate. They said that lower discount rates implied the system was even more progressive. Steven Caldwell, Melissa Favreault, Alla Gantman, Jagadeesh Gokhale, Thomas Johnson, Laurence J. Kotlikoff, "Social Security's Treatment of Postwar Americans," *Tax Policy and the Economy*, Vol. 13, ed. James Poterba, January 1999, 112, http://www.nber.org/chapters/c10923.pdf. Earlier studies came to similar estimates, e.g., Peter Ferrara and John R. Lott Jr., "Rates of Return Promised by Social Security to Today's Young Workers," in *Social Security: Prospects for Real Reform*, ed. Peter Ferrara (Cato Institute, 1985).

28. Eugene Steuerle, "Marginal Tax Rates, Work, and the Nation's Real Tax System," Statement before the Joint Hearing of the Subcommittee on Human Resources and Subcommittee on Select Revenue Measures Committee on Ways and Means, June 27, 2012, http://www.taxpolicycenter.org/UploadedPDF/901508-Marginal-Tax-Rates-Work-and-the-Nations-Real-Tax-System.pdf.

29. Katherine Bradley and Robert Rector, "Confronting the Unsustainable
     Growth of Welfare Entitlements: Principles of Reform and the Next
     Steps," Heritage Foundation, June 24, 2010, http://www.heritage.org/
     research/reports/2010/06/confronting-the-unsustainable-growth-of-
     welfare-entitlements-principles-of-reform-and-the-next-steps.

30. See the Compilation of Patient Protection and Affordable Care Act,
     as Amended through May 1, 2010, available on Housedocs.house.gov,
     http://housedocs.house.gov/energycommerce/ppacacon.pdf.

31. Senator Jeff Sessions, "CRS Report: Welfare Spending The Largest
     Item In The Federal Budget," United States Senate Budget Commit-
     tee, http://budget.senate.gov/republican/public/index.cfm/files/
     serve/?File_id=34919307-6286-47ab-b114-2fd5bcedfeb5.

32. Ellinorianne, "Speaking of Entitlements . . . Big Oil has to GO!" Daily
     Kos, July 10, 2011, http://www.dailykos.com/story/2011/07/10/993242/-
     Speaking-of-Entitlements-Big-Oil-has-to-GO.

33. President Barack Obama, "Transcript: Obama's Speech to Congress
     on Jobs," *New York Times*, September 8, 2011, http://www.nytimes.
     com/2011/09/09/us/politics/09text-obama-jobs-speech.
     html?pagewanted=all.

34. Ibid.

35. "Republicans 'flabbergasted' by call for more spending as part of fis-
     cal deal," Fox News, December 3, 2012, http://www.foxnews.com/
     politics/2012/12/03/republicans-outraged-by-call-for-more-spending-
     as-part-fiscal-deal/.

36. "2012 Annual Report," Boards of Trustees of the Federal Hospital
     Insurance Trust Fund and the Federal Supplementary Medical Insur-
     ance Trust Fund, Centers for Medicare & Medicaid Services, April 23,
     2012, http://www.cms.gov/Research-Statistics-Data-and-Systems/
     Statistics-Trends-and-Reports/ReportsTrustFunds/Downloads/
     TR2012.pdf. Obama Administration's Office of Management and
     Budget, "Fiscal Year 2013 Budget of the U.S. Government," budget.
     gov, 210, http://www.whitehouse.gov/sites/default/files/omb/budget/
     fy2013/assets/budget.pdf. Chris Cox and Bill Archer, "Cox and Archer:
     Why $16 Trillion Only Hints at the True U.S. Debt," *Wall Street Journal*,
     November 26, 2012, http://online.wsj.com/article/SB1000142412788
     7323353204578127374039087636.html.

37. "'This Week' Transcript: Treasury Secretary Timothy Geithner," ABC
     News, December 2, 2012, http://abcnews.go.com/Politics/week-tran

script-treasury-secretary-timothy-geithner/story?id=17838
601&page=11.

38. Robert Pear, "Efforts to Curb Social Spending Face Resistance," *New York Times*, November 26, 2012, http://www.nytimes.com/2012/11/27/us/politics/politics-in-play-over-safety-net-in-deficit-talks.html?pagewanted=all&_r=0.

39. Paul Krugman, "The Twinkie Manifesto," *New York Times*, November 18, 2012, http://www.nytimes.com/2012/11/19/opinion/krugman-the-twinkie-manifesto.html.

40. William Kristol, "Kristol: A 'Mistake' For GOP to Fight Over Bush Tax Rates," RealClearPolitics Video, November 13, 2012, http://www.realclearpolitics.com/video/2012/11/13/kristol_a_mistake_for_gop_to_fight_over_bush_tax_rates_.html.

41. Binyamin Appelbaum and Robert Gebeloff, "Tax Burden for Most Americans Is Lower Than in the 1980s," *New York Times*, November 29, 2012, http://www.nytimes.com/2012/11/30/us/most-americans-face-lower-tax-burden-than-in-the-80s.html?pagewanted=all.

42. The figure for corporate income taxes shown in the text uses OECD data for thirty-four countries, but that data are not available for all years. A smaller set of twenty countries has data for all years. The figure on page 308 shows that the two sets of numbers reveal similar patterns.

43. When a company doesn't pay out its profits in dividends but keeps the money, the value of the company's stock increases by the amount of money that is retained. So whether the investor receives the profit as a dividend or as a capital gain, he still faces the same double taxation problem. "Historical Capital Gains and Taxes," Tax Policy Center, November 20, 2012, http://www.taxpolicycenter.org/taxfacts/display-afact.cfm?Docid=161.

44. The problem is somewhat more complicated than described in the text because as the share of the work force composed of women has increased, their labor supply elasticity has declined. But if one compares the 1950s to today, the net effect is still clearly to make the labor supply for the economy more elastic. For a recent survey of the literature see: Olivier Bargain, Kristian Orsini, and Andreas Peichl, "Labor Supply Elasticities in Europe and the US," IZA DP No. 5820, June 2011, http://ftp.iza.org/dp5820.pdf.

45. The regression results are as follows:

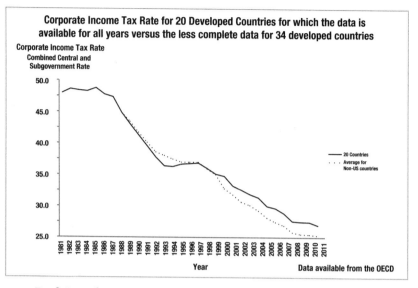

Real Cumulative GDP Growth = -1.153 (3.34) Corporate Income Tax Rate + .581 (5.75)

Adj-R-squared = .2353 Prob > F = 0.0021 Number of Observations = 34

Real Cumulative GDP Growth = -0.925 (3.90) Top Personal Income Tax Rate + .6289 (6.35)

Adj-R-squared = .3010 Prob > F = 0.0005 Number of Observations = 34

46. President Bill Clinton, "State of the Union Address," U.S. Government Info, January 27, 2000, http://usgovinfo.about.com/library/ref/blsou-full.htm.

47. "Monthly Budget Review: Fiscal Year 2012: A Congressional Budget Office Analysis," Congressional Budget Office, October 5, 2012, http://www.cbo.gov/sites/default/files/cbofiles/attachments/2012_09_MBR.pdf. For earlier years see "Fiscal Year 2013 Historical Tables, Budget of the U.S. Government," Office of Management and Budget, http://www.whitehouse.gov/sites/default/files/omb/budget/fy2013/assets/hist.pdf.

48. "The First Presidential Debate," *New York Times*, September 26, 2008, http://elections.nytimes.com/2008/president/debates/transcripts/first-presidential-debate.html.

49. The federal deficit reached $54.6 billion dollars in 1943. After adjusting for inflation, that would have been $669 billion in 2009. Yet, the

actual 2009 federal deficit was $1.41 trillion, more than twice as large. As to the increase in government spending, during World War II, federal government spending increased by $43.4 billion in 1943, the equivalent of $532.5 billion in 2009. Still, this increase was slightly less than the $535 billion in spending during Obama's first year. Office of Management and Budget, "Fiscal Year 2012 Historical Tables, Budget of the U.S. Government," Office of Management and Budget, budget.gov, http://www.whitehouse.gov/sites/default/files/omb/budget/fy2012/assets/hist.pdf.

50. President Barack Obama, "Text of Obama Speech on the Deficit," *Wall Street Journal*, April 13, 2011, http://blogs.wsj.com/washwire/2011/04/13/text-of-obama-speech-on-the-deficit/?mod=WSJBlog.

51. President Barack Obama, "Text of Obama Speech on the Deficit," *Wall Street Journal*, April 13, 2011, http://blogs.wsj.com/washwire/2011/04/13/text-of-obama-speech-on-the-deficit/?mod=WSJBlog.

52. Letter to the Honorable Daniel K. Inouye, "Preliminary Analysis of the President's Budget for 2012," Congressional Budget Office, March 18, 2011, http://www.cbo.gov/publication/22061.

53. Michael Warren, "CBO: We Can't Score Obama's Budget Plan Because It's Just a Speech," *Weekly Standard*, June 23, 2011, http://www.weeklystandard.com/blogs/cbo-director-we-dont-estimate-speeches_575464.html.

54. Data on publicly held debt are available here, "The Debt to the Penny and Who Holds it," TreasuryDirect, December 19, 2012, http://www.treasurydirect.gov/NP/NPGateway.

55. "Fiscal Year 2013 Budget of the U.S. Government," Office of Management and Budget, budget.gov, February 13, 2012, http://www.whitehouse.gov/sites/default/files/omb/budget/fy2013/assets/budget.pdf.

56. "Country Rankings," 2012 Index of Economic Freedom, Heritage Foundation and *Wall Street Journal*, http://www.heritage.org/index/Ranking.aspx.

57. "Explore the Data, 2012 Index of Economic Freedom, Heritage Foundation and *Wall Street Journal*, http://www.heritage.org/index/explore?view=by-variables.

58. "SIPRI Military Expenditure Database," SIPRI, 2012, http://milexdata.sipri.org/files/download/?key=06c22d95649cf4fa050108ff925d6b3e&file=SIPRI+milex+data+1988-2011.xls

59.   "Military Expenditure," SIPRI, Table 4.2, Expenditure, http://www.
        sipri.org/research/armaments/milex/resultoutput/milex_15/the-
        15-countries-with-the-highest-military-expenditure-in-2011-table/
        at_download/file. See also this link when the 2011 number was not
        available (in which case the 2010 number was used), "SIPRI Military
        Expenditure Database," SIPRI, 2012, http://milexdata.sipri.org/files/
        download/?key=06c22d95649cf4fa050108ff925d6b3e&file=SIPRI+m
        ilex+data+1988-2011.xls.

60.   "Databank," worldbank.org, http://databank.worldbank.org/data/
        Views/VariableSelection/FileDownloadHandler.ashx?filename
        =2f663be2-5ef0-4915-8add-f3d947b7f14e.xls&filetype=BULKEXCEL.

Conclusion

1.   Leigh Ann Caldwell, "With 19 days to go until Election Day, Obama
        stays vague," CBS News, October 18, 2012, http://www.cbsnews.
        com/8301-250_162-57534735/with-19-days-to-go-until-election-day-
        obama-stays-vague/.

2.   "Transcript and Audio: Vice Presidential Debate," NPR, October 11,
        2012, http://www.npr.org/2012/10/11/162754053/transcript-
        biden-ryan-vice-presidential-debate. Rebecca Kaplan, "A Timeline of
        Fiscal Cliff Meetings, Offers, and Counteroffers," National Journal,
        December 19, 2012, http://www.nationaljournal.com/congress-
        legacy/a-timeline-of-fiscal-cliff-meetings-offers-and-counterof-
        fers-20121219.

3.   Henry Decker, "Final Results: Obama Wins Popular Vote By 3 Per-
        cent," The National Memo, November 12, 2012, http://www.nation
        almemo.com/final-results-obama-wins-popular-vote-by-3-percent/.

INDEX

A

ABC News, 33–34, 37–38, 65, 133
abortifacients, 17
ACLU. *See* American Civil Liberties
  Union
Aetna, 11, 49–50
"Affordable Health Care for America
  Act," 11
African-Americans, 26, 28–29, 40
aggregate demand, 86, 89
agricultural building, 169
AIG. *See* American International
  Group
Airline Safety and Federal
  Aviation Administration
  Extension Act, 152
AK-47s, 128–29
Alabama, 45, 49–50
Alaska, 49, 118, 154
Ally Financial, 172, 178
Amanpour, Christiane, 124, 126
Amazon.com, 35
American Civil Liberties Union
  (ACLU), 186
American Customer Satisfaction
  Index (ACSI), 34–35
American Enterprise Institute, 53
American International Group (AIG),
  171
American Medical Association, 48,
American Revolution, 161
anti-poverty programs, 195
antitrust exemptions, 46
Antos, Joseph, 53
Apple, 187
Applebee's, 3
Apple-Metro, 3
AQR Capital Management, 172
Arab Spring, 70

B

Argentina, 139
Arizona, 143
Armed Pilots program, 131
Arnault, Bernard, 187
arrest rates, 138
Asness, Cliff, 172
assault weapons, 129–30, 134, 137–38,
  144
assault-weapons bans, 129, 137
  and crime rates, 137–38
  federal, 129–30, 137–38
  proposed by President Obama, 134
  state, 130, 138
Associated Press, 63
Attkisson, Sharyl, 142
Aurora, 128, 133–35
Australia, 27, 100–1, 106, 115, 201,
  205–6, 256
austerity measures, 93–102, 106, 110–
  12
Austria, 25, 27, 114, 136, 210
Auto Task Force, 174
Azana Salon and Spa, 135

background checks, 141
Baier, Bret, 7
bailouts, 172, 174, 216
  of auto industry, 174–77
  of banks, 106
  Ford Motor Company and, 180
  of Greece, 94
  TARP bailout, 176
balanced budget multiplier, 98
Bank of America, 178
banking, 155, 210
bankruptcy, 7, 52, 118, 120–21, 160,
  173–74, 176–77
banks, 88, 106, 174